PRINCIPLES AND METHODS OF TEACHING GEOGRAPHY

MAXWELL PRESS

PRINCIPLES AND METHODS OF TEACHING GEOGRAPHY

FREDERICK L. HOLTZ, A.M

Head of Department of Geography
and
Nature-Study Brooklyn Training School for
Teachers New York City;
Author of "Nature-Study Manual"

MAXWELL PRESS

Chennai Trichy New Delhi

MAXWELL PRESS

This edition has been published in india by arrangement with Carson Books, UK

ISBN 978-93-90877-66-9 Maxwell Press

All rights reserved No. 44, Nallathambi Street,
Triplicane, Chennai 600 005

MJP 1078 © Publishers, 2021

Publisher : C. Janarthanan

Publisher's Note

The legacy of a country is in its varied cultural heritage, historical literature, developments in the field of economy and science. The top nations in the world are competing in the field of science, economy and literature. This vast legacy has to be conserved and documented so that it can be bestowed to the future generation. The knowledge of this legacy is slowly getting perished in the present generation due to lack of documentation.

Keeping this in mind, the concern with retrospective acquiring of rare books has been accented recently by the burgeoning reprint industry. Maxwell Press is gratified to retrieve the rare collections with a view to bring back those books that were landmarks in their time.

In this effort, a series of rare books would be republished under the banner, "Maxwell Press". The books in the reprint series have been carefully selected for their contemporary usefulness as well as their historical importance within the intellectual. We reconstruct the book with slight enhancements made for better presentation, without affecting the contents of the original edition.

Most of the works selected for republishing covers a huge range of subjects, from history to anthropology. We believe this reprint edition will be a service to the numerous researchers and practitioners active in this fascinating field. We allow readers to experience the wonder of peering into a scholarly work of the highest order and seminal significance.

Maxwell Press

PREFACE

THIS book is designed for the experienced teacher and for teachers in training. It presents an analysis of the nature of geography as a science, and of the pedagogical principles involved. Upon this is based the discussion of the special method of the teaching of geography. The treatment is rendered concrete by examples from classroom experience.

While a general review of the subject matter of geography is out of the question in a book of this kind, there is considerable that will serve to review and impress at least the general principles of the science.

The book begins with the subject and method of home geography, and then proceeds with the discussion of the work of the higher grades, in such a way as to indicate the growth of the subject in the pupil's mind. This plan lends itself well to a logical development of the theory and method of teaching and to the organization of the science of geography.

TABLE OF CONTENTS

PRINCIPLES AND METHODS OF TEACHING GEOGRAPHY

CHAPTER I

THE AIMS OF GEOGRAPHY

The grand distinction between Man and other creatures is that he can take advantage of his environment, so as to modify his development in any desired direction. — MILL.

Practical value. — Geography has a place in the curriculum on account of its practical utility and cultural value. Its usefulness is apparent from the mere statement of the definition of geography as the description of the habitat of man, and of his physical and psychical adjustment to his environment.

Geography teaches place relations. This knowledge is applied in daily life in finding one's way about the home community, in reading and conversation, in sending letters or parcels, and in business.

The commercial world depends upon geographical information. The importer must know where his wares may be obtained, and by what routes they may be shipped most cheaply. The fruit commission man, for example, must be in touch with California, Florida,

Cuba, and Spain. From all these regions he can get oranges. He must know in what season in each country the fruit is ripe. Even to the fruiterer at the corner, and to the housewife who buys the fruit, such geographical knowledge would not come amiss.

The manufacturer must know the source of his raw materials, the markets for his products, and the routes of shipment. The exporter, likewise, must be familiar with routes and markets, else he might be "carrying coals to Newcastle." Knowledge of transportation facilities is immensely important in modern commercial life. The shortest and most economical routes must be chosen to meet competition.

Geography teaches us about our own country — its natural advantages, resources, and beauty; its greatness and possibilities, and also its limitations, which enables us individually or as a nation to make better adjustments to our physical environment. The study of foreign regions is but a complement of home geography. As citizens of the United States we should be acquainted with the geographical conditions of the countries with which we have commercial dealings, or historical and political association. Many useful lessons for home application may be learned from the study of foreign countries.

Geography teaches the interdependence of the different sections of our nation — how the East depends upon the West for its foodstuffs; how the West in turn gets most of its manufactured articles from the East; how the cities and the rural sections balance each other; in short, it teaches us "how the other half lives." In this way it tends to develop in the student a social sympathy, a feeling of relationship to others, a certain sense of civic duty that help toward good citizenship. The development of patriotism and good citizenship should be a chief aim in the teaching of geography. Moreover, a knowledge of world geography should broaden our international sympathies and make for universal peace. Countries that do not know each-other are suspicious of each other. On the other hand, a knowledge of geography encourages international travel, commerce, confidence, and interdependence.

Geography helps us in understanding and appreciating the frequent geographical allusions in our daily reading, in the newspapers, in literature, and history. Current events are meaningless in proportion as we are ignorant of the places where they occur, or of the geographical conditions affecting them. History depends absolutely upon geography to give it definiteness. When the geographical setting of an historical event is known, it has additional meaning and interest.

As a final practical aim of geography may be mentioned the ability to use geographical books, apparatus, models, diagrams, maps, and tables in after-school days in the pursuit of further geographical studies, or in occasional need of interpreting these data in general reading.

Cultural aims. — Turning to those aims of geography that consider something beyond mere utility, namely, intellectual pleasure, mental strength, refinement, and growth of character, the subject, it will be found, has much to offer. It should be noted that some of the preceding utilitarian aims have also a cultural side, as the development of the social sense and patriotism, and the appreciation of history and literature.

Geography contributes to the enjoyment of the natural elements and forces, the beauty of scenery, and the ways of life of the people, both in our local walks and in more extended travels. One should read the geography of the places to be visited, their history and literature, if one wishes to get the most pleasure and satisfaction out of travel.

The subject of geography is intrinsically very interesting. Books of travel, exploration, and of descriptive, general geography may be very pleasant and entertaining reading. In fact, in the beginning when geography had not yet been accredited as a distinct subject for schools, and efforts were made to introduce it, this was one of the chief arguments of its advocates. Sir Thomas Elyot, in the *Governour*, 1531, writing about cosmography (what geography was then), says:

"For what pleasure it is, in one hour to behold those realms, cities, seas, rivers, and mountains that uneth [scarcely] in an old man's life can not be journeyed and pursued! What incredible delight is taken in beholding the diversities of people, beasts, fowls, fishes, trees, fruits, and herbs: to know the sundry manners and conditions of people, and the variety of their natures, and that in a warm study or parlour, without peril of the sea, a danger of long and painful journeys. I cannot tell what more pleasure should happen to a gentle wit than to behold in his own house every thing that within all the world is contained." — WATSON.

Geography as a discipline tends to establish certain habits of thinking, a geographical method of looking at the relations of the earth and man. There is a great mass of facts for concrete reasoning, and much opportunity for working out the abstract relations that exist between these facts. The logic of the causal relation, the method of comparison, the grouping of geographical facts, the generalization of principles, are some of the forms of reasoning required in geography. These habits of thought should be valuable not only in the study of geography itself, but in history, and in the geographical experiences of daily life.

Geography is no longer something to tax the memory merely. The thought content is as great as in any other subject, affording the best of opportunity for inspiring the imagination and cultivating clear, logical thinking.

CHAPTER II

CHILDREN'S INTERESTS IN GEOGRAPHY

Arrangement of subject matter. — Textbooks of geography fall into two general classes. The first may be called scientific or logical, the other psychological or pedagogical. In the former the facts of the science are arranged according to their natural, logical sequence, in modern days chiefly along evolutionary or causal lines, beginning with the astronomical and ending with the human side. The other class of texts recognize that the scientific order is unintelligible and uninteresting to the beginner, and that since the child's mind is quite different in its range from the adult's, the subject must be adapted to it in scope, arrangement, and method of presentation. The growth of this principle was slow and is not fully in force to-day.

Adaptation of texts. — The earlier textbooks were lacking in any attempt to come down to the level of the child, the only difference being that a beginner's text must be smaller than the adult's. So textbooks were made for children by abridging those intended for maturer students. Such abridgment, however, is not satisfactory.

Since about a century ago, when the teaching process itself was first subjected to study, much has been learned as to methods of instruction. The greatest thing brought out by this study is that instruction must be adapted to the mental capacity and interests of the learner.

Mental stages. — It is agreed among psychologists and educators that children pass through several periods or stages of mental growth, and that the studies and methods of instruction for one stage are not necessarily suited to another.

So far as teaching geography is concerned, while it must be remembered that they overlap and shade into each other, these stages are as follows:

The observational or perceptive stage. — At this period the child learns through his physical senses and thinks objectively and concretely. This is also the stage of learning the names of things. The reflective or reasoning ability is not yet marked.

The memorizing and imaginative stage. — The child is now able to go beyond the range of direct experience. His memory is retentive, perhaps more than at any other period; and his imagination is active. He can take the facts in his memory and recombine them into new relations through the imagination. He is not so dependent upon observation for his knowledge, and pictures and books become intelligible to him, because he has acquired the necessary sense experience in the first stage.

The reflective stage. — In this the reasoning ability is more mature, and the tendency to reflect on facts and to seek their relations is stronger. At this stage the children want to know the " Why " of things, and the abstract is of greater interest.

The teaching of geography must follow this order of the child's development. Upon it, if the teaching is to be economical and efficient, both the subject matter and the method of instruction must be based. The great fault with the older books, and with much recent instruction, is that they force little children to think in the way of adults. We have given to little beginners textbooks on the technical, logical plan. The consequence is that the child does not appreciate the subject; it is unintelligible and dull. In this respect geography is " one of the worst taught subjects in school." (Gibb.) Dr. G. Stanley Hall calls it " the sick man of the curriculum." " As an example of a science which might be full of life, and which may be taught as a string of the baldest and crudest and dullest facts imaginable, geography is preëminent." (O. Lodge.)

Children's interests in geography. — It is a current maxim in education that in order to secure the coöperation of the pupil, and to teach along the line of least resistance, and at the same time most efficiently, it is necessary first to secure his interest. Real effort in study is proportionate to interest. Secondary interests, such as reward and punishment, are not meant here, but rather a liking for the subject itself.

Several profitable studies have been made by W. S. Monroe, Anna Buckbee, Sarah Young, C. Brodeur, David Gibb, and others to discover the geographical interests of school children. "If you could travel, where would you like to go, and why would you like to go there?" or an equivalent question has been put to thousands of children. The children ranged through all school grades of geography. Monroe found that out of 4000 children in Massachusetts, the greatest number preferred to visit cities, especially those near by and frequently mentioned. Of these 355 wanted to visit New York City; the second largest number, 72, Boston. The older children preferred foreign cities, Paris, Rome, London. The next strongest interest, again chiefly among the older pupils, was in states and countries. California, Florida, Canada, England, China, and Japan were the favorites. The reasons assigned for desiring to visit these places were: to see friends or relatives, to visit a birthplace, some national or historic interest, an agreeable climate, the fruit, and in some cases art and religion. Of the 4000 only 200 wanted to see physical features, such as the ocean, mountains, etc.

David Gibb made similar studies, in 1907, and found the interests for different grades were as follows:

Grade IV — People, land and water forms, animals, buildings, China, Japan, Holland, ships, relatives.

Grade V — People, water, animals, cities, buildings, land, products, Japan, maps, plants, occupations, manufacturing.

Grade VI — People, buildings, occupations, water, land, scenery, animals, products, manufacturing, climate, maps, ships.

Grade VII — People, land, cities, occupations, animals, products, water, art, buildings, history, plants.

Grade VIII — People, water, animals, cities, land, buildings, plants, occupations, products, manufacturing, art.

From these studies we may get some idea of what children think about in geography. These data, however, are not absolute. It is evident that interests vary with locality, nationality, current events, with other subjects in the curriculum, and with the treatment of geography in any particular school. There is no question that people and their ways appeal most in geography; and that to beginners, the life of children in other lands is especially attractive. Jane Andrews' *Seven Little Sisters* will long remain a children's classic.

Application of the principle of interest in teaching. — Geography throughout the elementary school must have a human center. To throw the emphasis where it belongs in the elementary school, it should be defined as A Description of how Man lives upon the Earth.

Beginners in geography should study about people, their customs, houses, clothing, sports, family life, and about land and water features of the vicinity which they can study observationally.

The commercial sense comes later (fifth, sixth, seventh grades), and then occupations, manufacturing, products, processes, should be studied. In these grades maps appeal. And since memorizing is easy, the great bulk of places and facts necessary for conventional and practical use in later life should be drilled on here. The imagination should be fed with descriptive geography rich in interest.

In the last years of the course the causal relation, historic associations, and the commercial principles of geography are of greater interest. The facts previously learned may here be analyzed and generalized. Physical geography can be used more fully as the basis for the political. The heroic side of geography — discovery and exploration — should be touched upon, and the biographies of great explorers read. The more complex relations of human life, as shown in art, religion, society, and government, are now more interesting and better understood.

As the pupils mature and feel themselves a part of society the social motive may be appealed to. This has more of a moral force. It is a sort of educational conscience, which makes the pupil realize he owes it to himself and society to learn those things that will give him a proper standing with his associates, and will enable him to do his share of society's work. In this respect geography is eminently valuable. W. T. Harris placed geography next to history in social importance.

By following the natural interest of the child, the study is more than mere task work. It is the psychological course. Any other method will make the subject unintelligible, therefore uninteresting and dull to the pupil. Interest lacking, the pupil resorts to the method of learning by rote even what he does not understand.

Keep alive the glow of curiosity. When ennui takes the place of lively curiosity, geography becomes drudgery. The wonder motive should prevail throughout the whole course.

CHAPTER III

THE OBSERVATIONAL AND ORAL METHOD OF INSTRUCTION

Real basis of geography. — Geography is so generally associated with a textbook that it is easy to overlook the fact that the foundation for the subject is not a book at all, but the real physical features and forces of the earth, the plants and animals and living people. It is these that a beginner should study, and these realities should be used throughout the course as a check on the books. Geography should be studied objectively, concretely, as far as possible.

Their natural curiosity prompts the children to note and examine the multifarious aspects of human life, occupations, industrial processes, natural phenomena, earth and water features, and scenery, to formulate some sort of definition of these things, and to create in their minds something that corresponds to a map of the home locality. These definite, concrete concepts must necessarily be the basis for studying the geography of inaccessible regions, which has to be learned through hearsay, especially from books. The only conception a child can form of a mountain, if he has never seen one, must be through the imagination, aided by pictures, and comparison with such elevations as he may have actually seen.

Concrete teaching. — This self-instruction through observation should constitute the method of Home Geography (Chapter V). The pedagogical value of this method is universally admitted, though by no means universally practiced, and is generally dropped after the first steps in geography have been taken. In every grade, throughout life, interest in the real world should be maintained by reference to the actual geography of daily experience.

The child comes to geography with a fairly large mass of facts gained thus from actual experience in his home locality in the years before school begins. This apperceptive basis is further increased by the nature-study of the first years of school. In learning these things books were not used. The method of instruction hitherto employed should be continued when geography is begun.

First instruction oral. — At the beginning, instruction in geography should be oral. This lends itself best to the observational method of learning. It possesses the advantage of the personal quality given it by the teacher. It is a more flexible method than the textbook, and permits of variations and quick adaptations to the exigencies of the recitation. A teacher who has thoroughly prepared herself and is gifted with a fair imagination can usually make a topic more vivid and impressive than the impersonal, impassive textbook.

Unfortunately, we give pupils, even in home geography, a text, and then the vicious effects of cramming are soon realized. In some countries, Germany for example, pupils do not have such large, finely illustrated textbooks. They may have a mere epitome, or probably none. The teacher presents the subject orally, elaborating, illustrating, explaining, and enriching by correlation with history, art, and science.

Children like the personal element in geography. A teacher should draw upon her travel experiences to make her teaching vivid and interesting. Short, simple word pictures of famous places or scenery, or sketches of human life in different countries, if based upon personal experience, are always entertaining to children. Likewise, pupils should be encouraged to tell what they have seen on their journeys. By so doing, the air of unreality possessed by the world in the book will, at least for the moment, disappear.

There is danger, however, that too much work on the part of the teacher will leave the pupils mentally passive. To prevent this they should be taught to think actively, to think geographically. They should use their own observations and knowledge to make inferences and judgments. They should be given little geographical problems to work out.

Eliciting. — To this end the usual method of eliciting can be admirably employed. Through appropriate, thought-encouraging questions pupils can be led to observe the natural environment, specimens, experiments, pictures, maps, etc., and to form their own opinions as to the geographical relations shown. In a field lesson on a Stream, the teacher can thus get the pupils to see for themselves that water runs according to the slope, fast or slow; that it gathers in its course sediment, which it drops again at certain places. The relation between the motion of the water and the occurrence of deposit may thus be worked out. The subject of Rain may be developed, without telling very much, by performing suitable experiments in evaporation and condensation. Or, by eliciting, alone, pupils may from a physical map determine conditions of topography, climate, drainage, and other features. It is, in general, better to let the pupil thus see or find out facts for himself, than for the teacher to do all the talking on the subject. If properly conducted, this method gives the pupil initiative, and power to attack and work out geographical facts and relations for himself.

Development with textbook. — Even when textbooks are used there is still much opportunity for oral instruction. The usual method of "reciting" on the book is only a pitiable apology for oral instruction. The teacher who is not a slave to her book, who has a wider knowledge of the subject through collateral reading, and a knowledge of broad underlying principles, will not teach thus. She will appreciate the fact that parroting of ill-digested or totally misunderstood book statements, or even giving back the words of the book though understood, is not sufficient. She will do more than just "hear recitations."

Supplementing the text. — There is plenty of chance and need for the teacher to do some real, oral teaching, even when the pupils have studied the lesson in a book. For what has been studied must yet be developed, explained, illustrated by picture or word description; comparison must be made with the concrete experience of the pupils; or cross references to previous lessons that serve to elucidate must be brought out. In other words, the recitation, though based upon a book, should be considered an opportunity for thoughtful discussion of what has been assigned. It is safe to assume, in the more difficult lessons, involving abstract principles, causal connections, and correlations, that such are not fully appreciated, and need further discussion and organizing. This is the teacher's opportunity. As far as possible, let the pupils work out their own salvation. But there will always be need for developing and organizing. It is not too much to say that the teacher should present, in addition to what is given in the briefer textbooks, as much more of material which has a proper bearing on the topic.

Oral development before book study. — Many difficult lessons should be taught orally before they are assigned in a text. In this case, presentation by development is usually best. The principles and data of previous lessons needed for appreciating the new should be recalled. By directions and questions, the pupils should be led to think out the new lessons for themselves. The teacher presents the illustrative material, guides the course of the lesson, and arranges the matter so that the pupils make the necessary inferences, find the geographical data desired, form definitions, or generalize the geographical principles involved. After that the textbook will be understood, and is useful for review and drill. This is the German method, and it is admittedly the best.

This discussion has been presented to emphasize the importance of oral instruction and to insist upon a rational use of the textbook. It does not mean that the teacher must plan courses or lessons outside of the book. She may follow exactly the order of the book, and yet carry out the above suggestions. No textbook can take the space, however, to recall the foundation facts for each lesson, nor give all the elaboration needful, or give the pupil the necessary application and drill. These must always be supplied by the teacher.

Oral work in topical study. — In the topical and type study method (Chapter XIX) in upper grades, however, the teacher (or supervisor) needs to make her plan different from that of the ordinary text. This suggests another opportunity for independence from the textbook and for oral instruction.

CHAPTER IV

HOW TO USE THE TEXTBOOK

Necessity for the textbook. — The limits of Home Geography are comparatively narrow. To know about the regions beyond the horizon of actual experience, dependence must be placed on hearsay evidence, that of eyewitnesses (explorers and travelers), authors (compilers), and teachers. This must necessarily remain the chief means of acquisition of geographical knowledge, and herein lies the main danger of geographical instruction.

Pedagogy of textbook.—Textbooks, to-day, are more than books on subject matter. They represent the methods and advice of the best instructors. This a teacher should bear in mind before trying to improve on the scheme and making out a course of her own. The approach to the subject, the general arrangement and order of topics, and the general relations and principles to be derived from this order, are all the result of practical teaching experience and wisdom. Many textbooks not only give explicit directions to the teacher as to teaching methods, but also take into account the pupil's difficulty, and provide for it by careful arrangement and typography, and sometimes by definite hints for study, suggestions for self-testing, questions and exercises to stimulate pupils to make applications, and references for collateral reading. Teachers will do well to follow these authors' suggestions seriously.

Shortcomings of textbooks.—The ordinary elementary school textbook in geography cannot, however, do justice to the subject. The science is altogether too comprehensive and rich in content to remain interesting after being condensed into the limits of books of the usual size. By the unavoidable compression, the living juice of the subject—that is, the incidental allusions to history, the references to science for explanation, the numerous cross-references needed to knit together old facts and new, — these must all be left out, and the result is the usual formal, terse, laconic, uninteresting textbook, the dry bones of the subject. The essential facts are all there, to be sure. But they need the living voice of the teacher to make them real and vivid. They must be largely supplemented to become interesting. There are some textbooks in use now that attempt to supply what these others lack.

Supplementary readers are a device to furnish additional matter, and to infuse life and interest. (Chapter XIII.)

The textbook cannot, moreover, do justice to the pupil. It is an unconscious, inanimate teacher which cannot see when a pupil flounders; which does not stop to permit reflection; which does not repeat, and in somewhat different language, to give the pupil another chance to grasp its meaning; which does not see when the pupil has forgotten, at least for the moment, some facts of a previous lesson necessary as an apperceptive basis for the new, and so does not make helpful cross-connections; which does not stop to clinch the facts learned by means of the necessary drill. The living teacher only can do all this.

The mode of presentation in a textbook of geography is usually a formal, rather dogmatic statement of principles, and a laconic, descriptive narrative. Rarely, unless it be by map study, does a textbook elicit or develop a lesson. The tendency, therefore, particularly with young children, is to read the text without reflection and judgment, and to rely too much on the easier and quicker method of committing to memory.

The textbook presents in clear, systematic, though usually uninteresting form, the essential facts of the subject. School geographies are generally mere epitomes. As a "Leitfaden," a sort of daily reference book with which to work out assignments for lessons, and for reviews of orally presented lessons, textbooks are highly useful. "After all, the textbook is as good or as bad as it is *allowed* to be." (Conwentz.)

The teacher should repeat often to herself and to her

pupils that the book is but a means; not an end. The book is not geography itself, but *about* geography, and it is necessary for the reader to project his imagination to the real people, the real occupations, the real scenery, and earth features and forces so meagerly and faintly represented by the printed page.

The geography the first information book. — It is a noteworthy point that the first book given to pupils, from which they are to get information or facts, is a geography. True, they have readers, spellers, and other books before this, but these are chiefly to develop the art of expression. Geographies are given for the study of facts. But the pupils have not yet learned to study for information. In fact, they still have their difficulties with the mechanical side of reading. Only in recent years has this matter of study been taken up in General Method. Some few of the later geographies have valuable hints to the pupil advising him how to use the text.

The introduction of the textbook should be gradual. Home geography requires no text. The first geography should be taught orally. But in the first course in general descriptive geography a book should be used. The first lessons in the book should be studied in the recitation, in school. Let the teacher tell her pupils the purpose of the book, and ask them to read silently, *for the thought*, a paragraph or so, and then aloud. The teacher should test the pupil to see if he has understood what he read by requiring him to repeat in his own words. It is important (some definitions excepted) to demand that the pupils paraphrase and not use the identical words of the book. The pupil should be taught to distinguish the difference between *words* and *ideas*. It is in such study that the true function of the teacher lies — to guide and assist the pupil in learning for himself. Sympathy, patience, skill, and ingenuity are all required for this.

The teacher herself should show an attitude of interest. This will make the pupils more enthusiastic. A teacher who "hates" geography and shows it cannot hope to succeed in interesting others in it.

During such study lessons the teacher should use illustrative material, appropriate stories, and descriptions drawn from outside the text. She should explain and elaborate and make thoroughly interesting what the textbook has treated so briefly.

Methods of study. — As the pupil gets older he may be permitted to base his preparation more and more upon the text and other books. By this time he should have learned to study independently. He should not try to memorize the words, but should seek to retain the information contained in them, the facts, the ideas. While reading a paragraph or a page he should consciously try to find out "what the author is trying to tell him." He should know how to read a portion thinkingly, then close the book and tell himself what he has learned. It is a good plan to note down a brief, logical memorandum of each portion as acquired. This should not be a copy, but the gist of the matter, in the pupil's own language. The teacher should show the pupil how to make outlines, synopses, or summaries of study. One reading is usually not sufficient to clinch the study. The first reading is to dig out the isolated facts; the second, to organize them into a whole or unity. This organizing is often best done in class with the aid of the teacher. Blackboard synopses or summaries are a useful help. The younger pupils cannot make these unaided, though older children should. The teacher should in the recitation help to bring out the relation of the various ideas of the lesson, arranging them in a synopsis, as main topic, subordinate topics, coördinate topics, etc.; or welding them all together into a general principle. This unifying work, so often sadly neglected or taken for granted, is the climax of the lesson. After all, the important thing is not so much to learn the thousand and one facts of geography, as their relations, and the principles they embody.

If geography is as serious business as this, no wonder that school officers often suggest that no home work be assigned in it, but that it be studied at school under the guidance of the teacher.

Methods of assignment. — The success or failure of the lesson is largely due to the way it has been assigned. In spite of ridicule, the practice of assigning the new lesson as "so many pages" still persists. Some of the old geographies of a hundred years ago were thus divided, without reference to the unity or natural relations of the subject, into "lessons," each about as much as could be mastered daily, the end coming anywhere, perhaps in the middle of a topic.

Time is not wasted in the careful assignment of a lesson,—in fact, just the reverse. For beginners, the teacher may very profitably read aloud through the lesson, dwelling on this point or that, to elucidate, or show which is the important, which the incidental, and finally briefly summarizing.

Or, if the pupils are older, as an aim or interest a sort of title may be given to the lesson, in the light of which it is to be studied: "In to-morrow's lesson you will learn how —— came to be located, and why it grew to be such a large city." "The next lesson tells you what the people do for a living." "This lesson tells you how irrigation is carried on."

Again, pupils may be given sets of definite, properly organized questions, the answers to which they are to find in the text: "Where is Alaska? To whom did it formerly belong? What native peoples live there? Learn about their houses, clothing, food, amusements, home life." Etc. This suggests the proper emphasis, and leads to definiteness in preparation.

A similar plan is to write a synoptical outline as a guide for study in which, through heads and subheads, the proper relationships may be indicated.

Older pupils should occasionally be given little geographical problems to work out: "The next lesson is The Rainfall of the Western Half of the United States. Study the rainfall conditions from the coast to the Great Plains. First review page —, which tells about the prevailing winds in that latitude; page — about rain; and page — about the topography of that section. Refer also to the relief map, page —. Then read the new lesson, from the bottom of page — to the middle of page —, connecting with the old lessons above-mentioned. Note where the greatest rainfall occurs, and find the reason; where the least, and why. Compare your reading with the rainfall map, page —. Also read page — of Supplementary Reader."

To these suggestions may be added that the lesson, especially if it is a difficult one should sometimes take the form of an oral development. After this the pupil may review the matter in the text.

In topical and type studies great care must be used to give definite directions as to what to study, and where to find it. Here the consecutive order of a textbook may not be followed, but the material may have to be gathered by the pupils from various parts of the textbook, from supplementary readers, magazines, encyclopedias, and other sources. The pupils should be taught how to use an index and table of contents; though, to begin with, references should be assigned definitely by page.

Such careful assignments not only tell the pupils what to study, but teach them to discriminate, and above all to see that the textbook is not an end, but a means. They do much to provoke interest in the new lesson, and prevent the textbook work from becoming purely memoriter, than which nothing can be more stupid and dull.

Relation of lessons to the course. — It is obvious that the method of assignment and presentation indicated require that the teacher do more than merely study each lesson at the same time as the pupil. It is a shiftless, hand-to-the-mouth policy, where the teacher assigns merely by so many pages, or the next section, without clearly knowing what these are about. It is disastrous to the children. The teacher owes it to herself and her pupils to have a wider view of her subject than this. Naturally, by teaching the same grade work year after year she gets the relations of the lessons in her grade. But in teaching a course the teacher should know its scope, order, and relation to the work of the grades below and above. She should read far enough ahead of her class to see to what to-morrow's lesson is leading. In this way the lessons are not isolated, and dislocated;

but are organized to carry out a definite scheme of presentation.

The suggestions here offered are not intended to increase the burdens of the teacher, but rather to assist her to systematize and economize her school energies. In the end, the methods that economize and make efficient the pupils' efforts are an economy and satisfaction to the teacher.

CHAPTER V

HOME GEOGRAPHY

"In the place where a child lives should he first find his orientation in reality and study the region in all its relationships." — RITTER.

Synthetic growth of geographical knowledge. — The earliest study of a child is getting his bearings in the world. Sight, touch, and hearing teach the child the first rudiments of space relations. The narrow circle of the horizon of the infant thus enlarges from the cradle to the home, then to the garden, in widening reaches. Then the home block is explored, and a mental map is made of it. The children on the block, and the grown people, their games and their work; the corner grocery; the blacksmith's and the carpenter's shop near by; the wagons and cars coming from outside his known world and vanishing again into regions unknown; the flowers, trees, birds, insects, and other life; the weather, pleasant and unpleasant; the winds for paper windmills and kites; the cold that makes good sleighing and skating; the beautiful moon and stars, — all these and many more — all true geographical matter, the little child gets acquainted with, and this for the most part without instruction from others, though frequently his irrepressible curiosity leads him to some unfathomable problem and he questions his elders, "Why?"

First geography by observation. — This early self-instruction through personal experiences and direct observation is the most vivid and real geography possible, and furnishes the concrete basis upon which the less tangible geography of regions beyond the reach of experience must rest.

This getting acquainted with the home region is Home Geography. We talk about beginning it in the third or fourth school year. The fact is, the child began it years before, and we but continue the study. Being a natural mode of learning, one in which the child is practiced, it should be continued in school to still further enlarge the view of the world.

Home geography is the study of the occupations, historic associations, and civic life of the community; it includes the first lessons on land and water forms — hills, valleys, brooks, rocks, soil, scenery; on the weather and the seasons. It is a very simple study, and there is nothing technical about it.

The scope of home geography varies according to the location and conditions of the school. The home geography of a place should have something *peculiar* to that place. The historic factor of one locality would differ from that of another; the industrial factor would show some difference; the physiographic features would be more alike, probably, though with differences. Home geography connects with and includes the nature-study of previous grades, the animals and vegetal life, and the natural phenomena. These all help to paint the local picture.

For knowledge of locality. — Home geography, a composite study of many local elements, is taught that the pupils may come to know their local environment, and so, even as children, and later as citizens, appreciate it the more, and adapt themselves better to it. One of the most powerful primal instincts is the love of home. Even national patriotism is but a phase of this feeling. It is therefore of the highest civic importance that the geography of the home be taught.

As a basis for world geography. — From a pedagogical standpoint, also, home geography is the only rational basis for advanced geography. Ziller was first to recognize this as a working principle of geography teaching. It is through what we know of the home district that we judge the world. By imagination, the wayside stream is expanded into a mighty river; the local hills become the Alps; the ordinary simple relations with the shop and store become manufacturing and international commerce. The simple concepts of home geography are the types with which we compare the features of foreign lands. Here the need of real observation and personal experience is clearly seen. The concepts thus formed are not abstract, hazy, vague, and unreal, but definite and real. By continuing the method of observational study, the school can add to such stock of definite notions. What the child has "picked up" untaught, or self-tutored, may be studied further in detail, and added to, and new relations may be shown therein, or new lines followed.

Home geography in upper grades. — A more intensive course in home geography should be given in the upper grades when the pupils can appreciate the more complex relations of commercial and civic life, and know more of history. It is true that local physiography is studied in the upper grades, but the human side is neglected.

The center of each person's world is the home locality. The rest of the world is important only so far as it is related to the home region. The place where people spend most of their lives is worthy of a deeper study than can be given it in the primary grades. It is a mistake to drop home geography there. In every grade it can be made use of to add vividness and reality to general geography.

In European practice home geography is realized more fully by studying geography on the radial plan; that is, starting from the home region along certain lines of historic, political, or commercial interest to more distant centers, and returning to start anew in some other direction to again connect with other centers more or less closely associated with the home region. A very practical unity is thus furnished for the subject.

The synthetic method in geography: Induction. In general, in home geography the child proceeds from the known to the unknown in enlarging, concentric circles, or lengthening radii. This is the Synthetic Method, building up a larger whole from the details. It is also Inductive: from a group of related facts the child makes simple generalizations, which he applies deductively to new cases. He may not be conscious of the logic of his thoughts, and just how he gets his generalizations, nor may he be able to state these in words, and yet he has some concepts and principles useful for daily application.

Field lessons. — The ideal way to teach home geography is without a textbook. The book habit usually vitiates its spirit. The best way to form correct concepts of real things is not to read about them in a book, but to observe the things themselves. Just as travel is the ideal and most pleasant way of studying foreign places, so travel at home is the ideal method of studying the home environment. Field lessons, excursions, visits to historic places, visits to museums and other places of interest, collecting trips, are under the right conditions delightful, proper, and very pedagogical methods of learning home geography.

Every one travels more or less about the home locality. Our walks and rides about town are, however, usually limited to our routine paths of business and occasional pleasure, and most of us could find many places of human or natural interest with which we are still unfamiliar. It is a common remark, especially in larger places, that visitors who come for sight-seeing know more of a place than the natives. Many delightful discoveries can be made by going out of our usual path occasionally, going to our destination by one route, returning by another. The exploring instinct, if kept alive, will do much to add pleasure and interest, to vary the monotony of routine, and to increase the appreciation of the home community.

Field lessons in country and city. — In rural districts field lessons on earth features and earth forces, on vegetation and animal life, and the country industries will be most feasible. In cities the human phase of geography is most easily observed, though the physical is by no means lacking. It is surprising, when one seeks for it, to find so much of nature in the heart of a big city. The city-bred teacher is apt to overlook it. We see that in which we are most interested. The city inhabitant is most interested in man and his ways. Perhaps that is all the more reason for teaching a city child how to find nature also.

Field lessons are not necessarily far afield, and are not

difficult to give. The following lessons can be taught in the schoolyard, the street in front of the school, a vacant lot near by, in the school garden, on the school roof, or a park close at hand; weather and sky studies, different kinds of plants and animals and the conditions of their life, rocks and soil, processes of tillage and cultivation, weathering, erosion and deposit, the story of a pebble, history of glaciated rock, minerals, land and water forms, etc. The neighboring streets display a wealth of topics from human geography, — races, nationalities, customs, costumes, various trades and shops, many products and manufactures, intercourse, transportation and commerce, evidences of the civic organization, etc. It is a mistake to go miles for what may be found close at hand.

Since near-by field lessons will entail no difficulties as to time, permission from school authorities and parents, long distances and carfare, dangerous crossings, etc., there is little excuse for teachers in cities near large parks or in the outskirts, or in village and country schools for not giving field lessons. But it is well to remember that the mechanical difficulties of mass teaching, and the ordinary routine of a large school system, render field lessons at a considerable distance well-nigh impossible. Much is usually made of the European practice of taking pupils on long walking trips, or even excursions of several days. This is, however, generally only in the smaller places and special schools, and with older students. It is absolutely foolish and dangerous to undertake long field trips with little children through large cities. Every parent knows the responsibilities of trying to manage his own flock on such occasions, and has a perfect right to refuse to let his children go on a long trip with a large class, under the management perhaps of only a single teacher. It is highly commendable, however, for a teacher to chaperon a small, enthusiastic group of pupils who are especially desirous of making a field trip.

Much is also made of visiting shops, factories, and other industrial places. This also is desirable, if done without compulsion and with real interest, by small parties. But if the practice should become universal, these industrial plants, and many public institutions, must close their doors to such visits because of too great interference with the regular business. So long as the thing is not overdone, such visits are usually not denied, and often welcomed. It goes without saying that permission should always first be sought to visit places not generally open to the public. This avoids disappointment and trouble, and often secures a pleasant reception, official guides and instructors.

Again, it must be remembered that a visit to a flour mill, for example, is not only a very risky thing on account of the many dangerous belts and cogwheels of the machinery, but is generally absolutely worthless from the standpoint of a study of the process. Here, as in many another modern industrial plant, the process is so specialized, and divided up, and carried on in so many different parts of the mill, that a child, or even a grown person, would get practically no concept of the actual process, except of its marvelous complexity and system.

In visiting museums and collections, too much should not be attempted. The visit should be for the study of a limited portion of the exhibit of special geographical interest, related to the current work.

So it is necessary to use common sense about field lessons. Where it can be done easily and safely, and does not require too great a sacrifice of time, they should be given occasionally. Otherwise, they had better be dispensed with.

Observational geography without field lessons. — It is fortunate that the average child, even a city child in the most congested section, is in the habit, and has been for years, of using his eyes and ears, and has already, on entering school, a foundation of real geographical experiences so great that all the field lessons possible under *adverse* conditions would be but "a drop in the bucket" in comparison. It is the accidental and incidental observations of daily life that furnish the child his real geography. Children should be encouraged to be interested in what goes on around them, to watch the life and the occupations of the community, and to note the local physical features. The show windows with wares on display (sometimes showing processes of manufacture); the open door of the blacksmith's, shoemaker's, and carpenter's shops; the ships at the docks; the drays hauling the merchandise of the world through the streets; the bridges, ferries, trains; the telephone and telegraph; public parks and pleasure resorts; zoölogical gardens and museums; the local hills, valleys, and streams, all appeal daily to the child's curiosity. He knows, perhaps, where the Soldiers' Monument is, and the flour mill, though he may not know the history of the former, nor the process in the latter. But the history of the monument may be just as well taught in school, and the process of making flour can be shown, even more clearly than in the mill itself, by the simple experiment of grinding some grain, according to the primitive method, between two stones.

Illustrative material in classroom.— Even where field lessons cannot be safely or economically given, reliance should be placed on the pupil's store of direct knowledge, and with this foundation of reality, the topics of home geography should be further developed by means of specimens, experiments, pictures, and other illustrative material. Thus the teaching may be still concrete, and not by the book.

Sometimes "the mountain may be brought to Mahomet," — experiments on evaporation and condensation bring the rain into the schoolroom, teaching, in fact, something not so clearly seen in the natural process outside. A river may be made in a sand tray, and would show, more easily, because under much better control, than the Hudson or the Mississippi, the processes of erosion, transportation, and deposit. True, a sand tray river and mountain are pathetic imitations of the real thing, but are the next best thing when the real river or mountain is inaccessible. Better these symbols than word symbols alone. A sand model of a mountain, of course, would be out of place in a Swiss school, or in Denver. In the country, where a brook flows near the school, or in the city, if there is one in an easily accessible park, or suburban district, the schoolroom brook would be a farce. The wise teacher would wait for a rainy day for observation of the brook in the gutter.

Preparation for a field lesson. — Field lessons require careful preparation. The teacher should know her subject matter. She should visit the place and note the best ways and means of getting there, the difficulties to be encountered, the abundance or absence of data for observation, etc. She should plan the order of study to give it unity.

A definite aim should be given for the trip. "We shall look in at the shoemaker's shop to see how shoes are made." "It has stopped raining. Let us go outside and look at the water running in the gutter to see what it can teach us." "We have been reading about the Indians. We are going to the museum to look at Indian weapons, tools, clothing, etc." Such a prelude will focus attention, and give a definite purpose.

Management of classes. — The shorter outdoor lessons may be given in school hours. Longer ones had better be taken after school, or on Saturdays. Some school authorities set aside certain days to be used for field lessons. Sometimes the last period of the day is used and the time extended to after school hours. For trips out of school hours no compulsion as to attendance should be exercised. For trips involving any responsibility the parents' consent should be secured, and any trips after school hours should be announced beforehand to the parents. In the poorer communities carfare and other expenses must be taken into account.

Children should not be taxed beyond their strength on excursions. If the distance is too great for walking there and back with ease, it must be abandoned, or transportation provided. In large cities this is a special problem. It is possible to charter special street cars, sight-seeing automobiles, or boats. Otherwise there is always the liability of a large party being divided in trying to secure passage in public conveyances.

It is useless to try to take a class of forty or fifty pupils, except on shorter trips in the immediate vicinity of the school. For more extended trips, the teacher should have assistance, or the class should be divided into manageable sections. Sometimes mothers may be invited to help supervise the children. This stimulates interest in the trip.

A good disciplinarian will have no special trouble on field trips. Naturally the pupils will feel less restraint on such occasions than in school, but they should attend strictly to the business in hand, and remain in a more or less compact body near the teacher, ever ready to respond to her directions and her discussions of the topic of study.

Unless the trip is planned with care and executed with promptness, firmness, and common sense, and with its purpose always in mind, it is apt to turn into a "lark" for the pupils, and, as Samantha Allen would say, "a pleasure exertion" for the teacher.

Method of instruction. — The presentation of the outdoor lessons may be less formal than in school, but should follow in general the same practice. The pupils should be led to see things for themselves, and to think about them. Questions and directions by the teacher should guide the observation and reasoning. Physical features and forces are best studied thus by development. Industrial and historical topics are better treated in a simple lecture by the teacher. The children should be allowed to contribute whatever they can. Field lessons should be reviewed and amplified in school after the trip, and application should be made of what was thus learned. Textbook study and supplementary reading should follow a field trip.

Theoretically, a field lesson should precede the study of the topic in school. Then the trip is one of discovery. Practically it is common to take a class on an excursion after one or several topics have been studied, and an interest in them has been aroused. Then the trip becomes one of verification or corroboration of the previous study. This method economizes in the time spent on the trip. A considerable amount of subject matter can thus be covered.

CHAPTER VI

LESSONS IN HOME GEOGRAPHY TO ILLUSTRATE METHOD

A few concrete examples of subject matter and method of presentation are given below, not to furnish a course, but to illustrate the foregoing chapters, and to bring out special points in method.

Points of the compass. — The sun is the most common means of orientation used in life. Note the place of sunrise and sunset, and the direction of the sun at noon. Also find north. Fix the names of these directions. The directions may be marked in the schoolroom with letters on the walls, or with crosslines on the floor or ceiling. A weather vane on the school, or on a pole in the yard, helps to make a habit of getting one's bearings. Locational ideas in geography rest upon this basis of orientation. In home geography application of the points of the compass should be made in pointing towards familiar places, or in going to them.

An interesting exercise is to determine the noon shadow of a vertical stick placed in a south window, or in the schoolyard. The north and south line can thus be determined with fair accuracy.

The pupils are old enough to be interested in the magnetic compass. This should be shown and its operation taught. The pupils would like to make their own compasses from magnetized knitting needles, watch spring, or other hard steel. A compass used on a field trip would add interest and assist in mapping out the district. Finding the north by the North Star is also an interesting exercise. The well-known fact that moss and algæ grow more abundantly on the shady, damp, north side of trees, rocks, walls, etc., may also be brought out by observation.

Bird's-eye view. — In many cases it is possible to get a general view of the locality from some high hill or building, perhaps from the roof or upper windows of the school. This is a very instructive lesson for locating the different sections of the community, prominent local natural features, buildings, etc., and for getting relations otherwise not easily seen. Use the points of the compass. This study is excellent as a basis for the conception of a map.

Occupations and trades. — Children know enough about the commoner occupations to serve as a basis for an indoor lesson. The aim is not so much to learn a special trade as to teach certain principles of geography, — about raw material and the finished product; division of labor; interdependence of people; value of invention, labor, and money, in industry; need or demand (market), buying and selling; communication, transportation, and commerce. It must be remembered that some of these terms may be out of place in home geography. The principles they stand for need not be forced upon the attention of the children. The teacher, however, should keep them in mind, as the geographical purpose of these industrial lessons. These generalizations will not come all at once, in the first lesson. Only after many lessons, perhaps only after months, do these facts gradually dawn on the pupil's mind. Even though the tools, materials, and processes are soon forgotten by the pupil, he will retain a useful residue for the further appreciation of other industrial studies.

To the child, carpentry, blacksmithing, bread-making, are not as interesting as the carpenter, the blacksmith, and the baker. It is the personal element, the human element, that appeals. Therefore such lessons should be presented for the most part, or at least introduced, from the personal side.

These lessons should be based on the previous experience of the children, perhaps on preliminary, individual observations, under direction, or, if convenient, by the whole class visiting the place of the trade or occupation. Specimens of the commercial materials used, possibly tools and pictures, add to the reality of the schoolroom lesson. Some of the processes may be illustrated by simple experiments.

Primitive methods of primitive peoples appeal more to the child than the highly specialized modern processes. Nothing could show more clearly the making of flour than the simple schoolroom experiment of crushing and grinding wheat between two stones, and sifting the flour from the bran, as some Indian tribes and other races still do. This is the process of the modern mill in epitome. The threshing process is just as simply shown by rubbing some heads of wheat in the palm of the hand, thus shelling the kernels. Then by blowing away the chaff the winnowing is illustrated. A child would get very little from a visit to a spinning factory, yet the process may be nicely shown by twisting some parallel fibers of cotton or other material between the fingers till a firm, strong yarn or thread is formed. The complicated modern weaving process can be beautifully typified on the ordinary school hand loom.

Sometimes these primitive arts are appropriately studied in correlation with studies of primitive peoples, as, for example, the story of Hiawatha. A natural and artistic setting is then given to such a study. Children also like to make believe they are primitive people, or Robinson Crusoes, and their imaginary necessities may be used to stimulate their inventiveness in working out experimentally these simple arts.

Nature-study and geography should be correlated in these industrial studies. Through the former, the pupil should learn the origin and nature of the more common animal and vegetable materials used in commerce, — wheat, corn, pine, flax, cattle, sheep, iron, copper, granite, marble, etc. (See Chapter XXI, Correlation of Nature Study and Geography.)

Begin the teaching of industries with the study of local types like the following:

The blacksmith. — Where is the shop? Describe the smith; appearance, strength, clothing. Why "black" smith? Quotation from Longfellow's *The Village Blacksmith* to interest the children in his personality. Do you like to look into his shop? Why? What is it like? What does he do? Describe the forge and bellows (drawings), the anvil, tools. The melody of the anvil. The sparks. Why must the iron be heated? (Experiment with sealing wax, glass, or pieces of iron wire.) What does the smith make of the iron? Process of making a horseshoe. (Show shoe, nails.) How a horse is shod. For whom does the blacksmith do this work? Why does not every man shoe his own horse? How do other people serve the blacksmith? Why is a blacksmith shop likely to be found at country crossroads? (Illustrate the study with appropriate anecdotes.)

The grocer. — In this study of foods begin at the home: The family need. Trace foodstuffs from the grocery back to the market; to the truck garden outside of the town; to the farms; perhaps to other parts of the nation; and even to foreign lands. Ideas of ultimate sources of food supply, shipment, means of transportation, commerce, are taught by this lesson.

Transportation. — Study the delivery of packages from the store. What is a delivery boy? A truckman? An express company? Assistance from beasts of burden. Importance of the horse. Other animals used in other lands. The need of good roads and streets. Simple sketch of road-making process. Brief study of some principal roads leading out of town. Whither do they lead? Are roads always straight? Why not? Hills, lakes, rivers, as obstacles, and how avoided or surmounted. Why does a road often go around a hill? Why located in valleys of rivers or mountains? Sketch of traffic as observed by children. Different kinds of vehicles, and their uses. Different kinds of things transported. Trace some of these staples from farm, forest, or mine to city; from shop and factory to homes and stores; from the steamboat landing and the railroad station to the factory or store, etc. Follow with the study of shipping and railroads.

Such lessons should at least teach the worth of labor, and the interdependence of man and man. Keep the local color — do not teach in an abstract, colorless way. Try to get children to call up in imagination the familiar places referred to.

The fruit stand. — Ask the pupils to observe the variety of fruits and nuts offered for sale. Let them note the labels, or inquire of the dealer as to the source of various fruits. Thus they will discover oranges from Florida, figs from Turkey, dates from Algeria, blueberries from Cape Cod, nuts from Brazil, pecans from Louisiana, apples from New York, etc. Perhaps the pupils will bring specimens of fruit to school for an exhibit. The materials should also be used in the nature lessons. This study of fruits may be used as an approach to foreign geography. Many a child, like Mignon, has longed to fly to the land where the oranges grow.

Civics from home geography. — Children are not old enough to appreciate the subject of local government in its official and legal aspects. There is, however, a side that appeals; and through this, rudiments of civics may be presented. The administrative side interests pupils. The policeman on his post, the firehouse around the corner, the postman who brings the daily mail, the street cleaner, the ash man, etc., mean more to the child than mayor, treasurer, aldermen, judges, etc. They come more directly and frequently into the child's life, and the work of these public servants may teach pupils a respect for law and order, and simple duties as little citizens. The heroic element in the lives of these men should be shown. The instinct of hero worship in the child will respond to it.

Historic studies. — These should be based upon visits to historic places of the locality, historic buildings, and monuments. There is no place so young that it does not have something of a past, though it may glory chiefly in its future. The early, primeval condition, incidents of its founding, reason for its location, brief sketch of great events in its history, simple sketches of its great men, buildings of historic interest, monuments to commemorate men and events, are topics to be studied.

The study of history has not in these grades gone very far, and the teacher must be careful not to take the pupils beyond their depth into events they never heard of, and in which they are not interested. The reality of the scenes and incidents must be preserved by constant attachment to familiar objects and places, familiar names of families still represented, by relics and heirlooms loaned for the occasion, by facts the children may be able to gather from their parents, grandparents, and " the oldest inhabitant." It should be the aim to develop through such lessons a sort of local patriotism.

Hills and valleys. — These should be studied in a field lesson, if convenient. Hills and valleys give the child a notion of topography, " the face of the land," " the lay of the land," so important in the map study later on. The actual climbing " up hill and down dale " gives the child muscular sensations useful in appreciating the geographical side of the matter. The bird's-eye view and the expanding horizon are also valuable. To children who have never seen mountains, hills must stand as prototypes.

Follow a street, road, or path among the hills. Note how it conforms to the valley. Why? Leave the valley and climb a hill by the shortest route. Note the exertion. Change the ascent to a zigzag and note greater ease with gentler slope. Note how the roads choose the lowest grade or zigzag up the slopes. The study will emphasize the fact that hills are obstacles to travel and traffic. Note where the town is situated. Some towns for a special reason are located on the tops of hills, but most towns are on lower ground. Why?

As the hill is climbed, note the water courses. Whither do they lead? Perhaps a stream occupies the lowest part of the valley, certainly in rainy weather. Let pupils trace the drainage. Let them see how the tributary streams come down the side valleys. Note the hills that separate one such tributary from its neighbor. The term divide or waterparting may be used.

Arrived at the top, survey the landscape, the lay of the land as a bird sees it. Locate familiar places. Find directions with compass. Note the relation of the city to the surrounding farm lands. Note how "all the roads lead to Rome." Refer to the travel and traffic.

Note the enlarged horizon. Suggest idea of distant

towns beyond the reach of vision. Perhaps a train may be seen winding out of the town. Where is it going?

The sense of freedom, the stronger breezes, the beauty of the landscape, the sky and atmospheric effects, should all be enjoyed. Is there any difference in vegetation on the north and south sides of a hill? Why?

Note the hillside industries, — wood chopping, grazing; orchards and farms on the lower slopes; perhaps quarrying or mining.

As the descent is finished, again note the beauty of the hills, and the valleys between. Note the more imposing height, the sky line, the restricted horizon, the shadows and light effects, the beauty of forest-clad hills as compared with the balder heights from which the forests have been cleared.

On the level prairie this lesson would be impossible. In the heart of a metropolis likewise. Yet here too, in less æsthetic fashion, the idea of slope may and must be taught. The land is nowhere so level that water will not run off. In cities the paved streets are graded so as to slope from the middle to the sides, and toward the end of the block. These "hills," or slopes, together with models of sand and pictures of real hills, must be used to develop the idea of topography.

The brook. — This is a good subject to stimulate the imagination. The average city child and teacher is more apt to think of Tennyson's *Brook* than of the real thing; of the brook "in the country" or "in the mountains," but not in the city.

If the school is conveniently situated near a brook, the best way is to take the class to it. In a congested city district, however, this is impossible. Fortunately, there is everywhere at hand a concrete, though prosaic, example of a "brook"; that is, the rain or snow water running in the gutters. Æsthetics aside, nothing better can be found than this to teach the essential geographical notions about streams, — source, slope, divide, watershed,. tributary, velocity, erosion, sediment, transportation, deposit; and even falls, rapids, deltas, and lakes. The children of the city play in the gutter-brook, wading; floating imaginary ships and toy boats; making bridges, dams, waterfalls; and even setting up miniature water wheels. Thus the childish play in the gutter is the basis for ideas of navigation, water power, commerce, and the physiography of streams. The city field lesson should be started at the gutter, and not in imagination in the country.

The prosaic features of a brook may be farther represented in a sand tray. If the teacher semi-seriously suggests, "This is a hill," "This is a rain storm" (sprinkling on water), "And this is a river," the imagination of the children will make believe that a larger example is before them. This classroom experiment shows finely all the physical features of running water.

The physiographic side of a brook should not be taught too technically, in the abstract, nor should it be left unconnected with the human side. The study should be very simple. " What a brook can do," or " The work of the brook," suggest the treatment better than " erosion, transportation, and deposit." The main physiographic facts to be learned at this stage are: that water flows downhill, and faster down the steeper slopes; that running water can wear off and wash away mud, sand, and gravel, and that these are dropped here and there when the water stops flowing, or flows slowly; that valleys are dug out; that hills are worn down, and lakes filled by the sediment; that waterfalls are formed by certain natural or artificial obstructions. The ordinary map terms applied to streams in common geography should be learned.

As before stated, the inanimate side of geography is not as interesting to children as the living. A technical study of such things as drainage conditions, erosion, transportation, etc., would be a rather bare picture to the child. The human and the scenic or æsthetic side need to be emphasized to complete the picture.

There is a peculiar fascination in running water. Children and grown people feel its spell. The picturesque setting of most natural streams; the variable motion of the water; the different sounds of ripples, falls, and clinking pebbles; the distinct unity of character, or individuality; its coming from "somewhere" and going "somewhere" catch the fancy. It is a curious and significant fact that streams are described in terms of human life, — a stream has a head and a mouth. It can run and fall. Streams pay each other tribute, or rob each other of their watersheds. A brook laughs. A stream even typifies the career of human life. From time immemorial streams have been associated with the life of man. No wonder they have a peculiar influence and interest. Poets and painters have always found their muses by the banks of running water. A little of this sort of thing should pervade the lesson on the brook in home geography.

After the notion of what a stream is has been developed, and the ordinary map terms used in connection with it have been taught, then the brook should be given its natural setting "in the country" or "in the mountains." Let the pupils relate their vacation experiences with brooks, and have them tell what they like about it. Show numerous pictures of brooks in various moods and of different types. The study should not be limited to the water and bed merely, but the banks, valleys, and surrounding scenery; the rocks and cliffs; the trees, flowers, and ferns; the birds and other animal life associated with the stream should all be connected with the brook to make a unity such as the brook usually presents. Its relations to human life should by all means be brought out: the uses of the stream as a water supply for man, or a drinking place for cattle, for fishing, boating, water power, and its scenic value. Before leaving the subject, the stream should be enlarged to the dimensions of a river, and further uses suggested, such as navigation, irrigation, etc. The reverse of the picture, the flooding and destruction of land and other property, and the necessity of fording, ferrying, or bridging, should be shown.

These relations to life should not merely be summarized as a conclusion to the lesson, but should be dwelt on in a study of concrete, local examples, and developed from the study of pictures and through supplementary reading. Considering the vast importance of streams as geographical factors, such study is by no means excessive.

Weather study. — There certainly is no excuse for not studying this observationally. The weather cannot be escaped. It is everywhere. The purpose of weather study in the nature work of the primary grades is chiefly æsthetic, and should remain partly so in the upper grades. But there the informational side predominates. There should be enough study to appreciate the æsthetic elements of even bad weather, to be familiar with various weather phenomena, and to know their relations well enough to judge when to carry an umbrella, or when it is a good day for the wash, and when to make hay. Also, the purpose is to teach some general principles of weather and climate so necessary for the understanding of the biological conditions in different parts of the globe.

In home geography weather vane, thermometer, rain gauge, and calendar should be taught through use. The simpler weather phenomena, heat, cold, rain, snow, wind, clouds, and the changing seasons, are suitable topics, and these should be taught by observation outdoors and by indoor experiments. The work must, however, be kept simple.

It is customary to make weather calendars or weather charts. These are useful in showing how such records are made, and in stimulating observation of weather and the use of weather instruments. This study should not be carried on too long. Very often these tables are a waste of time, dull and unprofitable. It is a mistake in the elementary school to make records throughout a whole term. A few weeks of consecutive observation will serve the purpose. To continue it invites lack of interest. The beginning of winter, the coldest period, windy March, and showery April are the most interesting times for weather study.

Through the simple weather study of home geography should be taught certain generalizations as to the association of temperature, wind direction, and the state of the sky, as indicative of different kinds of weather. The south wind is hot and muggy. The east wind and overcast sky mean rain. The indications for each locality should thus be learned. A little can be taught about the work of the Weather Bureau, and pupils may be encouraged to look up the forecasts as shown in the daily press, and to become familiar with the local signals of flags and whistles.

CHAPTER VII

ILLUSTRATIVE MATERIAL

Geography should be concrete. — The more vivid and real the subject can be made, the more it appeals to the children, and the better it is understood. To children of the plains, mountains are hard to realize without models and pictures. And the unlimited view of the plains is just as difficult to imagine for children shut up in narrow mountain valleys. Geographies tell about locks and canals, but few pupils can understand how a ship is locked through, without the aid of pictures. The cotton gin is rightly given an important place in commercial geography. But how many children know just why it has to be used, how it is constructed, and how it works? Reference is made to a host of natural products, manufactured articles, etc., that are mere empty names to one who has never seen them. Occupations, customs, dress, architecture, interest the child in the study of foreign lands, but only in so far as he is able to picture them.

From these examples is seen the necessity of assisting the imagination to form concepts of those facts in geography which cannot be seen and studied at first hand.

To bring before the class adequate and suitable illustrative material is as much a duty of the teacher as "reading up" on the lesson. The amount and character of the material for visualizing the lesson may be taken as an index of the teacher's earnestness and ingenuity, and even of her appreciation of the subject.

In the chapters on home geography, the purpose and treatment of the field lesson were considered. There now remains to be considered the following kinds of illustrative material, some of which is actual and some only representative:

Pictures, next to the real thing, stand foremost in interest and usefulness. Children are always fond of them, and study them to the least detail. By the modern photo-mechanical and color-printing methods results of marvelous accuracy and beauty are obtained. Being photographic they may generally be considered authentic, and are so regarded by children. The half-tones in the text corroborate the words of the book. Not only that, but they often teach more. They should, like the text, be assigned for study, and should be used in the recitation. The teacher, however, should select pictures from other sources to supplement those of the text; and, better still, display larger views that may be placed before the class and seen by all at once. European schools are provided with large type pictures of races, occupations, physiography, and scenery which are immensely useful.

But there are no such type pictures made in this country. Such as are used are imported. There are, however, numerous medium-sized pictures obtainable from various sources. Some may be purchased from view companies. Many may be gathered from magazines and newspapers. Frequently excellent pictures used for advertisement may be obtained from commercial houses, real estate companies, steamship lines, and railroads. The picture post-card fad, also, is a good thing for geography.

The teacher should be on the lookout for pictures, and make a collection. Pupils are usually glad to help. This collection should be made useful and available by a proper method of classification and filing. They should be mounted on stiff paper, and properly labeled. Looking for a picture in an unsorted collection is like looking for a needle in a haystack. Some teachers paste their pictures in a scrapbook with reading matter. This plan is not so good as keeping them loose and classified in pigeon-holes, drawers, or envelopes.

Study of pictures. — It is not enough to simply display a picture to the class. It should be studied and described by the pupils, and a lesson should be drawn from it. Perhaps the picture is an Eskimo scene: What sort of clothing do the people wear? Why? What else in the picture shows that it is cold? Are their houses made like ours? Of what are they made? Why do you think they use snow? Look at the scenery. Do you see trees? Now can you tell why they make houses of snow? What else do you notice in the picture? Yes, the Eskimo is a good boatman. Notice his boat. Would that be made of wood? It is made chiefly of skins. Where do these come from? Yes, that is a seal, and that a polar bear. What has the man in his hand? What is it used for? What uses would he make of the animals he kills? Etc.

In this lesson the picture serves as the basis for the development of the facts to be brought out.

It is a good practice for cultivating observation and expression to have the pupil describe a picture at length, so far as he is able.

Children like to listen to a good description of a picture. Sometimes the teacher should do the describing, using plenty of descriptive words and phrases, not neglecting the scenic or beauty aspects, and remembering the children's natural interests. This description should be lively, vivid, and picturesque. It should not be merely a passive description of static appearances, but should suggest life and activity, and the thoughts and emotions naturally aroused in such situations as are depicted.

In some studies a single picture cannot show all that is needed. A series should be used, particularly with such topics as represent action, development, changes, processes, — as, physiographic changes, manufacturing processes, agricultural processes, etc.

Blackboard drawings. — In this connection it should be urged that teachers use every opportunity to sketch on the blackboard as an aid in teaching. Simple outline drawings may be made of natural earth features; maps may be sketched from memory; diagrams showing relationships, processes, development, etc., may be drawn. Even though these pictures, maps, and diagrams are in the book, there is an advantage in reproducing them. They are a wonderful help in creating and holding attention, and in teaching many topics. They should, as a rule, be drawn at the moment they are referred to, and comments should be made upon them by the teacher as she draws them. Colored crayons help to differentiate the parts of a drawing. Pupils also should be taught to reproduce the simpler diagrams, and to make necessary maps on the board.

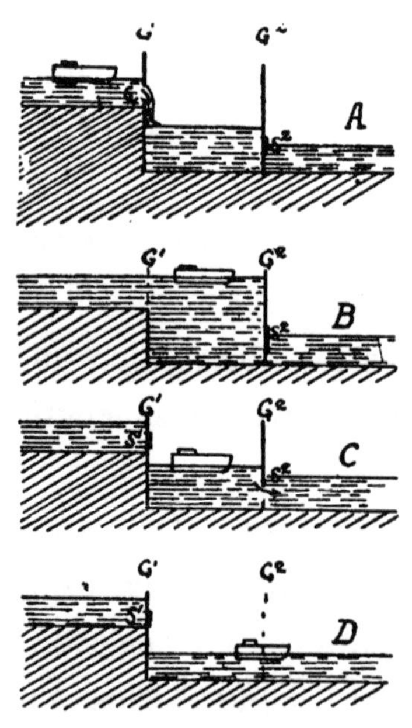

Fig. 1. Diagram showing operation of a canal lock.

Visual memory. — The psychological reason for the high teaching value of pictures is that they enable the eye to convey impressions to the mind, which in simply listening or reading must depend on the imagination and memory to construct the objects of the scene. The picture does this much more quickly, vividly, and accurately, and, what is very important, a visual memory persists with most pupils longer than any other. The popularity and educative value of pictures is attested by their almost universal use in every kind of book, paper, advertising, etc.

The lantern slide and moving picture are also very popular. Where facilities permit, both of these should be used in teaching geography. In this way much "tarry at home travel" may be accomplished. Such pictures, where the necessary facilities exist, may be shown by the regular teachers. School authorities should provide for this purpose more liberally than in the past. Rooms should be arranged with dark shades, and projection lanterns of the simpler types should be installed. Many teachers give a personal touch, which pupils generally like, by having slides made of their own photographs, taken on their travels. Sometimes outsiders, as high school teachers, travelers, and lecturers, may be induced to give a travel talk with pictures. The travel lectures given to the general public by accepted authorities should be recommended to the pupils for attendance. These lecturers have contributed much toward the popularizing of geography. It is the realistic character of the large pictures on the screen, particularly if colored, that make them so valuable. The geography teacher should attend these lectures to get out of a rut, and to learn not only the art of popular exposition, but some very good pedagogy. The intensely human treatment of geography by the public lecturer will be noticeable.

Lantern slides may be rented from view companies, and often large loan collections are under the control of the school authorities.

The opaque projection lantern is another means of adding interest and pleasure to the work. By this, without going through the labor and expense of making slides, one may take a photograph, postal card, or even a picture in a book and project it upon the screen in original colors.

The stereoscope produces the most wonderfully realistic effects by combining two pictures of the same object, from slightly different angles of view, similar to what occurs with binocular vision. This instrument, with sets of views, should be found in every school. They are inexpensive. The disadvantage of these stereographs is that the work with them must be individual, not collective, as with the lantern slide. To allow group work, schemes have been proposed for providing sets of ten or more of each series of views. The plan is too expensive and cumbersome. It is better to place the stereoscopes and stereographs in the classroom or the library, where they may be looked at by the children individually. Or particular views may be sent singly around the class.

To avoid oral repetition, it is a good plan to write a brief description or explanatory remark on an attached card, calling attention to the principal points to be noted Stereographs may be obtained at book stores, photo supply houses, and view companies.

Children delight in making collections. — This tendency should be turned to good account in getting them to assist in collecting pictures from all sources. It is an excellent plan to let them illustrate geographical exercises or notebooks with clippings and pictures. In making a book of geographical views, the pictures should be classified by topics, — river scenes, mountain scenery, cities, buildings, people, products, etc. When a foreign country is studied, or any other topic, the pupils might make a book of pictures of that topic. It is also well to suggest a more systematic arrangement of the pupils' private postal card albums.

Geographical specimens. — A touch of reality is given to the study of a foreign country by having some material object from that land. A piece of granite from the top of Mt. Washington, a shell from the South Sea Islands, a coconut from Brazil, a piece of sugar cane from the plantations of Cuba, a Chinese newspaper, a Japanese fan, etc., are worth having at the time related topics are studied, if only to catch the attention and hold the interest. But specimens do far more than this. They take the subject matter out of the realm of the abstract, stimulate the imagination of the pupils, and help them to project themselves in thought to the regions whence these objects came.

Sometimes a specimen is simply employed incidentally for the sake of interest; and sometimes it is essential, in order to get a true conception of the topic under study. When China is being studied, a Chinese teacup, though not necessary, adds interest. But a cotton plant from the South, when the Southern states are taken up, is a real aid to the appreciation of the staple industry of that region. And it is practically useless to discuss the composition and appearance of granite without the rock and its constituent minerals. Here the specimens teach the lesson. Geographical specimens may play a large or only an incidental part, but they always add interest and serve to make the subject tangible.

A teacher on her travels should collect geographical specimens and souvenirs for use in teaching. By a little questioning, pupils may be found who have at home interesting geographical material, which they would be only too glad to lend the teacher for use in class. Here, again, advantage may be taken of the children's collecting instinct in the formation of a school collection.

A geographical collection or cabinet is a useful adjunct.

This may be gathered through the teacher's and pupils' efforts, and through purchases by the authorities. There ought to be a common collection for all the classes of a building. Thus the classroom collections may be pooled, and a larger stock secured. In fact, as material for one is often useful in the other subject, the nature and the geography collections should be combined. Among suitable articles for such a collection are: historic relics (books, papers, weapons, pictures, etc.); raw materials and different stages of manufactured articles (foods, fabrics, metals, etc.); botanical and zoölogical specimens or products not perishable in nature (grains, fibers, pressed plants, ivory, horn, mother of pearl, starfish, etc.); rocks and minerals, to illustrate physiography.

Such a collection should be classified and labeled. The labels should state the name of specimen, where obtained, and by whom given. The collection should be kept in neat order, and clean. If possible it should be placed so that pupils could observe it in their leisure hours. Finally it should be *used*.

Geographical experiments. — An experiment is a question addressed to nature. In an experiment things are put under certain conditions " to see what will happen." There is need and opportunity for experimentation in geography, especially in physical geography. Sometimes it is inconvenient or impossible to observe certain phenomena or relationships in the field, or to wait for their natural occurrence. Then, often, they may be artificially reproduced in the classroom.

The process of rock disintegration and soil formation may be nicely represented by rubbing two stones together and grinding off particles. The porosity of stone and absorption of water may be shown by immersing a brick or a piece of sandstone in a jar of water. The solvent action of natural waters may be suggested by the effect of acid on marble. The action of running water may be illustrated in a sand tray. The study of the convection of air (winds), the evaporation and condensation of vapor, and the pressure of the atmosphere can only be made clear by simple experiments in physics.

Some of the industrial processes can be elegantly demonstrated in their simplicity by classroom experiments. Flour making, cotton ginning and spinning, tanning, dyeing, weaving, making pottery, etc., may be thus shown. Agriculture, irrigation, and some of the principles of forestry may be represented in the school garden.

In mathematical geography experimental possibilities are indicated by the shadow stick, the noon altitude of the sun, and the compass.

The experimental method is excellent to develop the questioning attitude on the part of the children. They are too prone to accept the dogmatic statements of teachers and books. The experiment shows them that they can find out something independently.

When experiments are used to discover facts and principles, the reasoning is inductive. Often, however, the experiment is used to prove the word of the teacher or the book, in which case the deductive method is used.

Geographical concepts increased by illustrative material. — In conclusion, the teacher has, in pictures, specimens, experiments, and field observations, an invaluable aid in geographical instruction for rendering it realistic, vivid, and entertaining, and for making it more concrete and more easily understood. At the same time pupils get the benefit of personal observation and inference, and learn to depend not wholly upon the teacher and the text. This illustrative material may be used as effectively in the upper grades as in the lower. The stock of concrete geographical concepts may be continuously increased thereby, and a surer foundation laid for that portion of the subject which cannot be actually seen.

CHAPTER VIII

PHYSICAL GEOGRAPHY

Definition. — That portion of geography dealing more particularly with the forms of land and water and the states of the atmosphere, with the natural forces acting upon them, and with the relation of plant and animal life (including human) to their environment, is called Physical Geography. The emphasis in this phase of geography is usually on the inanimate side, and Man receives a rather brief consideration.

The natural environment of man must ever be of concern to him. It is that which sustains him, and largely determines his occupations and habits of life. A proper understanding of physical geography is, therefore, the best foundation for the appreciation of political.

The greatest advance in geography as a science in recent times has been in this field. The older geographers confined themselves to a static description of the earth; that is, to locative and scenic descriptions of physical features, especially coasts, rivers, and mountains. But since the development of the sciences of geology, mineralogy, and biology, physical geography has become dynamic; that is, the earth is no longer treated as permanent and unchanging, but as constantly subject to various modifying forces. The evolutionary or developmental conception of the earth has been grasped, and mountains, valleys, rivers, etc., are no longer treated as everlasting, and unchanging in form and character. These features are now considered as having a growth or development. The forces or agencies that made them are now taken into account. Mountain folds are thrown up by the stress of forces within the crust. But they are subject to erosion and decline. Rivers tend to grade toward sea level. Lakes fill up and disappear. In short, the earth is no longer considered as an inactive, inert thing, but pulsating with mighty forces, alive, as it were.

Modern physical geography teaches far-reaching relations; for example, topography and drainage, altitude and temperature, mountain trend and rainfall, climate and vegetation, and the dependence of man upon his physical environment. In order to teach geography well the teacher should know at least the rudiments of these great principles. This branch of geography is considered so important that many schools for the training of teachers make it a requirement in the course.

Place of physical geography in the elementary school. — Geography, so far as the elementary school is concerned, is a study of how man lives on the earth. This involves a study of those features that influence or control his distribution over the earth, his occupations, and very civilization. Descriptive geography should be taught in the light of this fact. This may seem too philosophical by far when we consider children's interests and mental ability; but it is not necessary to force the pupils to see these great relations all at once or all together. Certainly very little toward this can be accomplished in primary geography or home geography, and even in the eighth grade, pupils are incapable of grasping the whole truth. The teacher, however, should know these principles, and teach the subject in the light of them, and should try to have the pupil ultimately appreciate something of them. The facts of geography should be presented in their natural relationships. Beginners will for the most part note merely the facts, and not their relationships. But older pupils care also for the abstract relations and principles involved, and these from repeated examples will gradually dawn upon them.

One thing must be remembered, physical geography by itself has no place in the grades (except possibly in the uppermost). It may be properly taught as a separate science in the high school, but in the grades below, whatever physical geography is taught should be connected with the political side.

The "advanced" geographies of the upper grades

usually begin with an introductory sketch of the fundamental physiographic facts and principles, which are then deductively applied in the following descriptive geography.

In the grammar grades the pupils gradually formulate the relations of man and nature, and get a philosophic glimpse of the organization and unity of the science impossible in grades below. Here pupils are old enough to appreciate somewhat the causal relation existing between location, surface, elevation, drainage, climate, vegetation and animal life, and human beings. The physical features may be used to develop or interpret human industries, mode of life, dress, and other human activities and characteristics. See Chapter XI.

The Great Plains. — An excellent example of the value of physical, as an explanatory basis for descriptive geography, is the study of the Great Plains of the United States.

Topography and climate. — The Great Plains are a high, fairly level plateau extending north and south through the United States, just east of the Rocky Mountains. They slope gently toward the Mississippi Valley. Their vast extent and levelness gives them their name.

The United States lie in the belt of prevailing westerlies, which bring moisture from the Pacific Ocean. Owing, however, to successive mountain systems, which begin at the very coast, and rise higher and higher farther inland, the moisture of the westerlies is condensed as the winds rise over the mountains, so that by the time they pass the Rockies they contain comparatively little moisture. As the winds descend on the eastern side of the Rockies they become warmed by compression and by the warmer temperatures of the lower altitudes, their moisture capacity is increased, and they become drying winds instead of rain-bringing.

The precipitation on the Great Plains is therefore very slight, from ten to twenty inches per year. There are long periods of drought, especially in the summer. The climate is semiarid.

The consequence is that the vegetation of this region is limited to such species as are able to withstand the excessive dryness of the soil and atmosphere. Sage brush covers large areas of the plains, especially in the north. Farther south, in the warmer belt, cacti of various kinds flourish. Only along the streams can trees exist. Even the grass is not able to produce a continuous sward, but grows in tufts here and there, and hence is called bunch grass. This grass, owing to the dryness of the air after the middle of the summer, dries up quickly and retains its nutritious quality. That is, it becomes cured into natural hay, which the light snows of winter do not completely cover.

Ranching industry. — This peculiarity of the climate and vegetation have made possible the great cattle or grazing industry of the Plains. Upon these immense stretches, where in days past the bisons and antelopes roamed in vast numbers, thousands upon thousands of cattle, sheep, and goats find a fair pasturage. But owing to the sparseness of the grass, these grazing grounds, or ranches, must be large. This makes the homes of the settlers far apart, and the region is thinly settled.

Farming, as it is carried on in moister lands, cannot be practiced here on account of the aridity. The United States Department of Agriculture has introduced drought-resisting plants from other countries, such as alfalfa, macaroni wheat, millet, etc., and has tried to develop native wild species, the cactus, for example, into more useful forms. Such crops can be grown by the dry-farming method, and much progress has been made in the West in their cultivation. Another method of farming in this dry land is by means of irrigation. By this method water is drawn from rivers into canals and distributed over the fields. Thus the water supply is sure, and many kinds of crops can be raised. Irrigation from rivers in this way can be carried on only in their valleys.

By means of dry farming and irrigation many more people are enabled to live on the Great Plains than by ranching alone, and many towns have developed in the more agricultural sections. Still, the general aspect of the Plains is that of a semidesert. The treeless, grassy lands stretch away monotonously to the horizon.

The ranchers live a seminomadic life, as they drive their herds about for new pasturage. There are farming communities and towns in only the more favorable locations, oases along the water courses.

Physical geography, in home and primary geography, requires a different treatment. Here the physical features are first studied to familiarize the child with the local environment. Owing to the immaturity of the pupils, the relation between causes and consequences cannot be very thoroughly studied. The work should be chiefly descriptive of the static aspect of land, water, and the atmosphere, leaving for higher grades the origins and results of natural forms and conditions. Here and there the more obvious of these relations may be studied. Thus it is customary in primary geography to study a little about the origin of soil, the effects of running water, and the causes of wind and rain.

Specific, concrete, and human interest. — The approach and general treatment of the physical features in home geography should be from the human standpoint, even from the child's, and the study should again find an application in life. For example, in studying a brook, begin with the child's experiences with a brook (perhaps only a street gutter during a shower). The childish play has taught definite ideas of the motion of the water, its force, ripples, waves, eddies, rapids, falls, the melodies of running water, the beauty of light and shade. The sport of playing at ships, bridges, dams, water wheels, etc., is basal for appreciating later the commercial utilization of streams. The study must not stop with the physical treatment merely, but should be brought into relation with man again in the study of the practical uses to which streams are put, and also by reference to their detrimental qualities.

In the physiographic description, care should be taken to use untechnical language, and to make the reasoning about causes or results very simple and practical. The local flavor should be retained. Instead of learning about brooks in general, some local stream should be taken specifically. The study should be observational, based upon actual field observations, well-remembered facts, classroom experiments, diagrams, models, and pictures.

It is best in home geography to teach physical geography in connection with some concrete example, as incidental to a description of the same, than to present it in the abstract. Thus erosion may be studied in connection with The —— Brook of the neighborhood. Weathering should be studied in connection with local soils in the school garden or near-by fields. It is better to study the facts of physical geography as they are needed. Let them be used in explanation of the political and industrial features of the vicinity.

Physical geography explanatory of life conditions. — In the Primary Course of Descriptive or General Geography physical geography should be subordinate. The human or life side, national occupations and characteristics, is the main thing. Instead of introducing a study of a country with topography, climate, rivers, etc., in systematic order, it is better to start with some trait of the people, some historical association, some occupation, a description of the plants or animals. The scenic aspect, though physiographic, depends upon the subjective impressions of the beholder, and is an interesting approach at times. The introduction to a country might vary. In Australia the curious animal life, in England the historical connections with the United States, in the Southern states the cotton industry, in Japan the silk industry, in Switzerland and Scotland the scenery, might be the first topics.

The physical geography should come in as explanatory of the political, and should be brought in only for this purpose, or else is better left out. Just enough physical geography should be brought in to answer the few Whys the pupils will be likely to ask at this stage. Why the climate is as it is (latitude, altitude), why the streams take the course they do (topography), why the people live mostly in certain regions and not in others (topography, climate, resources), why certain plant and animal industries are possible in certain regions (topography, climate, soil), why cities were located at certain places and have developed (ports, falls, resources), and similar queries.

Study of Holland according to this method. — Holland is a favorite country with children. Why? It is not the delta of the Rhine, but the Dutch people, that appeals. Reference to stories about the Dutch, Hans Brinker, etc. Study interesting costumes. In New York City there would be a special interest in the *Half Moon*, the early settlement, and the Dutch gabled houses still existing. Study of pictures of Dutch village scenes, canals, and windmills. Some Dutch industry, such as pottery, etc. The Dutch dairy industry. Why good pasturage (level land, sufficient rainfall). Why the land is so flat (delta). Why easy to dig canals. The peat industry. Why the land is marshy (low). Compare with local tidal flats and marshes. Building of dikes to keep back the sea. Why the windmills. Why called Netherlands, etc.

The scenic phase of physical geography is important. — A knowledge of the physical geography of the scenic elements in the local landscape, or of the scenery in travel, adds greatly to an appreciation and enjoyment of the same. The older pupils can get a deeper insight into the earth, but younger children enjoy the superficial elements. In home geography they should be taught to look for and enjoy the sky in calm and in storm, at night and in the morning; the wind effects of drifting clouds, swaying trees, and billowing grass or grain fields; the enchantment created by mists, haze, or distance; the colors of the landscape, and how they change with varying lights; the horizon line of the plain, or the hill country; the boldness of the hills, and the dreamy vastness of the plains; the beauty of the lakes and the grandeur of the ocean; the life and action of running water; these and many other elements of scenery should be appreciated. If physical geography did not add something to the pupils' power to discover and enjoy these things, it would scarcely have fulfilled its function.

Teachers should learn to describe in vivid word paintings different types of scenery to impress them upon the pupils, who should cultivate the power to image them again behind the words of the text, or the symbols of the map.

Pictures are a great aid in presenting the æsthetic aspect of geography. Some of them should be displayed for days, and the larger and finer ones permanently, if possible.

The teacher will find enjoyment and inspiration in this phase of geography by reading such authors as Scott, Irving, Bayard Taylor, Sir John Lubbock, John Muir, Burroughs, Russell, S. E. White, J. C. Van Dyke, and other writers on scenery.

CHAPTER IX

ILLUSTRATIVE MATERIAL IN PHYSIOGRAPHY

That physical geography should be studied directly, if practicable, goes without saying. Certain topics, such as weathering, the action of running water, weather phenomena, earth and water forms, glacial soil and glaciation, the adaptation of vegetation to the environment, should be studied outdoors. Previous outdoor observations and experiences of the children should be recalled. Many natural objects, such as minerals, different kinds of rocks, ores, and various physical phenomena, such as the action of frost, water, and friction in wearing down rocks; erosion and deposit, evaporation and condensation, convection of air, etc., should be shown in the classroom as specimens or experiments.

The function of the field lesson was discussed on page 34, and illustrative lessons suggested. The field lesson is particularly valuable in physical geography, not only rendering the subject concrete, but providing the opportunity of studying the earth features on the imposing scale of nature. Book study cannot impress size, distance, and magnificence like field study. The duration and fatigue of one walk will impress distance better than the use of the map scale and verbal description. The grandeur and beauty of the local environment can only be fully appreciated and enjoyed by actually experiencing it.

Physical geography of home locality. — It is fortunate that physical geography thus requires the study of the real thing. In this way the home geography of the lower grades is continued. The local features have to be taken as examples in these field trips, and thus physical geography is brought home, and not left in the abstract. This local study of physiography is made very practical by connecting the familiar landmarks of hills, valleys, streams, etc., with the local history, the industries, and the life of the community.

Sooner or later, however, inaccessible regions must be taught, and some representative illustration has to be employed.

The model. — The most effective of these is the model. This, for certain purposes, is more valuable than a map or a picture, in that it is in three dimensions, and the up and down, the high and low character of the surface, can be represented. Models should be used very early. Let the children reproduce the hills and valleys of their home geography. The home locality may be modeled by the teacher and the pupils, a very interesting piece of creative imagination. By such local studies the pupils become familiarized with the interpretation of models in general.

Relation to map study. — Models are generally used as the basis for the study of the continents. They are excellent for showing the great plains, plateaus, and slopes, and for developing the drainage. The eye memory is greatly helped by the construction of even a very crude sand model of a continent. The model should precede the map, and helps to interpret it.

Accuracy. — Models are most accurate in elevation and general detail when representing small areas. The larger the area modeled, the more do the minor elements in the relief disappear. A mountain five miles high, if correctly represented on a globe four feet in diameter, would be hardly noticeable, being only about one thirtieth of an inch above the general spherical surface.

In order, therefore, to represent large areas, like continents, in appreciable relief, it is absolutely necessary to exaggerate the same. In some of the best relief models of the United States the elevations are magnified ten times.

There is no very great harm done if younger pupils have an exaggerated notion of relief as drawn from models, or even from their own imagination. Older pupils should have these incorrect notions modified. The teacher, of course, must know the error in the model.

Expert and homemade models. — There are excellent and instructive models on the market, but most of them are as yet too expensive for the common school. Such models may sometimes be made available for children by visiting geographical laboratories in high schools or museums.

For ordinary purposes, however, a homemade model will serve very well. This may be made by the pupils, or if something better and more permanent is desired, by the teacher.

Sand model. — The best material for a temporary model is moist sand. The clay-modeling trays, common in elementary schools, may be used for holding the sand. Shallow tins, or oilcloth, or heavy paper, to protect the desks, may be used. Any clean sand will do. Dry sand usually slides and rolls too easily, and must be slightly moistened, but should not be wet and soggy. Place a double handful of sand on each pupil's tray.

Modeling a continent. — Write the directions below on the board, or, for younger children, give orally and let them imitate step by step the teacher's modeling. See that they follow the order:

1. Flatten out the sand to a thin layer, about an eighth of an inch thick or less, all over the tray. Put the excess of sand in one corner.

2. From a wall map or textbook map of simplified form, trace the outline of the map to be drawn in the

sand. With a stiff piece of paper remove the excess of sand.

3. Copying the model or interpreting the physical map, next build up the plateaus, *not the mountains*, using care to keep the various plateaus roughly in proportion as to area and altitude (follow color scale). The plateaus may be quickly built up by dropping double handfuls of sand along their general location, and then smoothing down gradually with the hand. Plateaus, plains, and slopes are the main features to represent in a model, hence care should be used in their representation.

4. (If time permits, or it is deemed desirable.) Put on the principal mountain ranges. This is best done by gently scraping a little of the plateau between the fore-fingers into a *slight* ridge. Be careful not to make the mountains too steep or too high, a common tendency with beginners. The usual practice of making mountains by sticking on dabs of sand held between the thumb and fingers is sure to make them too high, jagged, and steep. Few mountains have a slope exceeding thirty degrees.

5. The rivers and lakes may be traced with the pencil, but should not be dug down through the sand to sea level. Bits of blue yarn and pieces of blue paper may be inserted for the rivers and lakes to heighten the effect.

Such modeling is a useful exercise in review. Older pupils might reproduce a model from memory as a test of their knowledge of general topography. General relations of height, not accuracy of outline, should be the criterion.

It is not worth while for the pupils to model every continent. Enough should be done to give them a muscular and ocular appreciation of what relief is, that they may interpret more readily relief and physical maps.

Sketch models. — The teacher, however, should model maps more frequently. These generally need not be more than mere sand sketches thrown together in a few moments, while she is teaching the topography.

The children enjoy the manual exercise of modeling for its own sake, and welcome it as a relief from the routine of book work, but it may easily be overdone. Where there is sufficient time, a few more permanent models may be made of better material. The following **plastic media** have been found useful:

Paper pulp: Tear old newspapers into bits and soak in water for a day. Stir and churn till reduced to a pulp. Squeeze out the water, and it is ready for use.

Salt and flour: A mixture of these, two measures of flour to one of salt, is stirred together with enough water to make a paste.

Plasticine, used for art work, though somewhat expensive, is an excellent medium.

Putty makes good, durable models.

These materials should be used on stiff cardboard,

or on wood as a base. They often last for years and serve very well for demonstration purposes. A good size for class use is about eighteen by twenty-four inches. A rim or frame should be made around the model to protect it from injury.

Modeling according to scale. — A more scientific yet simple method, which the teacher might employ for making a permanent model, is the following:

From a contour map, or from published tables of elevations determined in public surveys, the heights of many points all over the map may be obtained. Draw the map on a board. Determine on some arbitrary scale, say, one tenth of an inch to a thousand feet. Drive wire brads or small nails into the map, at the places the elevations of which have been determined, leaving the nails exposed to a height equaling, according to the scale, the elevations to be represented. Then carefully work in the plastic material flush with the nails. The surface will need retouching, grooving, and peaking to render it more realistic. When dry, the model should be given several coats of paint, and streams, lakes, boundaries, etc., represented in appropriate colors.

Physical maps far exceed models in general usefulness and convenience. Models are effective for topographic features, but are not of much use if they represent a large area on a small scale, and if large, they are too heavy. Maps are light and compact. In the causal study of geography of the upper grades, physical maps are the foundation for the study of the descriptive geography.

Photo-relief map. — One form of physical map is the photo-relief map, made theoretically by photographing a relief model placed so as to show one-sided illumination of the mountains, thus causing them to stand out bright on one side, dark on the other. They are usually represented in half-tone. A common way is to paint a relief map in black and white so as to get the photographic effect. Such relief maps are almost like a picture of the naked earth seen in bird's-eye view, shorn of the vegetation and the works of man. The half-tone color also strikingly brings out the bare earth effect, so that they are excellent maps for teaching the fundamental relief features of the earth. They are often used to show drainage also.

The color-physical map represents relief by different colors, a particular color for a certain range of elevation: from 0 to 500 feet, green; 500 to 1500 feet, yellow; etc. In modern methods of cartography some beautiful color-physical maps are produced. Unfortunately, all makers do not use the same color scheme, though there is a movement toward international agreement. Children should be taught to refer to the legend or explanation on the map, and to estimate elevations thereby.

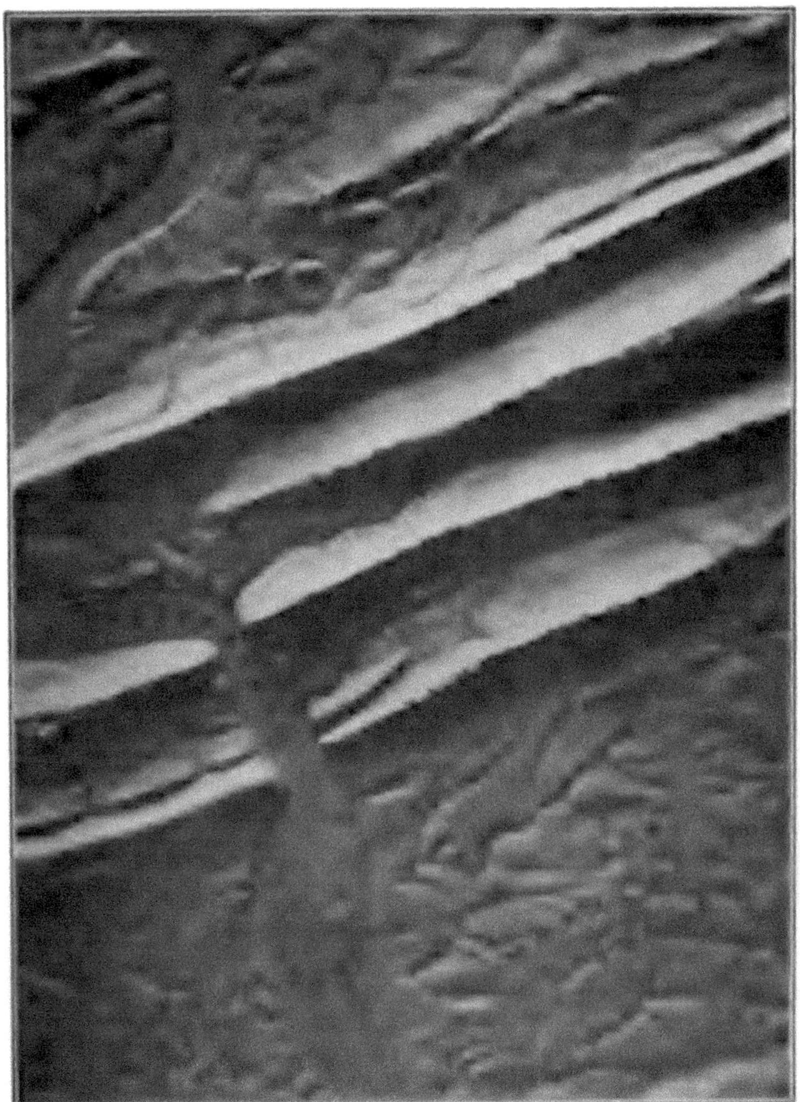

FIG. 2.—Photo-relief map showing relief and drainage.
From Keeler's Model, by permission of the Central Scientific Company.

At any rate they should appreciate the general meaning of the color scale, and be able to pick out at a glance the highlands or the lowlands.

Contour map. — The chief objection to the color-physical map is that the colors are not shaded or blended to correspond with the gradual change of elevation. This is overcome in a measure by the use of the contour map, in which, beginning at sea level, all points of certain equal altitudes are connected by lines. Thus

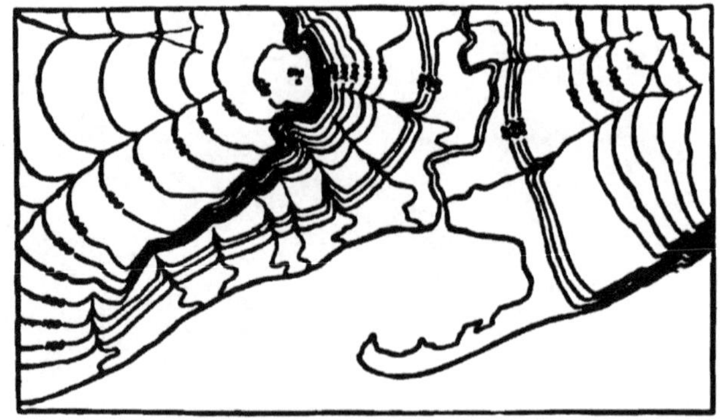

Fig. 3. — Representation of relief by contour lines.

there may be the 100-foot level line, the 200-foot line, etc. Such lines are called contour lines. The explanation on the map states the value of the contours, varying according to the purpose, 10, 100, 1000 feet, etc. By contour lines the relief can be very accurately represented. Where the lines crowd together, there is a steep slope; but where they are far apart, the ascent is gentle. Ravines, valleys, ridges, and peaks stand out beautifully on a contour map. Contour maps are the highest perfection in the art of relief representation. Yet they are rather complex in appearance, and somewhat difficult to translate, and therefore hardly in place in the elementary school. In the seventh and eighth grades pupils should be taught that such maps exist, and should be interested in their use, and learn how to read them; but no general use need be made of them. Most elementary school books do not contain such maps; yet the dividing line between two different adjacent colors on a color-physical map is a true contour line.

There is a combination of color-physical maps with the contour map, which is a beautiful and excellent form, used chiefly in some government surveys of this and other countries.

Features besides those of relief may also be shown by the physical map. — On the same map are generally found the surrounding waters (sometimes showing depths), lakes and rivers, latitude and longitude. Also divides, isotherms, ocean currents, winds, and vegetation limits are sometimes shown. It is customary, however, to show most of these on special physical maps for the study of only one or a few related features. Thus we have rainfall maps, temperature maps, wind and current maps, maps showing zones of life, etc. In this way overcrowding is avoided. But a short time ago one and the same map combined all the physical and political features.

Order of different maps in study. — It is customary

Pacific Ocean
Coast Range
California Valley
Sierra Nevada Mountains
Great Basin
Wasatch Mountains
Rocky Mountains
Great Plains
Central
Mississippi
Plain
Alleghany plateau
Appalachian Mountains
Piedmont Plain
Coast Plain
tic Ocean

Fig. 4. — Profile of the United States along the parallel of 39° N. The vertical scale is many times the horizontal. The fore the elevation is much exaggerated.

to present a continent or country in a photo-relief map, color-physical map, and political map, in the order given. In addition there are usually other maps for special features. In this way an otherwise very complex map is analyzed and simplified and made easy for reference, and at the same time irrelevant features are excluded, and do not distract from the main point.

The profile is a diagram showing a vertical section through a region, or the elevations of the surface line along a certain route, as, for example, a cross section of North America in the latitude of San Francisco, a longisection through the Panama Canal, a plan showing the rise and fall of the Erie Canal. The idea of profile may be taught by cutting through a sand model and viewing the edge. Cuts thus made through North America through various latitudes and also in a north and south direction are very instructive.

Profiles are not used sufficiently in the elementary school. Teachers will find in them a valuable aid in teaching relief. Pupils should be taught to interpret profiles, and likewise to draw them. The pupil who can make a fair profile of the United States in various latitudes shows that he knows well the relief map or model. Profiles are the quickest way of sketching the general relations of relief. They are excellent for showing the direction of slopes, for grades of railroads, canals, and drainage levels (as the Great Lakes). Naturally they are exaggerated vertically, but, with the necessary caution, are not misleading.

CHAPTER X

MATHEMATICAL GEOGRAPHY

Overemphasis of mathematical geography. — The reason for the great stress usually laid on mathematical geography does not lie in the pedagogical usefulness of this branch in the elementary school, but rather in its history and in its relation to astronomy in the higher schools.

In ancient times geography and astronomy were not separated. Geography was a part of astronomy. Mathematics was employed in the service of astronomy in determining the space relations of the earth, its movements, and its form. In the Middle Ages geography had fallen so low that it was taught as a part of geometry. This mathematical emphasis prevailed to the beginning of the nineteenth century, and, unfortunately, has not quite disappeared at the present time.

Mathematical geography too abstract for the beginner. — So far as the elementary school is concerned, very little mathematical geography is needed for a basis. It is unpedagogical to begin the study of geography with the astronomical or mathematical phase. This may be the logical beginning of the science of geography, but the child, not the logical requirements of the subject, must be considered. It is destructive of any real interest, and is forcing a child beyond his capacity, to compel him to begin geography with what is abstract and to him far from his experience. The space relations of the earth, conceptions of its size, conceptions of its motions, are, on the whole, beyond his comprehension. Latitude and longitude and degrees are to the beginner unintelligible, because, for one thing, he has not had the necessary arithmetic.

It is futile to teach these things to beginners, and judging by the very meager results from much effort, it is often futile to teach them in upper grades. Children readily learn to parrot off the usual bald statements about mathematical geography in the ordinary texts, but do not really understand them.

Child study has accomplished one excellent thing, the reduction of the amount of mathematical geography to be taught, and its postponement for a time. The child now begins with something concrete, tangible, and capable of direct observation; that is, with home geography, and not with something abstract, imaginary, "unreal," and difficult. This does not mean that the simple, observational study of the sun, moon, and stars may not be taken up even in primary grades, under nature-study. But the abstract and mathematical treatment of form, space relations, time relations, and motions are not for beginners.

When to introduce mathematical geography. — A time arrives when some reference must be made to the earth as a whole. Even in home geography there is mention of places beyond the horizon of the community, of countries beyond the seas, and of the uttermost parts of the earth. The idea of the world as a whole dawns upon the child, and he then needs some information about it. At this point mathematical geography usually begins.

The essential facts in mathematical geography in the primary course are the spherical form of the earth, some concrete notions of its size, the poles and the equator for orientation, the points of the compass, rotation and its results, revolution and its results. Zones are usually included, but in these grades heat belts are really meant by this term. If the dimensions of the earth, distance from the sun, axis, astronomical zones, latitude and longitude, meridians and parallels, and the study of the seasons based upon the inclination of the axis were not taught until the seventh year, nothing would be lost to the pupil.

Little of this is subject to direct observation. — Day and night, and the phenomena of the seasons, the appearance of the sun, moon, and stars, and a little of their change of position in the heavens, are all that can be observed directly by the pupils. The rest must be taught dogmatically, and backed up by argument, or "proof," that appeals to young minds.

The rotundity of the earth, for example, is really a fascinating topic, owing largely to the dramatic history of Columbus and Magellan. Their voyages make an excellent introduction to the study. Children by the seashore, or by the Great Lakes, have the opportunity others do not have, of observing the "proof" of rotundity in the gradual disappearance of a ship sailing outward, the mast being the last to disappear over "the shoulder of the earth." Elsewhere the children must be satisfied with models (globes), and the "proof" is still further weakened by being only an argument by analogy. The best proof of rotundity capable of being grasped by beginners is that of the shadow of the earth on the moon during an eclipse of the latter. It is first necessary, however, to explain the phenomenon of an eclipse. Of the many arguments for the rotundity of the earth some are only analogies, and some are incomplete proofs.

Conceptions of dimensions of the earth. — To say that the earth is eight thousand miles in diameter, and twenty-five thousand miles in circumference, is meaningless to a child. These numbers may be memorized, but are not really conceived, nor are they of great use till much later in the course. But if they must be taught, it is far better to let a child figure out some concrete example, such as how long it would take a train to go around the equator at a certain speed, say, fifty miles per hour; or tell how long sailing vessels or modern steamers (average rate, fifteen miles per hour) require for an actual circumnavigation. Tell about Jules Verne's *Around the World in Eighty Days*, and more modern records. In this way some sort of a concrete notion of the earth's greatness will be given.

The poles and the equator are to a beginner chiefly climatic in meaning, and should be mainly taught by a description of the temperature and life conditions there. The locative notion can only be derived by analogy from globe study. Spin a ball or orange. The point in which the spinning sphere turns is a pole; and directly opposite is another. The idea of equator is readily grasped, as an equal divider.

The term axis is really of no use in primary geography, and when introduced here serves only to confuse. The usual way of teaching the idea of axis is to compare it with an *axle*, which leaves a bad picture in the eye memory, hard to eradicate and to correct. An unpivoted ball, orange, or other round object, set spinning, will much better teach the abstract character of the axis.

Latitude, longitude, parallels, meridians, and prime meridian are out of place in primary geography. An examination of two of the most recent and foremost textbooks of primary geography revealed that one does not teach the terms at all, and that the other defines them, but makes no application of them in the text. The map studies and map descriptions in neither refer to latitude or longitude, and yet all the maps, except a few relief and sketch maps, show these lines. They would be simpler without them.

Day and night. — The effects of one-sided illumination and rotation may be nicely shown by means of a globe experiment. The books generally recommend a darkened room and a lamp for the experiment. This is usually impossible, or out of the question. Excellent results may be had by drawing all the ordinary shades but one, and this also partially, thus preventing cross-illumination. A black globe is very effective.

In spite of a general acquiescence in the principle, the pupils will find it difficult to imagine the earth actually in rotation, and are rarely conscious of its direction. A good way to realize this is to watch the sun near the horizon at sunrise or at sunset, and then "forcibly" to make one's self think of the earth as doing the moving. The sensation of rotation is thus quite marked.

In the study of the change of seasons pupils should note the varying phenomena of changing length of day, the changing temperature, the response of vegetation and animal life, and how man's life is regulated by these conditions. This side, rather than the mathematical or astronomical, should be impressed.

During early spring or early fall some observations

may be made with the shadow-stick on the height of the noon sun from week to week. (It does not pay to do it daily.) From this it may be shown that the sun is higher or lower on successive dates, and this should be correlated with the changing temperature. A further

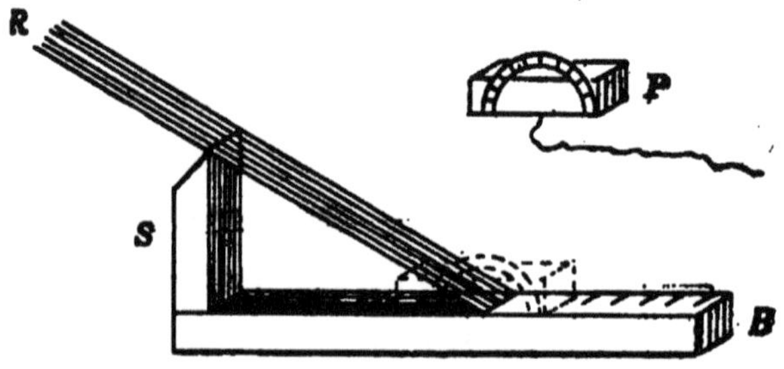

FIG. 5.—Shadow-stick and protractor.

causal study involving the inclination of the axis and revolution is out of place in primary geography.

Heat belts *vs.* zones. — The customary picture of the earth divided into five zones is an easy one to remember, and as heat belts, fairly correct for beginners. Zones are, however, strictly speaking, not heat belts at all, but light belts, or astronomical divisions. The true heat belts are much more irregular, and are not constant in position on the earth, while the light zones are fixed. Zones are determined by the position on the earth of certain light rays from the sun on certain days of the year, and by the inclination of the earth's axis. The boundaries of the zones do not vary. But the boundaries of heat belts are shifting isotherms of great irregularity, owing to the changing seasons and the modifying influences of land and water. The term zone should disappear from primary geography and heat belt should be substituted.

The best way to present the idea of heat belts to beginners is to tell or read stories of the climate, the vegetation, the animal life, and the human life of typical climatic regions. The reason for the unequal distribution of heat, if any be given here, would have to be given dogmatically, as by citing the varying height of the sun above the horizon as one proceeds from the equator to the poles.

Mathematical geography in upper grades. — Further than this in mathematical geography, it is not profitable to go with beginners. The pupils of the seventh and eighth grades are, however, more interested in, and better prepared for this subject. Here the subject is usually extended and reviewed. But even here too much is generally expected. The explanation of the change of seasons, based upon the inclination of the axis, and represented by diagrams, is beyond the capacity of the average child in the eighth grade, and is a severe tax upon the high school and college student. Even here the result is generally not a concept of the real earth swinging along its orbit in space, but simply a mental image of the seasons diagram in some book.

The fact of the varying length of day from the equator to the poles should be taught, but the reason therefor is

The international date line also is beyond their capacity.

The moon's phases do not belong in geography at all.

With these eliminations the subject of mathematical geography becomes an easy one for both pupils and teacher. It has always been a bugbear to teachers because of the inward realization that the pupils do not really comprehend much of it.

Observational basis. — Because of its abstract character it is necessary to present the subject by means of observations, models, diagrams, and pictures in as concrete a fashion as possible. As above suggested, some direct observations on the appearance of the heavenly bodies, the daily course of the sun, and the changing altitude of the sun during the year are possible. These observations should be made some time before a topic is to be considered in class. Thus, leading up to a study of the seasons, pupils should make a weekly record of the noon altitude of the sun for perhaps a month in advance. The accompanying changes of temperature, and the adaptation of plant and animal life, should also be noted. Thus an interesting, solid basis will be laid for the more abstract discussion of the seasons.

The globe is invaluable in the study of mathematical geography. A six-inch paper globe serves very well. Larger globes are attractive, but more expensive and unwieldy. There is a fascination about a good globe, and it should be left where pupils may examine it at leisure. They will discover much for themselves. A good globe, however, should not be soiled, or marked with pencils.

A black globe is very useful, especially for teaching day and night, and latitude and longitude. Such a one may be obtained from school supply establishments, or readily made by painting a common globe with a flat black paint, or better still with black slating. A wooden ball dipped in black ink does very well.

Expensive mechanical **solar models** are out of place, and also out of the question in the elementary school. The relation of the sun and the earth may be well represented by holding two globes or balls in the proper relation, and moving them in the proper manner. Such a physical representation by models should always precede the use of diagrams and abstract descriptions of the topic.

Diagrams in mathematical geography are themselves symbolic and represent relations and motions which to the child are imaginary. The model must therefore act out these relations and motions to interpret the diagram. The season diagrams as usually given, if they do not leave erroneous impressions, are too difficult for the average pupil, unaided by models. Yet diagrams, once understood, are beautiful representations. They may be used to emphasize certain features, or to represent what the mind, as well as the eye, sees. It is this last characteristic that makes them especially useful.

With the caution above given the teacher should be free to make much use of diagrams, more in the upper grades than in the lower. Diagrams should be drawn while the topic is being discussed. They are a sort of graphic shorthand that expresses a good deal. Pupils should be taught to explain or interpret diagrams, and also to draw them.

Inductive development before textbook study. — These lessons in mathematical geography are perhaps the most difficult for pupils to get from a textbook. They should therefore be first orally developed or explained by the teacher before being assigned in the book. They ought to be taught inductively as far as may be; that is, the pupil should *discover* these important relations, rather than have them presented dogmatically, either by the book or by the teacher. Care should be exercised that the technical terms have a real meaning for the pupil.

The points in method outlined in this chapter may be illustrated by the following lessons.

Latitude and longitude. — On a black globe make a mark (an island). Ask a pupil to tell where it is. It will be impossible to locate it except by reference to some other known fixed marks. The pupils have learned poles and equator. The above mark (island) may be located then with reference to these. But more accurate locating is needed. How shall this be done?

Construct parallels (one every 10 degrees); note their relation to the equator, and to each other. Give their names. What do they help to indicate? (Distance from the equator.) Now that the pupils have the concept, give it a name (latitude). How shall we designate or distinguish the parallels? Here review the necessary arithmetic, that is, circular measure. Draw a circle around the globe through the poles. How many degrees in it? How many degrees from pole to pole? From equator to pole? How far is the first drawn parallel from the equator? (10 degrees.) Etc. Now how may we distinguish the parallels? (By stating the number of degrees each is from the equator.)

Show how parallels may be drawn in both N. and S. latitude; how both sets are numbered from the equator. What is the latitude of the equator?

Where is the island drawn at beginning of lesson? Locate it by latitude. Can it be definitely located now? Why not? (It may be anywhere in the parallel.) Refer to the way in which we locate houses in a city by giving street and cross street, and suggest advisability of having another set of guide lines than parallels to help locate on the globe. Such lines may be drawn. The circle already drawn through the poles is such a one. Now proceed in a similar way to draw, say at every 15 degrees, other lines (meridians) from pole to pole, to number in degrees, from one selected (principal) meridian. Compare with numbering of parallels. Briefly explain why the meridian of Greenwich (London) was chosen. What do the meridians help to show? After the concept of longitude is attained, give its name. Now locate the sought-for island by longitude; by longitude and latitude.

Now, for clinching, compare the two sets of lines. In what direction do they run? How far? Their distance from each other? What does each indicate? What is the greatest latitude? Greatest longitude?

Then apply in simple exercises in locating places on a globe.

Pass on to a map. Discover the two sets of lines. Show pupils how to estimate between the lines. Practice use.

Show how the parallels and meridians are further used as state or international boundaries; as the basis for the United States Land Survey, and even for laying out the streets and lots of a city; how used as the basis for making a record of discoveries and making maps of these records. Such facts will impress on the pupils the reality and usefulness of these lines.

Are these lines visible on the surface of the land or the sea? How, then, does the mariner know his latitude and longitude? Emphasize the fact that the schoolroom is traversed by parallels and meridians. Can they be seen? They cannot be seen on the earth, but by looking at the sky.

Give a simple explanation of how latitude may be found from the altitude of the North Star. (See any text in mathematical geography or astronomy.) Pupils in the eighth grade can get a notion of this. They may find the latitude from the sun at the equinox.

The explanation of how longitude is found will have to be deferred till after the lesson on Longitude and Time.

Fifth grade lesson on the seasons. — This is most appropriately studied at the turning of the year, in spring or autumn.

The lesson should be begun a month beforehand by the pupils making preliminary observations on the sun's altitude at noon with shadow-stick (Fig. 5), its horizon position, the length of day and night (obtainable also from almanacs), correlated with weather study (temperature changes), and observations on the responses by nature to the changing seasonal conditions. Figure 5 shows a simple form of shadow-stick. Place in a south exposure at noon with vertical stick, *S*, toward the sun. *S* will then cast a shadow along the base, *B*, which may be measured on the scale. The angle of the rays, *R*, with the horizontal may be measured by placing the center of the protractor, *P*, at the end of the shadow and drawing the string over the top of the stick, *S*. The angle may then be read on the scale of the protractor.

Refer to present season. Name all. Let pupils characterize each as to temperature, length of day and night, the state of vegetation (budding, full leaf, flowering, fruiting, harvest stage; leaf coloring, leaf fall), the response by animals (migration, hibernation, thickness of plumage or fur, storing of food, building homes). How does man adjust his life to the changing seasons in the city? What games are played in different seasons? How does the farmer in the country vary his work during the year? The close relationship of life to the seasons will be emphasized by these references. Pictures will greatly add to the interest.

What is the source of the heat on the earth? Prove heating power of sunlight by holding hand first in sunbeam, then in shade. Why do we take the shady side of street in summer? Why carry parasols?

Compare temperature at night, morning, noon, evening, and connect with position of the sun and

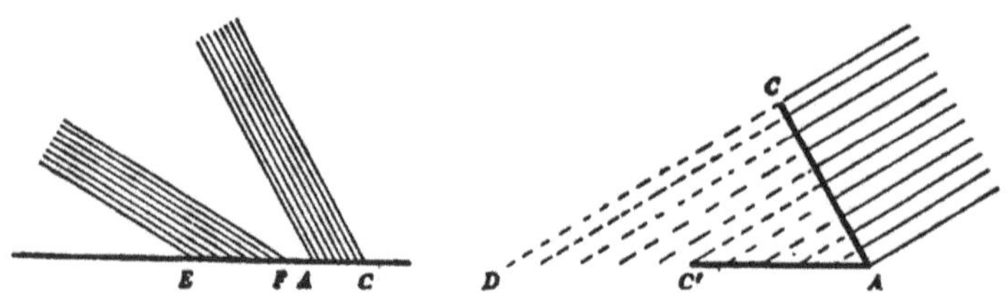

FIG. 6.—Diagrams to explain varying heat effect of rays of light at different angles of incidence.

the *slant* (*angle*) of the rays as they fall on the earth. Use the diagrams (Fig. 6) to explain heating value of sun's rays. In the diagram on the left two sunbeams of equal size (cross section) are represented, one falling on the surface, *EC*, at a smaller angle than the other. There is the same amount of light and heat in both, but the more nearly vertical beam covers less surface, *AC*, than the other. The light is thus more concentrated, intense, and the heating effect greater than on *EF*.

In the diagram on the right, the same thing is shown in another way. *AC* is a surface on which eleven rays fall at right angles. If this surface is now turned into the position *AC′*, so that the light falls at a small angle, only six of these rays strike it. The amount of light or heat received by *AC′* is thus only $\frac{6}{11}$ that received in position *AC*. This diagram gives a more mathematical demonstration than the other, and is easily comprehended by the children.

When is the heating effect of rays the greatest? (When striking perpendicularly.) How does the heating effect of the rays vary with the slant? Now make application to the variation of temperature during a day and connect with altitude of sun above horizon during the day. Consider next the shadow-stick data. These show that the shadow at noon is getting shorter in spring (longer in autumn). Why is it getting shorter? (Because sun is higher in the heavens.) How does the angle of the noon rays compare with the angle several weeks ago? (It is greater in spring.)

Connect with the preceding about relative heating

effects of rays more and less slanting. Why is it warmer in May than in April? (Because the rays are more vertical.)

Briefly explain revolution, using models. Do not refer to axis. Tell of duration of journey around the orbit. Refer to the four seasons. Give the first day of each season. How far apart are the successive dates? Place the earth (globe) in these relative positions. Also represent in diagram. Explain that as the earth goes about its orbit the slant of the sun's rays varies from season to season. The reason for this (position of axis) should not be given in this grade, as it is too difficult.

Another reason for the variation of temperature, which children of this grade can appreciate, is the changing length of day and night. How would the heating effect of the sun when shining only 10 hours in December compare with the effect shining nearly 15 hours in June?

Correlate with reading of stories of the calendar, and the naming of the months.

Eighth grade lesson on seasons.—It is customary to assign this topic in the textbook. This is pernicious, as the pupil will in this way very probably get no true concepts of the terms employed, nor of the problem as a whole. The topic should be presented in class, illustrated concretely with models, experiments, and diagrams, and developed or explained step by step by the teacher. After this it may be safely assigned for drill in the textbook.

The new terms, revolution, orbit, ellipse, plane of orbit, axis, direction and parallelism of axis, should all be made clear and concrete before attempting the explanation of the seasons. Introduce with a sketch of the relation of the earth to the sun. By concrete comparisons give some notion of the immense distance to the sun. By use of model first, then diagram, show the manner of revolution, and the path, the orbit. The usual picture of a very long, narrow ellipse for the earth's orbit with the sun at the center is misleading. As a matter of fact, the orbit is so slightly elliptical that its difference from a circle is not very noticeable. The sun is not at the exact center, but eccentric, yet so slightly that it need not be referred to. Children are apt to use this eccentricity of the sun as a reason for the seasons. So it had better be omitted. Try to get the pupils to picture the plane of the orbit.

The next point to teach is the inclination of the axis. Visualize this by means of rulers placed on the table (used as plane of orbit). While the inclination is referred ultimately to the plane of the orbit, it is really measured by the angle between the axis and a *perpendicular* to the plane of the orbit. Next refer to the northern end of the axis always pointing approximately to the North Star (how find this?) during a revolution, with the consequent *parallelism* of the axis to all its positions. This may be illustrated by means of rulers properly held, also by revolving the earth about a stationary object (sun), but care must be taken by the teacher to keep the axis in correct position; a diagram may also be used to show this. The discussion of the lesson proper may now proceed. The demonstration should be presented from that side of the room which will place the axis of the globe in its correct position (pointing toward North Star), and yet give the class a view of the inclination of the axis, or else the globe may be frankly placed so as to give this last view, and the North Star may be imagined directly in line with the axis. Have some object for the sun. Place first in either summer or winter position. Compare northern and southern hemispheres. Do they face the sun equally? Which is turned away? (Say the northern.) Place in the northern summer position. How is the northern hemisphere placed now with reference to the sun? (Turned toward.) In which of these two positions does it get more light and heat? What season would this be? What season for the northern hemisphere in the other position? Place the globe in the autumn or spring position. Note that the northern hemisphere is turned neither toward nor away from the sun. What would be the conditions of light and heat in this position? (Intermediate.) What season might it be? If passing from winter to summer? Drill on seasons for this hemisphere all around the orbit.

Next compare the southern hemisphere with the northern in relation to the sun. How do the seasons compare? When the northern hemisphere has summer, the southern hemisphere has ——? Why? Etc. When we in the northern hemisphere have spring, the southern hemisphere has —— ? When we have June, the southern hemisphere has ——? (*June* also.) We celebrate Christmas in December. When do the people in the southern hemisphere celebrate it? (Same month and day.)

Another reasoning is based upon the distribution of the vertical rays of the sun. With a device holding a number of knitting needles parallel, to represent the sun's rays covering half the globe, the slant of the rays in the two hemispheres may be made clear. Refer to the fifth grade lesson in seasons and review relative heating capacity of more slanting and less slanting rays. (Fig. 6.) Note in the northern summer position where the rays fall most vertically; least so. Conclude as to seasons here. Note even distribution of light in the spring and autumn positions.

After the models have been used to teach the above, diagrams may be used. The teacher should be sure the pupils understand them and the point of view from which each represents the earth and orbit.

The diagram (Fig. 7) is the best for the eighth grade. Though distances and size are necessarily out of proportion, the general relations are correct. The orbit is shown, as should be, practically a circle. The sun is slightly eccentric, nearer to the earth in northern winter.

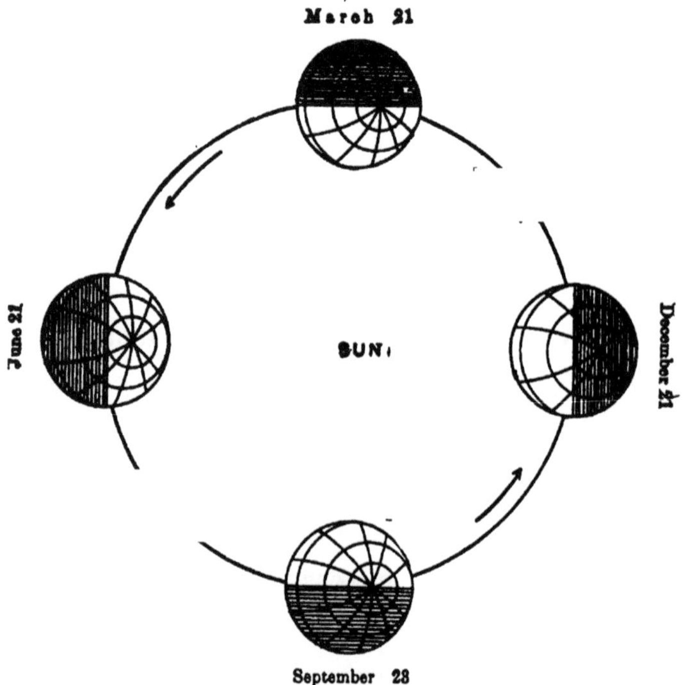

Fig. 7.—Seasons diagram representing the earth as seen from a point in space directly above the center of the orbit.

It is better to represent the sun by the word Sun, or by *S*, than to draw a circle for it, as it would be too much out of proportion with the earth.

The diagram shows the earth, etc., in a bird's-eye view, from directly above the center of the orbit, at a very great distance. The northern hemisphere is here shown. The inclination is represented by the eccentricity of the pole and parallel circles, they being shifted in each position of the earth toward the right in the diagram; that is, the axis must be imagined pointing to the North Star.

This diagram is particularly good to show the tilting of the northern hemisphere toward the sun in June, and away from it in December, and the non-tilted position in March and September.

It is also excellent to show the illumination of the northern hemisphere. It shows the unequal division of each parallel circle by the circle of illumination (line between night and day) in summer and winter; the equal division in spring and autumn. From this can be seen why daylight is longer in summer, shorter in winter; and why days and nights are equal in spring and autumn.

Furthermore, the diagram is good to show the conditions of illumination in the polar region in the different seasons. By means of it the polar night and day can be explained. The relation of the Arctic Circle to the sun can thus be brought out.

The diagram (Fig. 8) shows the earth as viewed from an immense distance, from a place in the plane of the earth's orbit, that is, directly from the side. It is particularly good to show inclination of axis, the tilting of the hemispheres toward or away from the sun, the parallelism of sun's rays, the angles at which they strike the earth, the illumination of the polar regions, and the contrast of the two hemispheres. It is easy to draw. It shows well the relation of the tangent ray to the Arctic Circle, and of the vertical ray to the Tropic of Cancer

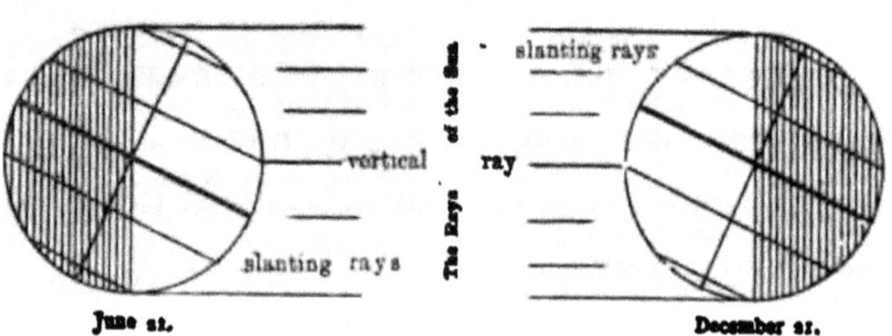

FIG. 8.—Seasons diagram showing the earth as seen from a point outside of the orbit but in the plane thereof.

and Tropic of Capricorn. Its disadvantage is that it cannot be used to show the light relations in spring or autumn.

The diagram (Fig. 9) is often used, but is apt to be misleading unless the point of view is explained, and

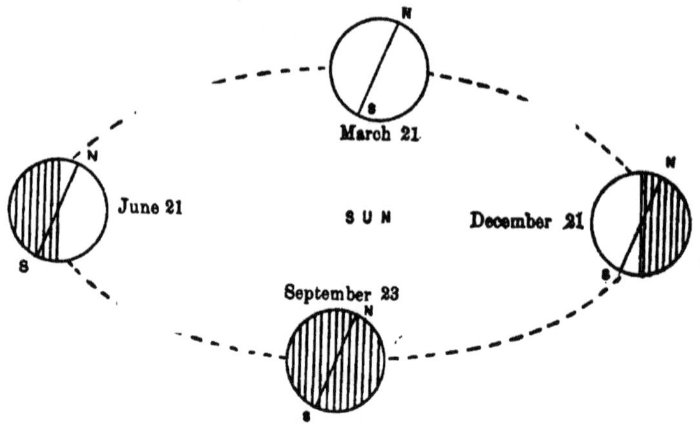

FIG. 9.—Seasons diagram showing the orbit in foreshortened perspective as seen from a point beyond and a little above the orbit.

unless it is used after the two preceding diagrams. It represents the earth and sun as seen from a point in space off to one side of the orbit, and a little above it. It shows the orbit therefore in foreshortened perspective as an ellipse. Pupils should be warned on this point not to picture the orbit thus, but rather as a circle.

With these cautions the diagram may be used, though it does not really contribute any more or as much as the other two. As usually shown in the books, like the diagram, the spring and autumn positions are represented, and the illumination of both poles at the same time is indicated. (The perspective is, however, violated here.)

With such explanation of the diagrams, after or in connection with the demonstration with the models, they become somewhat intelligible to the pupil, though it is a question whether the average eighth-grade pupil ever thoroughly grasps them. But they are found in the books, and some attempt should be made to render them meaningful.

The teacher should practice these diagrams with care so as to be able to reproduce them with fair accuracy.

NOTE. — The subject of zones, polar night and day, length of day in different latitudes, etc., should be left out of the lesson on seasons, and taught in a following lesson, if necessary.

CHAPTER XI

THE CAUSAL RELATION

Comparison of the old and the new geography. — Modern geography is more than a mere catalogue of facts; it is also a study of the relationship of these facts, which to the maturer mind makes the subject so interesting. The old "sailor's geography" answers the questions What? and Where? the modern geography, also the question *Why?* The first two questions call for the exercise of the memory chiefly; the last, for the exercise of the reason also.

Causal relation in geography. — The great principle underlying the science of geography is that of the Causal Relation, also variously called the Principle of Cause and Effect, Geographical Sequence, Geographical Consequence, and Geographical Control or Influence.

This modern phase of geography has been brought about by the application of the scientific method. This was made possible by the marvelous development of geology, meteorology, biology, anthropology, and sociology during the last century. The study of earth forces, earth structure, and life conditions and interrelations has applied far-reachingly to the explanation of geographic facts, such as the origin of surface features, scenery, climate, distribution of vegetation and animal life, and the characteristic adaptations of man to different regions.

The cause, origin, or explanation of geographic facts is a chief feature of the modern science of geography. The principle of origin, growth, development, modification, — in short, the Principle of Evolution, — has been applied to geography. The dynamic character of the earth and its life have been recognized.

Geographical consequence. — Not only are the causes or the origins of things looked for in geography to-day, but the mind is also directed forward to the results or consequences. Every present fact is, in a measure, the cause of some consequent fact, as well as being itself the effect of some preceding. The new geography traces this chain of cause and effect as far as may be. The observation of previous causes operating to produce certain results, leads us to predict of the future what has been true of the past. Thus we may anticipate.

The explanatory principle unifies geography. — It is this explaining of geographical events and features, and this anticipation of future developments, that renders modern scientific geography so fascinating. From a mass of chopped-up, inchoate facts, geography is transformed into an organic whole by this unifying principle. Instead of requiring the memory to retain a mass of unrelated facts and incidents, the principle of causal relation stimulates the reason to seek out the relationship of these facts, and to reduce them to some common principles, to simpler terms, or to classify them in categories more easily kept in mind.

The human significance of geographical relations. — Geography is distinguished from physiography and geology by the emphasis of the human element. To be sure, the extra-human part of geography is also studied, but this is only with regard to its importance in explaining or understanding the relations of human life to the earth. This puts a different aspect upon the relationships of geography. River action has its geological consequences, but in geography the question is, What is the significance of these consequences to man? Mountains are the result of crushing, folding, and uplift, due to the contractional forces within the earth. But this statement has, strictly, no place in geography, unless employed to bring out some feature of human life, as, for example, that mining is made possible by the resulting exposure of the strata; that mountains are obstacles to travel and intercourse; etc.

Geographic influence. — This peculiar geographical aspect of the principle of the causal relation is commonly called the Principle of Geographic Control, or Geographical Influence, referring to the bearing of geographical conditions upon human life. In other words, the features and forces of the environment are studied in relation to man's life. The same thing is expressed from the human standpoint by speaking of the adaptation of man to his environment. In modern geography, then, the environment is studied that the lives of the people may be understood. A national costume, a national occupation, racial stature, and even a racial, spiritual trait may find an explanation as the direct or indirect influence of the environment, or as the adaptation of man to the natural conditions of his habitat.

Examples of geographic influence. — The following few examples of this close causal relationship between man and nature may illustrate the foregoing:

Rivers, since man began, have played an important part in the history of his civilization. In ancient times, as to-day, rivers were used as the seat of human settlements. The mere physical necessity of water to drink would keep man near the streams. Streams erode valleys and deposit flood-plains, both of which are useful to man. Valleys are the easiest routes of travel because of the gentle natural grade. Even to-day the railroads follow the river valleys. Flood-plains, being level, make communication easy.

The rivers abound in fish, and the valleys in game, which to primitive man or early settlers are the main subsistence. When agriculture began and animals were domesticated, the alluvial plains along the streams became still more useful to man. Through agriculture and animal husbandry many more people could live on the same area than before, and hence dense populations sprang up in the valleys of great rivers, as, for example, the ancient civilizations of the Euphrates and Tigris valleys. And to-day the Nile Valley, the Valley of the Yangtse Kiang, and of the Mississippi teem with people. Centers of trade or cities developed here and there, especially along the rivers.

Gradually manufacturing developed, fostered in some cases directly by the streams, as in the higher regions where water power was available.

The riparian races learned early the art of navigation as a result of their familiarity with the water. This was the beginning of river commerce. The commercial development of a nation depends much upon the number and the length of its navigable rivers. This was formerly more the case than it is in this age of railroads. Rivers are the natural arteries of trade, domestic and foreign.

Rivers, being more or less impassable, have long been used as political boundaries, and in this way have had much to do with the segregation of peoples. Segregation tends to conservatism in occupations, customs, dress, etc.

On the spiritual side it may be said that rivers have by their beauty, majesty, and mystery been the inspiration of painters, poets, and composers.

The *topography*, or the lay of the land, also very much influences the life of man. Travel and intercommunication are easier on the level than in the broken surface of a mountainous region. If the map of any country be examined, it will be noticed that the cities and towns are scarcest in the plateau and mountain sections, and densest in the great plains and river valleys. A map showing the density of population makes this still more apparent. A railroad map, likewise, clearly shows how the routes of travel avoid the rough country. In a broken country towns and individual settlers tend to live apart, sociability being attended with too much tedious travel. The result is conservatism, a backward and backwoods type of civilization, out of step with the progress of the plains people. This simplicity or backwardness of civilization is seen in many places, the plateau of Mexico, the mountains of Spain, the plateau of Thibet, the Cumberland Plateau of Tennessee, the Highlands of Scotland, etc.

On account of the diversity of topography in a land or different lands, there arises a differentiation of industries, and a division of labor. The industries of the plains are agriculture, herding on a large scale, manufacture, and commerce. The chief mountain industries are lumbering, grazing on a smaller scale, mining, and quarrying.

Nations of the plains are more open to attack and

pillage from their neighbors. This either leads to subjection, or to the strengthening of their military power. Large nations are eventually built up by conquest and fusion. In a mountainous region there is more of a tendency for a country to remain apart and independent. It is easier to defend a mountainous country from invasion. Hence we find interesting examples of small, independent countries surrounded by powerful neighbors, as Switzerland, Montenegro, and Andorra in Europe. Russia and the United States are examples of nations that have spread largely by annexing foreign territory.

Climate.—Some of the most far-reaching consequences are due to climate. If the world had but one climate, and one kind of weather, it would be very monotonous indeed, in plant and animal life, in the occupations and customs of man, in his dress, and probably in his very color and physique.

1. Sun, source of heat.—To trace the study in proper sequence, it is necessary to begin with the sun, whose rays of light are converted into heat as they strike the earth. These rays strike the equatorial regions more squarely, the polar parts more glancingly, the result being a gradation of temperature from the torrid equator to the frigid poles. The situation is complicated by the inclination of the earth on its axis, with consequent seasonal variations as the earth revolves around the sun.

2. Winds.—The unequal heating of the atmosphere

by the sun is the primary cause of winds. The water of the earth is evaporated by this same heat, only to be condensed in the cooler altitudes into clouds, and these are drifted about by the winds. In general, the winds blow prevailingly in a definite direction in a given latitude, their direction being primarily determined by convection and modified by the rotation of the earth.

3. The rainfall of a region depends upon the temperature and the prevailing winds. These climatic factors are much modified by the changes of the seasons, by the distribution of land and water, by local disturbances in barometric pressure, etc., but nevertheless there is a definite, though complex, relation between them.

4. The topography of a country affects its climate, for as the elevation increases, the temperature decreases. Also the trend of the highlands is an important factor in modifying the temperature, but especially affecting the distribution of the rainfall. The moisture of the atmosphere condenses on the windward side of mountains, leaving the other side more or less arid.

5. Climate and vegetation. — The temperature, wind, and moisture conditions being thus very complex and widely different in various parts of the world, the distribution of vegetation, which depends upon these factors, will be varied. Thus we have the tundra vegetation of the polar lands, the conifer belt next, then deciduous hardwoods, and finally tropical vegetation. Tem-

perature is the chief factor in this distribution from north to south. The factor of moisture affects this still more. The rainfall of polar regions is least, that of the tropics the greatest. The luxuriance of tropic vegetation is largely due to the moisture in the soil and the air.

6. In the United States the distribution of rain is unequal. This country lies in the region affected by the prevailing westerly winds. Owing to the north and south trend of the highlands in the west, the moisture is greatest near the Pacific Coast, on the windward side of the Coast Range and the still higher Sierras and Cascades. Descending on the other side of these last-named ranges, the winds are drying, producing as a consequence the arid conditions in the Great Basin. Only on the tops of the Wasatch and other high Basin Mountains does a little rain fall in this otherwise rainless region. Again farther east on the still higher and colder Rockies some more of the latent moisture of the westerlies is condensed. But the winds continuing eastward fall on the eastern side of the Rockies, and here again are drying, because they are warming up, and they render the Great Plains semiarid. Thus the western half of the United States is divided into a number of north and south belts of varying rainfall.

7. Variety of vegetation in the United States. — These variations in the United States of temperature from north to south, and of rainfall from east to west, have

brought about a great variation in vegetation. On the mountains near the Pacific are the densest and tallest of forests, with conifers flourishing more toward the north, native hardwoods toward the south, and introduced citrous trees. In the somewhat drier valleys of Washington and Oregon thrive the hardy fruits, hops, and grains; and in a similar valley in central California, grains, grapes, and semitropical fruits. In the desert of the Basin, toward the north, the sage brush abounds, while farther south the cacti are typical. Where little rain falls on the tops of the Wasatch Mountains there is a fringe of forest growth, and on the Rockies are extensive, though somewhat open, forests of conifers and hardwoods. Then come the Great Plains with their semidesert vegetation described on page 75.

The eastern half of the United States is more variable in climate, and the differences in temperature from north to south are more marked. The resultant vegetation differences are well indicated by the staple agricultural crops, — the small grains (rye, barley, oats, and wheat), hay, flax, and potatoes in the north, next the famous corn belt, then the tobacco belt, and then the subtropical cotton, rice, and sugar cane along the Gulf, where also flourish the orange tree and palm.

8. Climatic distribution of animals. — The animal life is affected directly by temperature and moisture conditions, and by the character of the vegetation. For

the sake of brevity, suffice it to call attention to the distribution of the fur-bearing animals and domesticated sheep in the north; cattle, horses, and swine farther south; and to recall the study of the grazing industry of the Great Plains, page 75.

9. Man in relation to climate.—Thus far in this causal study only the non-human side has been referred to. The whole purpose of the study thus far was to lay a foundation for the following study of the adaptation of man to the varying conditions imposed upon him by the differences of climate.

Climate is probably the most important geographic "control" that affects man. He is directly affected by the weather and climate, and seeks to shelter himself from the elements. While primitive races go naked in the tropics, in colder regions they clothe themselves in furs and fibrous fabrics. Possibly the very complexion of man is the result of climatic conditions, for in the warmer latitudes the world around the races of man are more swarthy.

(*a*) Shelter.—The severities of the climate cause man to seek a shelter, be it the protection of a tree, a cave, a skin tent, a dugout, an igloo of snow, or a house of logs, boards, brick, or stone.

Man must adapt his ways of life to the passing seasons. He "makes hay while the sun shines," and lays up a store for the winter. He is thus forced to be provident.

(*b*) Wind.—Of the winds man makes direct use in sailing, windmills, etc. Formerly, before the days of the steamship, routes of marine commerce were determined by the prevailing winds. Winds have to be taken into account in the blowing of dust in the streets, in the encroachment of sand dunes, the drifting snow in winter, in disastrous storms and hurricanes. They are beneficial to man in bringing rain from the sea, and in tempering the heat and the cold by circulation.

(*c*) Migration.—Man may modify his circumstances somewhat, or perhaps he can adapt himself better to conditions. Thus races may migrate to a more congenial climate, and individuals travel from one region to another to escape the severities of climate. Southern California, Florida, Bermuda, and the Riviera are favorite winter resorts; while Alaska, the Wilds of Canada, the Maine Woods, and Norway are sought for cooler summers.

Altitude has a minor effect on temperature, yet it is important. In all lands the mountains are sought during the heat of summer. The plateaus of Central Mexico, Ecuador, India, and Africa, even in tropical latitudes, are endurable, though the ameliorating effect may in part be due to the lesser humidity of the air. The trend of the Alps cuts off the cold winds from the north of Europe, and renders Cisalpine Italy delightful by contrast. The Himalayas act in a similar way.

(*d*) Weather.—The daily climate, that is, the weather, is of concern to everybody, affecting the routine of work, and the planning for pleasure. So important is a foreknowledge of the weather that the government spends millions of dollars annually in the study of the weather for daily forecasting.

(*e*) Rain, life conditions, industries. — Man may endure the heat of the equator, and the extremes of arctic cold, but water he must have, water to drink, water for his cattle and his crops, water for power purposes and for navigation. Therefore he avoids the deserts. In general, the map showing the distribution of rainfall would serve to show the density of population. Roughly speaking, the more abundant the rainfall, the more people may make a living in a region. More migrations have been caused by rainfall conditions than on account of temperature.

The rain is our ultimate drinking supply. Some may be caught directly for this purpose, but most of it is obtained indirectly from the off-flow and from underground sources. Locally great engineering works have been constructed for the supply of water for cities or communities. The Romans conducted water thus by means of an aqueduct, the ruins of which still stand. Modern New York City brings its water from the Catskill Highlands.

But more interesting, from the human standpoint, is

the indirect influence of rainfall through the determination of vegetation and animal life, and in this it is usually combined with other factors of climate, especially temperature. Natural vegetation and agricultural crops are impossible without water. Different kinds of plants require varying amounts of water. Forests require at least twenty inches of rain per year, and this mainly in the growing season. Where less rain falls, prairies, steppes, or deserts prevail. The prairies are covered with a continuous growth of sod of grass, aster, goldenrod, wild sunflower, etc. The steppes generally have a sparse grass growth in tufts here and there interspersed with other drought-resistant plants.

Where there is sufficient rain to maintain forests, the forest industries, lumbering, turpentine, rubber, tan bark, the furniture and implement industries, prevail. The forest regions are usually well suited for animal husbandry and ordinary agriculture, and so the trees are generally cleared away in the course of time to permit farming.

Different agricultural crops require different amounts of moisture, and can endure different degrees of drought. This, with the varying temperature conditions, chiefly determines what kind of crop shall be raised in a locality, whether rye, wheat, corn, macaroni wheat, alfalfa, tobacco, cotton, rice, sugar cane, coffee, rubber, etc.

The fact of irrigation emphasizes the controlling

power of water. By irrigation man attempts to modify otherwise unfavorable conditions, by artificially supplying water to his crops. In this way considerable arid land has been reclaimed and made habitable.

Animal husbandry, like agriculture, is conditioned strictly by climatic conditions. Grazing or herding can only be conducted where grass will grow. The cattle industry thrives well in agricultural regions, and is conducted in a small way by individual farmers throughout the world, as in Holland, England, New England, in the Central states, etc. But the cattle industry on a large scale, with herds of thousands, likewise the great sheep and goat herding, are carried on in regions too dry for ordinary farming, in the semiarid steppes of Argentina, Mexico, Spain, Russia, South Africa, Australia, and on our own Great Plains. This specialization of the agricultural and herding industries in different regions was brought about mainly by the difference in rainfall.

The forest, agricultural, and animal industries provide many of the raw materials required by the manufacturing industry. This is to a great extent independent of climatic conditions, and yet is influenced thereby. The success of the manufacturing occupations, of course, depends upon the production of the raw materials. The cotton manufacturer in England watches carefully the crop conditions (weather, etc.) of the cotton crop in the United States. The miller is concerned about the success of the wheat crop.

Some manufactories are located in the heart of the regions that produce their raw materials, as flour mills in the wheat country, and furniture factories in the hardwood section. However, the ease of modern transportation and market opportunities may interfere to keep the source of raw material and the factories that use them far apart.

Certain special manufactures require definite climatic conditions. The sun-dried bricks of ancient Babylon and the adobe of the Zuni require a dry climate to make them and to preserve them. In southern California there is a long dry season, which is utilized in the open-air drying of fruits. The niter industry of South America depends upon desert conditions. It is even said that the cotton industry of England developed on the western side of the Pennine Hills partly because here the greater moisture of the atmosphere made the cotton fiber less brittle and less liable to break in the process of spinning. The salt industry of many parts of the world depends upon the possibility of open-air evaporation in a dry climate.

(*f*) This study of the climatic control may be summarized in stating that the world is composed of many climes, which tend to create a great variety of industrial, social, and cultural conditions, a great variety of occupations, a grand division of labor, an interdependence of region upon region, class upon class, an interchange of commodities or commerce, and a mutual helpfulness.

Abuse of the causal principle. — Useful as this principle of the geographic influence is, it must be employed with caution. As a rule, geographic facts are not due to one simple cause, but to a combination of causes, the influence of each of which may be difficult to judge proportionately. Sometimes one factor works favorably, while others are adverse. The causal principle may be pushed too far. For example, a city may be situated on an excellent harbor. It may be far from the truth to say that this harbor determined the location of the city. The real reason may have been very different, and there may be other good harbors or better in the vicinity. We may say truly, though, that the excellence of the harbor contributed to the commercial development of the city.

The human equation. — Again, in trying to explain the human features of geography, the human reason, inclination, and even whim may be more important factors than the natural conditions. Ignorance and perversity even determine locations of industries or towns. The sociological factors governing some of these human institutions are often very far removed from the physical environment.

The establishment of some manufacturing industries

is sometimes seemingly out of place, when the physical conditions merely are considered. The saving factor is often the human qualities of good management, inventiveness, skilled labor, economy in production, and even patriotism (supporting native industry).

Again, there are cities with actually poor location which yet thrive. Harbors may be made artificially, power may be transported in the form of coal, or transmitted as electricity, tunnels or bridges may make the place accessible, etc. Countries are found where the mountainous topography has not been a hindrance, apparently, to development, as in the case of Switzerland. Isolation is not always a bad thing. England's insularity was for centuries a guarantee against invasion and permitted a peaceful development.

Care must be exercised not to make too sweeping generalizations about the influence of the physical environment. The case must not be pushed too far. Obvious physical influences should be noted, but the human factor must not be neglected. It is worth while in geography to appreciate the "effect of man on nature." Man makes some changes in his environment, and directs the course of nature somewhat along the lines of his choice. He is constantly changing the map of the world. To be sure, this is mainly a political feature, yet the distribution of races is thereby affected. He likewise affects the distribution of plants and animals by the extermination of game, forests, and harmful kinds of plants and animals; by the importation of foreign species to new regions. The small grains, and the domesticated animals, have been carried the world over from their original home in Asia, while American maize, tobacco, and potato have spread likewise.

Man's intellectual adaptation to his environment. — Man modifies the topography to a certain extent. He grades and levels the land for his cities and roads. He tunnels the mountains and rivers. He changes the courses of rivers, and makes canals that divide continents, constructs irrigation canals, deepens natural waterways, builds breakwaters, bridges chasms and streams. He modifies the climate by artificially heating his houses, and can even prevent light frosts in his orchards by means of smudge fires. Even distance is annihilated by the modern methods of communication and transportation.

Yet even in these human efforts the influence of nature is seen. The uneven topography necessitated the leveling; the insurmountable mountain had to be tunneled; the river barrier required the tunnel or the bridge; the narrowness of the isthmus suggested the possibility of the canal; the shoals of the river or harbor would not have been dredged had the water been deeper, etc. The "overcoming of nature" by man is simply another adaptation of man to nature, an intellectual or "psychic adaptation." Still, for purposes of history and human geography it is well to consider this adjustment as an achievement of man over his environment.

The general effect of man's efforts to modify his physical surroundings is concentrated locally, and, on the whole, is insignificant in comparison with what he cannot change. And yet, on the course of human affairs, these works of man may have a wonderfully great influence. The course of history is made as much by man himself as by the physical environment.

The principle of causal relation in teaching. — The discussion and illustration of the causal relation in geography in the preceding pages were intended for the benefit of the teacher. It is not intended, by any means, to suggest that children should study geography thus intensively, for this is beyond their capacity, and outside their interest. For children such a treament may readily become too speculative and too difficult. The teacher, however, should know these relationships of geography, and should present the subject, especially in the upper grades, with the whole organic unity of geography in mind. The most obvious and simple causal relations will appeal to the child, and should be pointed out. In the more complex relationships the facts should be presented in the causal order, but the pupil need not be pressed to work this out. Many such relations will gradually dawn on the pupil as other similar cases are considered, and the geographic consequence of facts studied many lessons back may be noticed in a future lesson. At any rate, if the subject is properly presented, a grammar grade pupil will get a general realization of the close dependence of man on nature, and should be able to point out specifically some of the more obvious geographic influences.

One method that helps to bring this about is to study a country by topics in causal sequence,—location, surface, climate, drainage, vegetation, animal life, mineral resources, industries, human institutions, and history. It will help pupils to learn and to remember. It will enable them to work out little geographical problems that may be set for them. Grammar grade pupils, at least, should be conscious of this causal sequence, which should be used in map study as well as in the text.

This logical treatment may become tedious even in higher grades. The non-human side is pressed too much to the front. Children are especially interested in the human aspect of geography. This is especially true of beginners. It is not wise, therefore, always to begin with physical geography. The discovery of the region, its history, the racial characteristics, interesting architectural features, national customs, national dress, etc., may often be a better starting point for a lesson.

The point to observe is that the physical and industrial geography of a country should be studied sequentially, and where profitable, reference may be made to other causal relationships, such as the effect of the physical features on history, or the relation between dress and climate, etc.

The place for the causal study of geography is in the upper grades. Still even in the lower easily perceived connections should occasionally be remarked, as, Why does the Eskimo wear furs? Why does he not make his house of wood? Of what advantage is it for a city to be on a big river? On a good harbor? Near a coal mine? Why are prairies good for farming? What use does a city make of near-by waterfalls?

Even where the statement of the causal relation is not required from the pupils, the facts should be set forth connectedly in that relation, as, "Chicago is situated on Lake Michigan, in the center of a great farming and manufacturing section, and has 2,200,000 people." "Cotton grows in the moist, warm region about the Gulf of Mexico." "On the vast treeless plains are great herds of cattle." "The people of the eastern states cleared away the forests for farming purposes." Later on the reason will appear.

CHAPTER XII

POLITICAL AND DESCRIPTIVE GEOGRAPHY

Political geography. — That phase of geography which deals with the division of the earth into nations and other political parts, with the races of man, and the various activities of human life, including the industrial, social, civic, and even educational and religious phases, is generally called political geography. This branch plays an important part in the elementary school. It does not stand by itself alone, however. In the preceding chapters the place and value of mathematical and physical geography have been considered. It was there shown that, in spite of their importance as distinct sciences, they were to be subordinated, in the elementary school, to political geography, or at least taught in connection with it.

Descriptive geography. — "It is unsatisfactory to rend apart geography into separate branches; it then becomes dry bones." (Mill.) The natural blending of the various branches of geography in the depiction of the appearance and conditions of a region or country, and in the account of the inhabitants, their mode of life, and their national characteristics, is known as descriptive geography.

The chief geographical interests of children, young or old, as was seen in the chapter on Interests, are human — such as racial and national peculiarities, various modes of living in different lands, occupations, adaptations of man to his environment, the life in cities, etc. Political geography presents this phase of the subject, and so conforms to the interests of children. The knowledge it teaches, of the social environment, is also very practical. For these reasons, textbooks in geography for children are chiefly political, or rather of the blended descriptive type. In this, physical geography is used to picture the location, topography, scenery, the climate, and resources, and to help understand the human life in that setting. The simple observational home geography of beginners is really descriptive geography.

Primary and advanced geography. — Descriptive geography for the elementary school is usually divided into two courses (sometimes three). The first is called primary or elementary geography. This generally begins with home geography. Then follows an application of its simple principles to a rough sketch of the world as a whole, in which the human side is particularly emphasized. In this "first round," except in home geography, the treatment should be a rather dogmatic presentation of facts. That is, the pupils at the age of eight to ten are not mature enough to reason out easily the relationships of geographical facts, and often would not appreciate them if pointed out. So the treatment should be chiefly a positive statement of facts put as interestingly and vividly as possible, in order that the memory may retain them better. Of course simple and evident relationships should be worked out, and facts regarding distant regions must be interpreted and judged in the light of the geographical knowledge gained through the direct study of home geography.

In primary geography all continents and principal countries are visited, and the general, great, striking, and interesting facts, from the child's standpoint, are considered. Through the study of human life in many lands, the essential facts of occupations, manufactures, natural resources, climatic conditions, and surface features are concisely treated. Instead of applying the causal principle rigidly, it is better generally to work back to the causes from their consequences in human life. In this way the perspective will present man in the foreground, with the physical features as a setting. The map work is, of course, to be associated with the descriptive text. (See page 172.)

The essential facts of the subject learned in primary geography. — It is important to remember the function of primary geography. Aside from details of fact, more extended correlation, fuller appreciation of the interrelations of geography, and the generalization of abstract principles, the pupil should have at the end of the primary course all the essential facts of geography that he will have at the end of the advanced course, — the distinguishing characteristics of the nations, their chief products, the general facts of world topography, and the chief locational facts necessary for daily use in life.

This is accomplished in the primary course by the conciseness with which it is taught, by the rather dogmatic treatment; and on account of the readiness of pupils in these grades to accept such treatment, and the ease with which they retain facts in the memory. This period is, therefore, the most suitable for acquiring the great mass of locative and distributive facts essential in geography. This does not mean a mere cramming by rote of the textbook. The main point to remember is that at this stage geography answers particularly the questions What? and Where? and every means should be used to add interest to the work, to awaken thought, to fix by means of thoughtful associations, and even to work out the more simple causal relations.

An example from primary geography. — The following, taken from a well-known text, is an example of the treatment of a country in the primary course:

SWITZERLAND

Language and government. — Switzerland is the only country of Europe, thus far studied, that has no seacoast. Neither has it a language of its own. Notice what countries surround it. Although it is very small, most of the inhabitants of the southern part speak Italian, those in the west, French, and those in the north and east, German. The most common language is German.

This is the only European country that you have studied, except one, that is not a monarchy. Its people, living among the mountains where they could easily defend themselves, or hide from their enemies, declared themselves independent of kings hundreds of years ago, and the country has long been a republic.

Agriculture. — The many lofty mountains seriously interfere with agriculture. The Alps extend completely across the country, and the Jura Mountains skirt the northwestern boundary. These mountains are so rugged that, except in the valleys, few people live among them. Between the two mountain districts, however, is a narrow plateau, where the surface is much less rugged. It is here that most of the people dwell.

One of the leading farm products is grain, raised mainly on the plateau. On the lower lands, especially near the German border, there are extensive vineyards. There is excellent pasturage for cattle and goats among the mountains, and these animals are raised there in great numbers. In spring and summer, as the snows melt from the mountain sides, the goats and cattle are pastured higher and higher. Such pasture is called an *alp*, and this is the origin of the name of the range, the Alps.

Lumbering and manufacturing. — Where the slopes are too rugged for farming, there is much forest. Therefore, lumber is an important product of the country.

Although there is no good coal in Switzerland, the Swiss do a large amount of manufacturing. Among the principal products are wine, butter, and cheese. Wood carving is also an industry in which many of the Swiss find employment. During the long winters, the wood from the mountains is shaped into toys, clocks, and other articles. Have you ever seen a Swiss clock?

The Swiss have become widely known for their manufacture of textile goods, such as lace, linen, silk, and cotton goods. They also make much jewelry, especially watches. In some of this work water power is used, for an abundance of power is supplied by the mountain streams. A great deal of manufacturing, however, is done by hand in the homes of the workmen, rather than in large factories. From these facts you can readily see that the Swiss people must be very skillful, progressive, and well educated.

Entertainment of tourists. — In the lofty Alps there is some of the grandest scenery of the world. Their snow-covered peaks, their glaciers descending into the valleys, and the lakes in their midst are wonders that many people like to view. Tens of thousands of people go to Switzerland every summer to enjoy the climate and the scenery, and one of the chief occupations of the Swiss people is to take care of such visitors.

Chief cities. — The capital of the Republic is Berne. Other important cities are Zürich, Basel, and Geneva, three manufacturing centers.

The advanced descriptive geography of the sixth, seventh, and eighth grades differs from the primary more in the point of view and the treatment, than in subject matter. The subject is that of the first course studied more intensively, in detail, and with the reasons for the facts (causal relation) generally considered; history, literature, and nature-study are more called upon (correlation) to enrich the subject, and to assist in its comprehension; the subject is also studied more formally (sequential order of topics); many principles of geography are developed as a working basis for further study; certain important, typical features are studied in detail as a standard of a class (type study); more use is made of the comparative method of study; and more use is made of other sources than the textbook, such as supplementary readers and reference books. In succeeding chapters some of these methods of presentation are taken up.

Some additional mathematical geography is introduced which was too difficult for the lower grades, and physical geography takes a much larger place in advanced courses, being used more in explanation of the political features. In fact, in some curricula elementary physical geography is introduced more for its own sake, in the seventh or eighth grade. Commercial geography is of greater interest to pupils of this age, and therefore industrial topics receive a larger treatment, and this is sometimes enlarged, in the eighth grade, into a separate branch. (See Chapter XVIII.)

Detailed study of a country in advanced geography. — The general difference of advanced and primary geography may be well seen from a comparison of the account of Switzerland, page 146, with the following taken from an advanced textbook. Note how the interest is aroused and held, the sequential order of topics, the causal relation, the emphasis of physical and commercial features, the comparison with other lands, the interpretation of the human facts by the physical environment, the correlation with history.

The study begins with a statement of the historical and the geographical importance of the British Isles and then proceeds to explain this position as follows:[1]

The prevailing westerly winds also partly account for the greatness of the United Kingdom. Two days out of three these winds blow across the British Isles; and, since they have crossed a vast expanse of warm water, they greatly temper the climate. Indeed, the winter season is milder than that in northern United States, and the summer is cooler.

The prevailing westerlies, bearing an abundance of moisture, so distribute it over the islands that no section suffers from drought. Yet the western portions receive more rain than the eastern, because the damp ocean winds reach them first.

As already stated, the mountains of Great Britain, like those of New England, are so old that they are worn very low. While these uplands rarely rise more than one or two thousand feet above sea level, there are occasional higher peaks of hard rock. For example, the granite peak of Ben Nevis, in Scotland, the highest point in the British Isles, is forty-three hundred feet in elevation. The *Scottish Highlands* are so rugged and barren that few people are able to live there.

Where the rocks are softer, and less disturbed by mountain folding, there are lower and more level tracts. . . .

The coast line of the British Isles is very irregular, as may be seen from the map. State the reasons. How does the coast compare with that of New England? Since the mountainous western portion had more deep valleys for the sea to enter than the level

[1] Maps, illustrations, suggestions, review questions, and title topics, as well as references to pages, maps, and illustrations, are omitted.

plains of the east, there are more good harbors on the west than on the east coast. On both sides, however, the mouths of the larger rivers usually make good ports. Why?

Another reason for the importance of the United Kingdom is the fact that these islands have great natural resources, and have therefore developed important industries. In our study of the United States we found that the people are mainly engaged in lumbering, agriculture, fishing, mining, manufacturing, and commerce. There is almost no lumbering in the British Isles, for, although in early times a large part of the land was wooded, little forest now remains; and lumber is, therefore, one of the leading imports. . . .

Since no portion of the British Isles is arid, the ranching industry is not developed there as in the western United States. Much live stock is raised, however, . . . and the British Isles are noted for their great number of fine cattle, sheep, and horses. . . . The Shetland Islands are famous for Shetland ponies; and on the three Channel Islands, — Jersey, Guernsey, and Alderney, near the French coast, — three breeds of cattle which are well known in the United States have been developed.

The importance of grazing is partly explained by the fact that much of the surface, like that of New England, is too rocky or mountainous to be cultivated. Besides this, some of the plains in eastern England, although too sterile for farming, make excellent pasture land. The mild winters and the damp air, which encourage the growth of grass, further favor stock raising. In addition, the cheapness with which grain is raised in other countries, like the United States, and carried to the British Isles, has made it less necessary for the British to use their land in raising grain.

The cool summer climate, of advantage in some respects, is unfavorable to many kinds of farming. For example, it prevents the production of corn, cotton, tobacco, and grapes, which require warm summers. More hardy products, however, such as oats, barley, and wheat, are easily raised. Turnips, potatoes, beans, and peas are other important crops; also hops, which, together with barley, are used in the manufacture of beer. Owing to the many towns and cities, truck farming is of great importance.

Since the early inhabitants had to cross the sea in order to reach these islands, and since most of their descendants have lived either on or near the coast, it is natural that many of the British should adopt a seafaring life. This sort of life has also been encouraged by the fact that food fish abound on the shallow banks of the North Sea and of the ocean to the north and west of the islands. More than one hundred thousand men and twenty-five thousand boats from the British Isles are employed in fishing.

Among the fish caught are cod, haddock, and herring, as off the coast of New England and Newfoundland. . . . Many fishing hamlets are scattered along the coast; but the fishing industry here, as in our country, is becoming centered more and more in the large towns, which possess the capital for large vessels and expensive fishing outfits. The chief fishing centers, like Boston and Gloucester in Massachusetts, are LONDON, HULL, and GRIMSBY in England, and ABERDEEN in Scotland.

One of the resources of the British Isles which early attracted people from southern Europe was the tin in southwestern England. This metal is not mined in many parts of the world, but has always been in great demand. Even before the time of Cæsar, ships from the Mediterranean came to England to obtain tin for use in the manufacture of bronze.

On the other hand, the abundance of two other minerals, coal and iron ore, reminds us of our own country. The one small island of Great Britain produces three fourths as much coal as all of our states together; and the United States and Great Britain are the two leading coal-producing countries of the world. While most of the coal is bituminous, that in southern Wales is more like our anthracite. Large numbers of miners in the United States are Welshmen who have come from that section.

Iron ore is also abundant and favorably situated. None of

the British iron ore is far from coal; and in some places the same shaft is used to bring both coal and iron to the surface. Limestone is also abundant and near at hand. This reminds us of the conditions at Birmingham, Ala., which is named after BIRMINGHAM, England, because they resemble each other in having an abundance of coal and iron ore near together. The extent of the mining industry in the United Kingdom is indicated by the fact that more than half a million persons are employed underground. . . .

Considering the abundance of coal and iron ore on the one hand and of wool from the millions of sheep on the other, it is clear that Great Britain has materials for extensive manufacture. As in New England, the hilly sections have abundant water power due to the glacier, and this also has favored manufacturing. Later, when the use of steam became known, the abundant stores of coal were of great importance. . . .

From the spinning and weaving of wool it was easy to turn to the manufacture of cotton goods; and on the western side of the northern mountains we find a great cotton-manufacturing industry. Dampness is one of the points in favor of that section, for in a dry air cotton is in danger of becoming too brittle to spin and weave easily. Another reason why this work is best developed on the west side of the island is the fact that it is nearer the United States, from which so much of the raw cotton comes.

Since the British climate will not permit the cultivation of cotton, it is necessary to import all that is used. It requires over two billion pounds a year to supply the mills. Although much cotton is now obtained from Egypt, India, and other parts of the British Empire, our Southern States still supply the greatest quantity. The center of the cotton manufacturing is MANCHESTER. What other cities do you find situated near by? . . .

The three industries connected with cotton, wool, and iron have made Great Britain one of the great workshops of the world. The most important is cotton manufacturing; iron ranks next, and wool is third.

What has thus far been said applies chiefly to Great Britain; but Ireland forms a striking contrast to Great Britain in several respects.. In the first place, it is mainly a country of farms instead of manufactures: . . .

First among the coastal cities to be noted is LONDON, on the east side, with BRISTOL opposite it on the west coast. North of London is HULL, with LIVERPOOL on the opposite side; and in southern Scotland is EDINBURGH, near the coast, paired with GLASGOW on the west. On the south side the two most important ports are SOUTHAMPTON and PORTSMOUTH. What are the two principal cities of Ireland? Locate each.

Steamships, railway lines, and canals connect the various cities, carrying immense quantities of freight. In Great Britain and Ireland there are nearly four thousand miles of canal and over twenty-three thousand miles of railway.

London, the capital of the empire and the largest city in the world, is situated on the Thames River. Like many other British rivers, the Thames has a wide, deep mouth, owing to the sinking of the land. London is located upon its banks as far inland as high tide allows vessels to go, or fifty miles from the open sea. The advantage of this position lies in the fact that, while it is in the interior of the island, it has direct water communication with foreign countries.

(Then follows a description of London, comparing with other chief cities.)

While we have learned many facts about the British Isles, some important questions are not yet fully answered. For example, why does this little country possess more colonies than any other nation of the earth? Further, why should it have the greatest foreign trade? And why, the greatest number of vessels upon the sea?

Some of the reasons in answer to these questions are as follows:

The fact that Great Britain is so small — no point in the island being more than seventy miles from salt water — is a reason why many of the British have become sailors. It is not surprising, therefore, that they have been great explorers.

Nor is it to be wondered at that, as these explorers discovered new parts of the world, they laid claim to them in the name of their mother country. In this way, and by war, Great Britain came into possession of the Thirteen Colonies of North America, and of Canada, India, Australia, much of Africa, and many other places. At present her territory includes about one fifth of the land surface of the globe, and one quarter of its inhabitants.

These colonies and dependencies help to explain Great Britain's enormous foreign commerce; for the colonies have found it more to their advantage to trade with the mother country than with other nations, which speak a different language and have less understanding of them or sympathy with them. The colonies sell raw products and foodstuffs to the mother country, and she sends to them clothing, steel goods, and other manufactured articles. It is largely the exchange of goods with these colonies that has made the foreign trade of Great Britain nearly twice that of any other nation. Next to her colonies, Great Britain's greatest trade is with the United States.

Some of the reasons why this little island owns more vessels than any other nation have already appeared. In fishing, exploring, and making settlements, a large number of ships have been needed; and many warships have been required for the proper defense of her widely scattered colonies. Another reason for so large a navy is the fact that the British Isles are cut off from all other nations by water. For defense, therefore, the British must rely upon warships rather than upon a standing army.

Further than this, the British are actually *forced* to own many ships. Here are over forty million people living on two small islands, from whose soil it is impossible to obtain the necessary food. They must send ships away for their flour, meat, sugar, tea, coffee, etc.; and they must send abroad for much of their raw materials for manufacture. Also, in order to pay for the raw materials and food, their manufactured goods must be shipped to all parts of the world; otherwise such extensive manufacturing would be impossible. From this it is plain why a very large number of vessels must be employed; and there are two reasons why the British, rather than other nations, should own them. In the first place, such trade is profitable; and secondly, when they own their own vessels, they can send them where and when they will, and are therefore independent in case of war.

These facts, coupled with the remarkable energy of the British, are the principal reasons why the United Kingdom greatly surpasses all other nations in number of warships and merchant vessels.

The comparative examination of primary and advanced textbooks by different authors would be profitable. Unfortunately some of them do not fully accord with the principles of pedagogy.

The need of an attractive presentation. —The interest aroused by the study of geography depends upon the inherent attractiveness of the facts to be learned; upon how they are told; how elaborated by association; how rendered vivid by description; how pictured to the eye; how humanized by allusion to human affairs; and upon how these facts are connected with each other, with other studies, and with daily life.

Baldness of most texts. — A mere summary of the facts to be learned in a course of geography would be about as interesting as the dictionary. Geography should read like a story. The chief reason why this subject has no interest for so many is that the ordinary textbooks are so meager and laconic in their treatment, and so little is done by the teacher to elaborate the text. If the teacher did her part, filling in the mere dry bones of the text with the life and blood of interesting matter, then such an epitomized form of textbook would suffice. This is the European method. In this country, however, geography is based too much upon the text alone.

Supplementary readers. — To furnish the additional subject matter, to infuse life and interest into the subject, we have supplementary readers. These are not written in the brief, categorical style of the textbook, but are often real books of travel, full of local color and human interest. They are specific, not general.

Some of these supplementary readers adopt the plan of representing children touring the countries described, which insures more the child's viewpoint of looking at the world. Many of these books take up special phases — the industries, the foods of man, domesticated animals, the dwellings of man, or the means of transportation. Some treat of the sky, of the weather, the land and water. Some are biographical, and some deal with discovery and exploration. A host of nature readers are useful in geography. There are also books of original descriptions by great travelers and writers.

Uses of the supplementary literature. — By correlating such literature with geography, the breadth of the subject is materially increased. Supplementary readers may be used in various ways. In primary geography only the simpler kind can be read by the pupil himself, and this should be done chiefly in class. The teacher should occasionally read from them to the pupils. The same thing may be done in upper grades, but here more independent reading should be expected. In the seventh and eighth grades a little reference work can be attempted, but the references should be very definitely assigned. This is good for the topical study and type study methods. Other texts, standard reference books, and encyclopedias should also be used in such reference work. Encyclopedias, however, should be used with care, as, for grammar grades, much in them is too abstruse.

School libraries should be well stocked with good supplementary literature in geography. Of such books as Carpenter's Geographical Readers there should be sets for a group or a whole class, for permanent use. Books of travel, discovery, exploration, etc., should be given to children for home reading, or for their leisure time in school. There are also good books of geographical fiction, such as *Robinson Crusoe*, *The Swiss Family Robinson*, *The Mysterious Island*, *Treasure Island*, *Around the World in Eighty Days*, and many others, that should be placed within the children's reach.

In upper grades, where it is likely to be more appreciated, descriptions of scenery, architecture, etc., may be read by the teacher from such authors as Cooper, Scott, Irving, George Eliot, Stewart Edward White, John Muir, etc. In this way the æsthetic appreciation of geography may be cultivated, an aim of no small importance when interest in the study is considered. The imagination is not greatly stimulated by the prosaic descriptions of topography in the ordinary textbook, and yet that is just what is needed to picture the beauty of physical forms, and to develop the habit of imaging the scenes described. See also page 284, on the æsthetic side of geography.

Current events taken from the daily papers and other journals are another form of supplementary reading. The special value of such reading, aside from developing the habit of reading the news, is that it impresses the reality of geography. The facts of the textbook seem so remote, rather unreal; but an interesting current event happening in a place previously mentioned in the book takes that place out of the book and gives it in the pupil's mind a definite existence it never had before. Again such reading is an application of school geography which gives the pupil a mental satisfaction, and a realization of the usefulness of the subject.

Various children's and youths' journals are either exclusively devoted to presenting current news, of interest to young people, or at least give some space thereto. In many classes of geography the pupils club together for subscription to such juvenile newspapers, which are used in connection with reading, history, and geography. By reading the news of the world the pupil enlarges his experience to a participation in the affairs of society at large and the world as a whole.

Current events may be brought up as they bear appropriately on the daily lessons. Or, a definite time on a certain day may be set aside for comment upon them. It is necessary to teach discrimination in such reading, and in this case only such news as has special geographical significance should be discussed in the geography class. Other news may be correlated with history. In the lower grades the teacher must guide in the selection of these topics, and in the higher grades this may be done by a committee of pupils appointed to edit the news items brought in by the class. An interesting plan is to have a weekly newspaper prepared in this way, to be read to the class, and to furnish food for discussion.

In treating current events it is not enough to simply read the news item and to tell where it occurred, or even to show it on the map. Enough more should be taught about the physiography, and the political conditions of the region, to give a proper basis for the full appreciation of the subject. For example, Peary's Discovery of the North Pole needs for a proper setting reference to latitude, longitude, polar night and day, the aurora, the gorgeous atmospheric effects, the ice field, the animals of this region, the Eskimo, the routes leading to the Pole, the hardships of the explorer, etc. Ordinary maps, polar maps, the globe, and pictures of the Arctic scenes should accompany the account.

It is profitable to take some progressive event, such as the cruise of the American fleet around the world, or even an automobile or walking race across the continent, and follow the course on the map.

For current events, sketch maps on the board or on paper will be found very useful, even better than regular maps. Special maps showing details which cannot readily be found on ordinary maps may often be found in the news journals. These maps should be enlarged.

An interesting method of treating current events is to make a scrap book containing news clippings, illustrated with newspaper and magazine pictures, postal cards, etc. Children always like to make these collections.

A comparative examination of the news items brought in by the children would reveal to the teacher the children's special interests in geography, and so might lead her to teach the subject more pedagogically and more successfully.

CHAPTER XIV

MAPS

"The root of all geographical ability lies in being at home with maps." — MACKINDER.

Maps are more or less symbolic representations of the earth on a flat surface by means of lines, characters, signs, and colors. A photograph, painting, or drawing may be made of some part of the earth's surface and show with much truthful detail surface configuration, scenery, the habitations, and the works of man. The smaller the area represented, the better the study of the detail. The larger the area, the more the details become lost in the perspective, and only the larger, general features, such as ground plan, topography, and distribution of land and water, can be shown.

Some maps are wholly pictorial, showing a bird's-eye view of considerable areas, a city, or a state, with suggestions of scenery, houses, ships at sea, etc. Such maps are frequently used for beginners, and also are much seen in popular magazines and newspapers.

From such pictorial maps one may proceed to others more and more symbolic. The houses and streets of a city are replaced by lines, dots, or circles; the pictures of hills and mountains by conventional characters or hachuring and shading; the variation in elevation is represented by different colors, or by contour lines.

Maps a shorthand record of geographical knowledge. — Maps are the chief aid of the geographer. Primarily they serve to show the form, extent, location, direction, and the internal and external relations of a region. Many other features regarding climate, vegetable and animal life, and human life may also be shown. Maps are the resultant record of actual discovery, exploration, survey, measurement, and development of a region, and depict in shorthand what would take many pages of text to describe. "The fundamental conceptions of the geography of a country should be built up from the data furnished by maps rather than from textbooks." (Geike.)

Political map. — The most common form of map is the political. This emphasizes the human relations. It shows the location of towns and cities, routes of travel and commerce, telegraph lines, canals, and the artificial divisions of the earth into nations and their civic subdivisions. The physical features of latitude and longitude, the shape of the region, lakes and rivers, the seacoast and mountain ranges, are generally shown also. Owing to the many place names such maps are apt to be overcrowded and confusing, and the physical features are often apparently lost, at least not conspicuous.

Special maps. — In commercial geography political

maps are much used to show the distribution of mineral resources, vegetation regions, crop areas, density of cities, railway systems, etc. These features are sometimes shown in special maps, each in a different map, being thus emphasized, to the neglect, perhaps, of the rest.

Physical map. — Since it is too confusing or impossible to represent everything on one map, it is customary to use the political map to show the artificial, human relations, and the physical maps (described on page 90) to represent topography, climatic conditions, etc. The physical features, also, are often analyzed and shown on special maps.

Comparative study of maps. — By means of these special maps, showing some one feature analyzed out by itself, that feature may be studied without any confusing irrelevancies. Care should be taken, however, that these separate maps are again superimposed mentally to bring out the proper relations between them, or to show their composite effect. Thus the rainfall map should be associated with the wind map, and with the topographical, the vegetation, and the industrial maps.

Introduction to the map. — The map being a chief means of learning geography, the pupil should be introduced to it early, and taught how to interpret it, to translate it into words. For this it is necessary to teach him what a map is, and what its various symbols mean.

A prerequisite for map study is an idea of direction. This is usually taught in nature-study before geography is begun. The simplest and oldest method of fixing the points of the compass is by reference to the rising and the setting sun, and the sun at noonday. The word orientation is derived from this. The Orient is the land of the rising sun. To orient oneself is to get one's bearings. See page 44.

The points of the compass being known by beginners, the first study may be made of a map. To make the map concrete and intelligible two common methods are employed: the first is to show the pupil a photograph or other picture of a region, one containing both land and water features being good, and then a map of the same region, requiring the pupil to discover the various features shown in the picture.

The other way to get the pupil to appreciate the map is to let him draw one for himself, a very simple one, the map of the schoolroom. The approximate dimensions of the room are found, the minor irregularities being disregarded. The points of the compass are noted. The pupils are told to draw a floor plan of the room. The teacher using a sheet of paper like the pupils' shows them or directs them step by step how to proceed.

As for scale, fourth grade children are scarcely ready in their arithmetic to appreciate its significance. All that is really necessary here is to see that the picture must be much smaller than the room. The teacher may tell the class to represent the length of the room by a certain number of inches. The rest will then follow according to scale, if proportions are observed. The pupils may need some assistance in placing the plan properly on the paper. Each wall is drawn as directed, and properly named according to the points of the compass. The teacher's and the pupil's own desk may then be sketched in, keeping the proper relations. The term *map* may then be used instead of plan. Each line and symbol drawn is now significant to the child. He knows the real things they stand for.

A further step is to draw the school block with the neighboring treets. By pacing the comparative lengths may be obtained. The block is drawn in proportion, and the school correctly located. In this study, again, the points of the compass should be observed.

Next a real map of the locality should be presented. First find the school block, the neighboring streets, and familiar objects; then streets and places farther off, perhaps seen or heard of; and then new and unknown features may be discovered.

It is important in this early map work, especially in home geography, to lay the map horizontally, with its directions corresponding to the points of the compass. That is, the north of the map should be placed toward the real north. Placed in this way the map may be used to find the direction of familiar or less known places. The pupils can then readily point to these places, or possibly go to them. If such a study of the locality were made on the roof of the school, from upper windows, or some high hill commanding a view of the surrounding region, it would be very effective.

The map is, however, for convenience hung on the wall. The pupils should learn how this changes the relations of the map to the real points of the compass. The map is least out of correct relation with the points of the compass when hung on the north wall. By comparison with the map in the horizontal and correct position, the fact may be brought out that when suspended, and also when placed in books, the north is usually at the top of the map, the south at the bottom, east at the right, and west at the left hand. Sometimes, however, maps are found with the north not at the top, in which case there is generally some guide, as a cross mark or other design showing the directions.

In locating and describing directions on the map pupils should not be permitted to say " up " when they mean north, and " down " when they mean south. Up and down may be used in map study only to refer to topography, elevations, slopes, drainage, river courses, and the like. The Nile flows down, north. The trunk railroads across the United States go from the Mississippi Valley up the gently rising prairies to the Great

Plains, and still higher up over the Western mountains, and then down to the Coast.

Imagination in map study.—In all map work, especially in the early home geography, the real geographical experiences of the pupils in the territory shown should be recalled in order to make the map meaningful and concrete. Begin the first map study with the vicinity of the home and school, then trace out routes of travel and well-known landmarks. Pupils should try to imagine, to see, the real streets, stores, factories, public buildings, streams, hills, etc., indicated by the symbols on the map, which is easy if he has seen them. In the same way he should try to picture the things shown on the map with which he is not so familiar. The use of pictures and vivid oral description by the teacher are an assistance in getting beyond the mere map.

In the more advanced geography it is just as essential to bring up in the mind's eye the lay of the land, the scenery, the vegetation, the occupations of the people, the architecture, etc. The map study of the outline of North America should leave the pupil with a picture of the level, frozen tundra of the Arctic Coast; the bleak promontories of Labrador; the "stern and rock-bound coast" of New England; the sandy pleasure beaches and the low and swampy shores from New York to Florida and along the Gulf Coast; the arid mountain shore of western Mexico and lower California; the narrow fringe of coastal plain with the snow-capped mountains beyond in the stretch from California to Alaska; the fiord coast of the Northwest with its thousand islands, the forest primeval of conifers, and the gleaming glaciers. Colonel Parker used to speak of "the terrible habit of not seeing beyond the map." The pupil who believes that the earth looks just like the map, or perhaps does not associate the map at all with the earth, has very barren results from his map study, — as barren as that of the author of a textbook mentioned by Rousseau, who defined the earth in this way, "The earth is a globe of papier-maché." Mere bounding and locating in map work is apt to be mechanical unless imaging the reality is practiced.

Thought in map study. — "Map reading is not finding names merely, nor knowing what the different characters stand for. The content, the thought, the *geistiger Inhalt*, must be read in: boundaries, natural and political, nature of the coast, islands, sounds, trend of mountains, declivity, drainage, passes, plateaus, plains, etc. Between the lines should be read generalizations and principles of physiography, commercial geography, etc." (Trunk.)

The wall maps and maps in the textbook for primary geography should be simple in outline, and should present only the most important physical and political features, not much more than is taken up in these years. Overcrowded maps are very confusing and time-wasting.

Conduct of map study. — The first map study should be conducted by the teacher to teach the children how to use a map, how to read it, and to show what may be inferred from it. The pupils may, or may not, have their books open at the map. The teacher points out and names the data to be learned. The pupils are required to find them again on the wall map, and perhaps also on their text maps. As new map symbols are used they should be explained. Pupils should be taught the use of the scale and the table or legend of explanations.

For purposes of drill and review blank maps and sketch maps, not giving the names of the places and physical features, are excellent. In using these, too great accuracy of location should not be demanded of beginners, approximation being sufficient.

Much of the map study consists in locating and bounding. This is an essential function of map work, but requires judgment in determining what is important and what is not, else it is apt to run into perfunctory, thoughtless routine. Much time may be killed in this way that should be devoted to descriptive study or to thinking out geographical relationships. The object of locating and bounding is, of course, to teach space relations, or situation, that the other geographical significance of the places thus treated may be better appreciated. That is, locating and bounding are not an end in themselves. They help to fix the mental image of the map, a very important thing, but that is not their whole function.

Memory-aiding associations. — In studying confines and situations, interesting and profitable associations should be brought in, both to make the work attractive and to give additional knowledge. A brief reference to the historic or commercial relations with a neighboring country, and racial differences; a suggestion of the appearance and character of the surrounding waters, or of the bounding mountains; the natural and political reasons for boundaries being where they are; the physical, political, and industrial effect of border mountains, rivers, etc.; the historical cause for the founding of a city; the advantages and disadvantages of the site chosen for a city, — are profitable allusions. It is not necessary for pupils to commit to memory these associations. It is sufficient for the teacher to make the commentaries or to develop these associations in passing. By doing this the map work acquires a significance impossible without it; it helps the memory to retain the map image; and pupils learn to look for broader geographical principles involved in locative relations. Also many of the associations brought out will be retained by the children without effort.

Telling the meaning of names is another good way to

attach interesting memory-aiding associations to the map work. See Chapter XVII.

Map study should be conducted logically and systematically. — Map questions should not be asked in promiscuous order, for thus a chaotic jumble will result in the pupil's mind. Physical features of location, extent, configuration, surface, climate, drainage, distribution of vegetation and animal life, and the mineral resources should be taken in sequential order, and should precede the study of the political features, location of cities, means of communication, etc. The map and the text description of a country should go together. By a systematic study like this an organized unity, a rational relationship, the influence of the environment, and the adaptation of man are more readily and clearly perceived by the pupil than from a "hit or miss" order of map questions. (Of course, for purposes of mere drill such a miscellaneous order is permissible.)

Causal relations in map study. — The map work should not be simply to answer the questions of the old "sailor's geography" of What? and Where? The question Why? should frequently be asked, especially in the upper grades. From maps alone many of the fundamental principles of physical and political geography may be developed. Why are there so few cities in Labrador? Why are there so few in Nevada? Why does the Southern Pacific Railroad go by way of

El Paso? Why has Chicago become so large? Etc. Such questions exercise the reason as well as mere memory.

Overemphasis of map study.—In the old geography there was much insistence upon a vast amount of map work, chiefly locational. It was assumed necessary to get the capes, bays, rivers, mountains, countries, cities, etc., fixed in mind before the description of the country was taken up in the textbook. In some of the older texts the map of the whole world was first memorized before any descriptive study was undertaken. In this day this is considered mere unthinking drudgery, and text and map are closely associated. Pupils should be taught to put the map work and the text together. Such a map habit, if well established, is useful in later life in locating current events, in reading history and literature.

The reaction. — The overemphasis of map work in former days has led to the present reaction toward simpler maps, fewer map questions for the sake of the map alone, and more association of map and text. In practice, however, there is danger that the very necessary map study may be slighted. Such work is fundamental, and must be done, or the descriptive matter will lose definiteness of location, and also the logic of many causal relations. Drill is very necessary, not only in locations of states, cities, physical features, and the like, but also in fixing the relation of the physical features to each other and their effect on human life.

Maps should be supplemented with globe study. — One criticism must be made of the use of maps: Through the unvaried use of the map representing the earth in the flat an incorrect and inadequate notion of the earth and the relation of the lands is given.

This may be corrected by the globe in connection with the map. It is a good plan, in general, when beginning the study of a new continent, to study its relations as shown on the globe. Location, extent, latitude, longitude, comparative area, and the relation to previously studied continents may thus be correctly seen.

The globe is useful also in many other lessons in descriptive geography, especially in the study of commercial relations, marine commerce, transoceanic telegraph lines, imaginary routes, polar studies, etc. Usually the globe is brought out during the study of mathematical geography and then relegated to the closet.

If we wish to get the pupil beyond the flat map to the round earth, we must use the globe. Ask pupils to point toward Europe and they will point out horizontally to the east, that is, in a line tangent to the earth, which would land them out in space, instead of pointing east and at the same time somewhat downward, so as to point through the earth. For Americans China is not simply west, but on the other side of the earth, down.

CHAPTER XV

MAP DRAWING

Purpose. — Map drawing is the usual accompaniment of the study of geography. It is done for two reasons,—as a means of map study, and as a means of geographical expression.

The pedagogical reason for requiring the drawing of a map for study is that in the reproduction of a map the pupil observes with more care the details of direction, proportion, relationship, physical features, etc., than by merely studying a book or wall map; that by such detailed observation he will know the map more thoroughly; that by such care in study and drill in drawing, the map will be impressed more indelibly on the eye-memory. "We all carry mental maps in our brains." (Trottner.)

Map drawing is easily overdone. — When this object is attained there is no further need for such careful, time-consuming work. There was a period in the last generation when map drawing was overdone. Pupils generally enjoy this creative handwork of making maps, and the temptation is to let them draw much. Very nearly as good map knowledge, however, may be acquired by the proper study of printed maps in books and for the wall, or by the use of printed outline maps. Moreover, a map may be drawn accurately and beautifully and still with so little thought on its geographical content that the pupil gains little or nothing more than the benefit from an exercise in drawing and painting.

The meridian net method. — Various methods have been suggested for drawing maps. Some would have maps drawn scientifically according to latitude and longitude. This is undoubtedly the best method for maturer students in high schools and colleges, and may be tried in a simple way in the upper grammar grades to teach more fully the meaning of meridians, parallels, surveys, and the principles of cartography. Some teachers require the memorizing of the latitude and longitude of the salient points of a map to be drawn so that memory or sketch maps may be quickly made with fair accuracy. Some have students construct their own meridian nets, and some use blanks with the meridians already drawn, and still others use blanks with the meridian net and the salient points of the map already checked in.

The method of squares. — Another method, not so geographical, but aiding in producing an accurate copy, is to rule the map to be copied with lines dividing it into squares, and then reproducing these on the desired scale on the paper on which the map is to be drawn.

The squares assist in getting direction and proportion more accurately. This method should not be applied to books not owned by the pupil, as the map is more or less ruined thereby. Printed outline maps may be substituted in such a case.

Construction diagrams undesirable. — Another formerly used mechanical method, having nothing to recommend it, except that it served fairly well for memory maps if the pupil could remember the scheme, was to construct arbitrary " construction diagrams " for blocking out the proportions of the areas to be drawn.

Simple copy method. — These methods are too difficult for the elementary school, or too mechanical. The best method is to let the pupil copy the map as he would a picture on a blackboard or in the drawing book in the art lesson. If drawing is taught in the school, as is most likely, the pupils already have the necessary principles of drawing, — getting directions and proportions, the two essentials in map drawing.

The simpler maps (such as in Frye's *Grammar School Geography*, Supplement) should be used for copy, or pupils may be advised to disregard the minor irregularities of coast and river, and of boundaries, but to note carefully the general lines of the outline, etc. The map should be neatly spaced on the paper. The drawing is begun, preferably, at the northwest corner, chiefly to avoid smearing, and that one may see the portion already drawn. The outline is sketched in very lightly at first. Before proceeding far, the lines already drawn should be compared critically with the copy map. Should this line go farther north or south? Does that line run exactly northeast, or more nearly toward the north? By asking oneself such questions the lines as sketched may be checked with the original, and if not correct, should be essayed again. After direction of lines, the next most important thing is their proportionate length. With beginners, nothing need be taught about scale. Simply the direction to make the map of a certain size, or as large as the paper will allow, is sufficient. The older pupils should learn to draw according to scale. To make a copy half or twice as large as the original, every line of the copy must be made half or twice as long as the original. The first line drawn determines the scale. The next line in a new direction should now be drawn in the same proportion or scale. By thus always judging proportionate lengths with the parts already drawn, and keeping directions true, the map will remain correct in shape.

After the outline is thus sketched in, and retouched lightly to satisfaction, it may be traced or lined in more heavily.

After the outline is drawn, the mountains should be put in as a guide for drawing the rivers. Rivers should be drawn carefully to conform to the slopes of the land, and special attention should be paid to their divides. The location of the other features involves no difficulty.

Great accuracy in map drawing should not be expected of children. Even the best of printed maps are far from accurate. For fixing the map relations thus by drawing, pupils should be expected simply to do the best they can.

The early map drawing should not be left to the pupil alone, but should be done under the supervision and direction of the teacher, who should guide and assist with the mechanical difficulties, and, what is important, at the same time teach the geographical facts of the map.

Progressive maps. — For a systematic study of a country covering several days, it is often a good plan not to finish a map all at once, but to spread it over the period of study, each day recording on the map, and thus organizing, what was studied that day. Such a slow-growing map is called a Progressive Map. It is one of the best means of summarizing and organizing in geography.

Coloring, shading, and finishing. — Maps are the most tangible evidence of a pupil's study of geography, hence they are always displayed in exhibits of school work. The temptation, therefore, is to embellish them more than is really necessary for the purposes of geography. An unconscionable amount of time may be wasted thus, in coloring, wave-lining, shading, lettering, etc., that might be better employed in reading the descriptive text. For most purposes a simple pencil drawing is sufficient. Sometimes for better distinction of political divisions, or for indicating elevation, or to represent distribution features, the map may be either shaded in black or painted. Care should be taken to select harmonious, rather neutral, tints. The color should not be applied too thickly, a common fault with beginners. If colored crayons are used, or shading in black is attempted, the work should be done smoothly, not in scratchy lines. In using water colors, care must be taken to avoid running over the edges, and to prevent water lines. The drawing of elaborate frills or ripples along the coasts should be discouraged. If the map is to be inked in and lettered in ink, this must be done *after* the coloring. For most purposes it will do to write the names in neat script. Printing is more difficult, and does not look well unless uniform. If many data are to be recorded, the writing must be small, to prevent a confused or cluttered appearance. As a rule, the writing or printing looks better if not written at all angles, but if written in parallel lines. This also saves space. Of course, this is not always possible. When a map is full of data represented by lines, characters, or colors, a legend or table of explanations should accompany the map. Sometimes to avoid crowding, cities, etc., are simply numbered or initialed, and the explanation given in the legend.

Printed outline maps. — The drawing of fine maps is such a slow, time-consuming process that it has rightly been reduced to a minimum in the school requirements. A great labor-saving device are the printed outline maps now in common use, though once condemned as much as Emmy Lou's system of drawing by tracing through tissue paper. They may now be obtained from various publishers for all the continents, the United States, sections of the United States, separate states, and even cities. The pupils line them in more heavily and fill them with the data studied. The advantages are uniformity, accuracy of outline, and saving of effort and time. They may be used for both the first studies of a map and for reviews. The disadvantage, which may be guarded against by thoughtful study, is that they may be filled in too mechanically, and that the visual image created by them is not as definite as that acquired through copy.

Maps to test the pupil's knowledge. — The other purpose of map drawing, besides that of getting the idea of the space relations of the map, is to express geographical knowledge. By means of a memory sketch map a pupil can give the teacher a fair idea of his understanding of the subject. Pupils should not only recite in words, but also by means of maps on paper or on the board.

Sketch maps. — Such maps should be either sketch maps from memory, or filled in on the printed outline maps. They should take but little time, great accuracy being out of the question. Yet this need not matter, so long as the map is recognizable, and the pupil has not been careless, and the general relations of things are fairly well observed.

Such sketch maps are very useful for illustrating topical papers, reviews, drills, and tests.

Blackboard sketches by the teacher. — The teacher herself should make much use of sketch maps on the blackboard during the recitation. Such sketches help to analyze difficult relations in the ordinary wall maps, or emphasize special features, serve sometimes as excellent substitutes for wall maps when these are not handy, take the place of printed blank maps for purposes of drill and review, and are in general indispensable.

CHAPTER XVI

CARTOGRAPHY

"Ninety-nine out of a hundred form their idea of geography from the map, not the globe, yet do not know the inaccuracies of the map." — MORRISON.

There are no correct maps possible except on the globe, and here only theoretically, for globe maps also may contain inaccuracies of human judgment in discovery, compilation, and construction. They are too small to take account of the minor details. The ordinary globe also does not allow for the oblateness of the earth. Still, globe maps are the most correct of all in principle. Flat maps are always more or less distorted, therefore untrue. Globe maps are the only kind that represent the meridians and parallels in their correct relations. On globe maps alone is the scale of distance the same in all directions and in all parts. Globe maps alone represent areas correctly.

Globes therefore are very valuable in geography. — Naturally they are the best representation of the earth for mathematical geography. Aside from such use globes show best the relations of the continents, their location on the sphere, their comparative areas, and their correct shape. The globe is best for showing the hemispheres, land and water, northern and southern, eastern and western. The globe is useful in studying commercial routes, and real or imaginary journeys around the world. It should find more frequent use in political geography than is the case.

Why flat maps are inaccurate.—The flat map attempts the impossible,—to represent a spherical surface in the plane. If one should peel off half an orange rind intact and then try to flatten it out, it would tear and split along the edges, or if it were elastic and tenacious enough, it would stretch around the margin. In either case the hemisphere would be greatly mutilated, modified, or distorted. The same thing happens in attempting to flatten out a globe map.

Maps, the ordinary flat kind, are at best makeshifts or approximations of the real map of the earth. Some sorts are nearer the truth than others. A brief sketch is here given of the commoner methods of designing maps and charts, illustrating various ways of getting around the difficulty of distortion. Only the maps commonly seen in school will be described, in order that the teacher may realize their defects and limitations, as well as their proper function.

Cartography is the art of compiling, designing, and drawing maps. A chart maker is a cartographer. Many learned men from the days of the ancient Greek mathematicians have suggested various designs or projections for representing the earth in maps.

The orthographic projection is an early form. Imagine a plane tangent to the globe, and lines to fall perpendicularly on this plane from every point of the globe. Where these lines intersect the plane, there are the *projections* of the points of the globe map. These

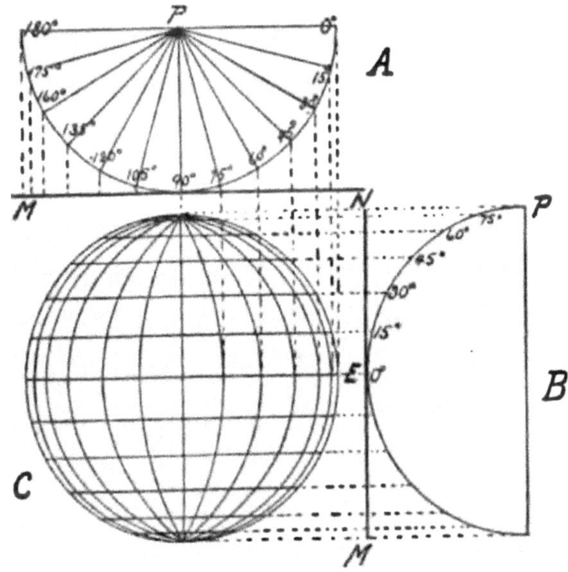

FIG. 10. — Construction of the orthographic projection.

projected points will constitute the orthographically projected map on the plane. The globe map may thus be thought of as being projected, transferred, or thrown direct upon the plane. In *A* (Fig. 10) the earth is seen from the pole and the meridians are projected on *MN*. *B* is the earth in equatorial aspect, with the parallels projected on MN. C shows the meridians and parallels on the projected map.

Another way to conceive such a map is to look at a globe with distinctly marked meridians and parallels, from a considerable distance, the line of sight being in the equatorial plane. The globe will look flat like a disk, and its lines will look as in the diagram (Fig. 10, *C*). Note that the parallels appear as straight lines, so also the central meridian, and that the meridians are more and more curved as they proceed outward. The meridians and parallels are also crowded by foreshortening at the margins.

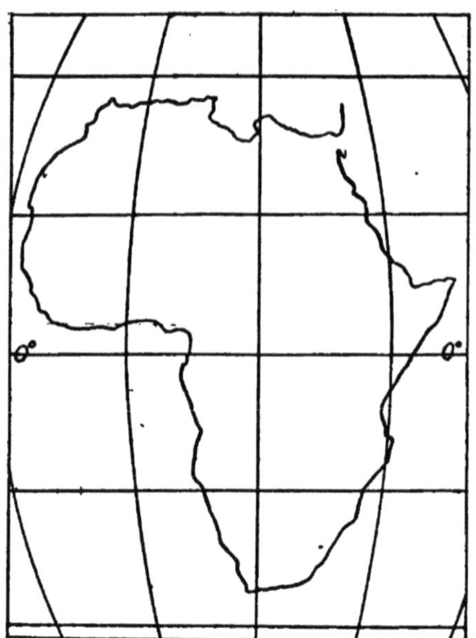

Fig. 11. — Map of Africa drawn in orthographic projection.

Limitations of the orthographic projection. — It is evident that regions in the margin of the hemisphere are contracted and distorted, and that only the middle portion of the map is fairly accurate. This form of projection is not much used for school maps, save for Africa, which is favorably placed in the center of the hemisphere, and for polar maps. This projection was invented by Hipparchus, a Greek astronomer and mathematician, who lived about 150 B.C.

The globular projection is the most common for hemisphere maps. It was devised by De la Hire, of

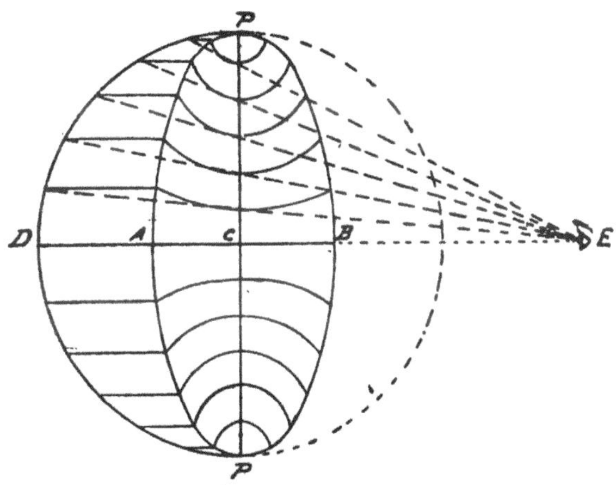

FIG. 12. — Construction of globular projection.

France (1704). Imagine a transparent half globe, with a transparent plane covering the cut surface, and the eye on the diameter at right angles to this plane, and at a distance from the plane slightly greater (1.7) than the radius of the globe. Project the points of the globe map on to the plane along lines passing from them directly to the eye. The eye would see the equator as a straight line, the parallels as half ellipses; meridians running naturally without crowding, both equally spaced. The projected map appears on the plane of projection as the eye thus sees the meridians and parallels.

Merits of this projection.—Such a map nicely simulates the appearance of a globe with its curving meridians and parallels, and suggests the rotundity of the earth. It is, however, not on the same scale throughout. It

FIG. 13. — Western hemisphere in globular projection.

will be noted that the distance between two parallels on the central and a marginal meridian are not the same, as is the case with real parallels. The error is about 1 to 1½. The marginal parts of the map are therefore stretched.

Mercator's projection, among many others, was devised by that brilliant Flemish-German, Gerhard Krämer (1512–1594), who revolutionized the art of map making, and started the great German school of scientific cartographers that has continued to the present day. (Mercator is the Latinized version of Krämer, a merchant. During the Middle Ages it was not fashionable for the learned men to use the vernacular in their writings, and they even signed their names in Latin, the language of science and culture.) Mercator's plan of projection may be considered as follows: Imagine a cylinder tangent to the globe at its equator (Fig. 14). From the center of the globe draw radii through the various points *A*, *B*, *C*, etc., of the globe map to the tangent cylinder. The places where these radii extended strike the cylinder are the projections of these points of the globe map. Now imagine the cylinder cut open along one side, and unfurled. The projected map will

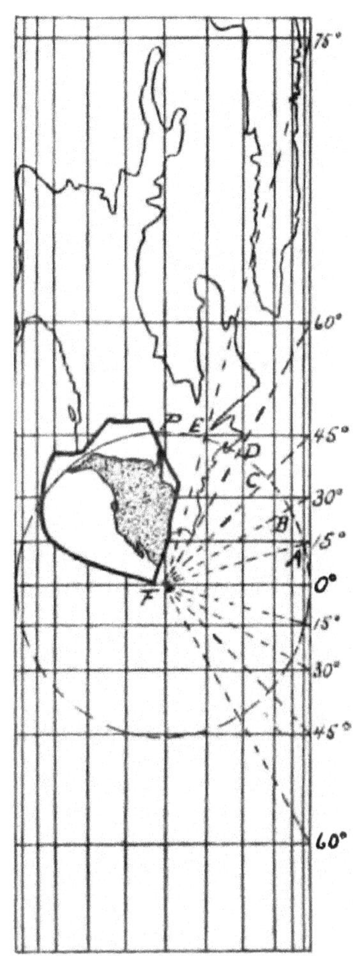

Fig. 14. — Construction of Mercator's central, cylindrical projection. The globe map within is projected upon the cylinder. Note great stretching, especially near the poles.

then appear on the outside surface in the flat. Parallels appear here as straight lines, and the meridians likewise, at right angles to the others.

Defects and merits of this projection. — The most glaring fault of the projection is at once seen in the fact

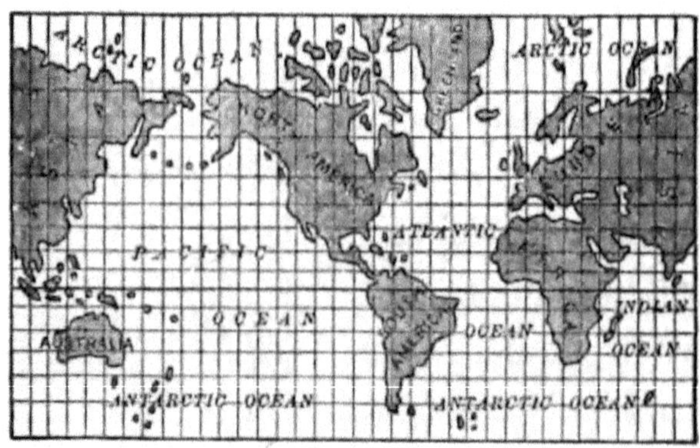

Fig. 15. — The world in Mercator's projection. Areas are distorted, but directions are correctly represented.

that the meridians do not meet, as they should. Hence the poles cannot be represented. Note how the spaces representing equal differences of latitude get larger and larger, indicating a great stretching polewards. This rapidly increases as points nearer the pole are projected, while the pole itself can only be projected at infinity. Also note that the polar regions are stretched out east and west as long as the equator, again a tremendous distortion. The Mercator projection, then, greatly exaggerates the higher latitudes in all directions, which, of course, increases their area unwarrantably. The extent of polar distortion is well seen by comparing

Greenland with South America on a Mercator map, and then again on a globe map. In the Mercator map it is represented larger than South America. In Fig. 14 the globe map of North America is represented thrown radially on the surface of the cylinder. The resultant stretching is evident from a comparison of the two maps.

In spite of this tremendous distortion the Mercator projection has its merits. The regions nearest the line of tangency of the globe and cylinder, the equator, are represented with fair accuracy. On the equator everything is placed in exactly the same relations as on the globe, for here projection and globe coincide. For points near the equator there is not much deviation from the truth. For a latitude embracing the tropics and most of the temperate belts, that is, the most inhabited part of the globe, the distortion is not unendurable. This projection is also called the central-cylindrical. Unmodified, this projection requires maps unduly long from north to south. Various arbitrary modifications have been devised to reduce the distortion in the higher latitudes. It was Mercator's distinction to invent a plan by which the distortion in longitude is kept equal to that in latitude. The result is that the Mercatcr projection gives the correct compass bearings of places with reference to each other. That is, what is shown directly east or southeast of New York City, for example, is really east or southeast. Hence this projection is much used for sailing charts for mariners.

Another advantage of this map is that it presents the whole world at once to view, which is very useful in studies of distribution over the world of physical features, such as heat belts, isotherms, winds, rainfall, ocean currents, etc.; and for other distribution studies, such as that of races, resources, industries, crops, commercial routes, etc. It is to be regretted, however, that it is used so much in

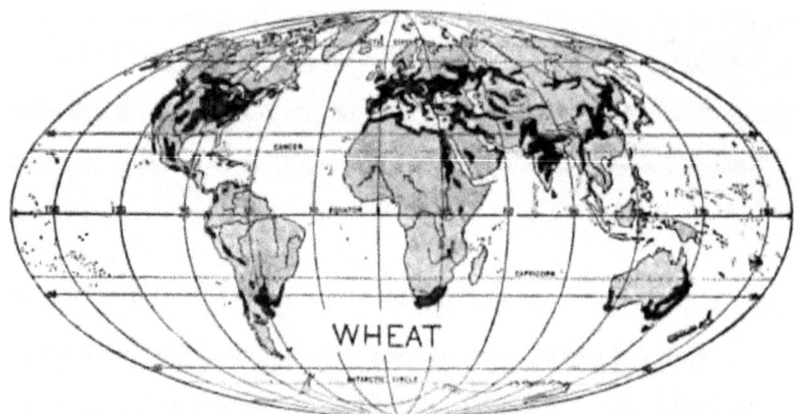

FIG. 16. — Mollweide's equal-area or homolographic projection. Shape is distorted, but areas are proportional. By permission, from Gannett, Garrison and Houston's Commercial Geography, American Book Co.

the texts of elementary schools, for through it very incorrect notions of shapes and areas are liable to become fixed. It goes without saying that such maps should never be used for the first study of the shapes of the continents.

Mollweide's equal-area projection. — There is a modification of the globular, called Mollweide's homolographic projection, Fig. 16, which uses a diameter about twice that of the globular and the parallels are not curved. This represents both hemispheres of the earth in one view, with the advantage over Mercator's projection in that areas are on the same scale throughout (hence it is also called equal-area projection), and shows comparatively little distortion of shape. This is being used considerably in recent books. It is a good projection where a comparison of areas is desirable, as in studies of distribution of natural resources, etc. The designer of this method was Mollweide, 1805.

The conic projection is similar to Mercator's, except that a tangent cone is used instead of a cylinder. When

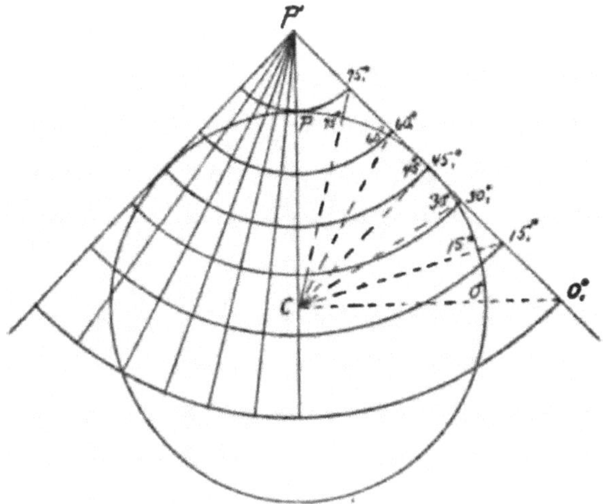

Fig. 17. — Construction of the conic projection.

the cone, with the globe map projected in a manner similar to Mercator's process, is opened and spread out flat, the meridians appear as straight lines radiating from the poles, and the parallels are concentric arcs with the pole as center.

Obviously this projection has limitations like the last,

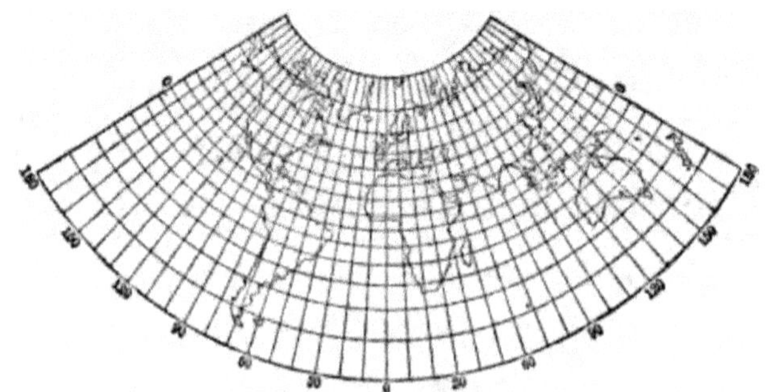

FIG. 18.— The world in conic projection.

though somewhat different. The region at the line of tangency of the cone and the globe is correctly represented, but the distortion increases on either side of this line. The flaring edge of the cone soon stretches the map in all directions, and towards the pole there is some east and west, but chiefly poleward, stretching. The conic projection is much used in school maps. The maps of smaller areas, such as

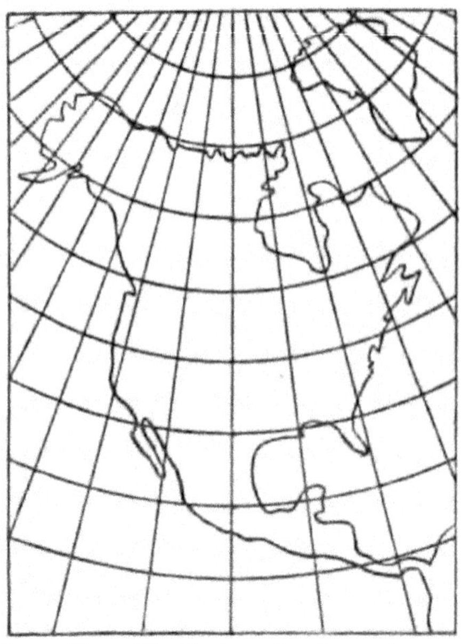

FIG. 19.— North America in conic projection.

the British Isles, Mexico, the New England states, Germany, etc., are generally thus represented.

Polyconic projection.—The conic projection has many modifications. One of much merit is the polyconic. As above stated, the conic projection is fairly correct

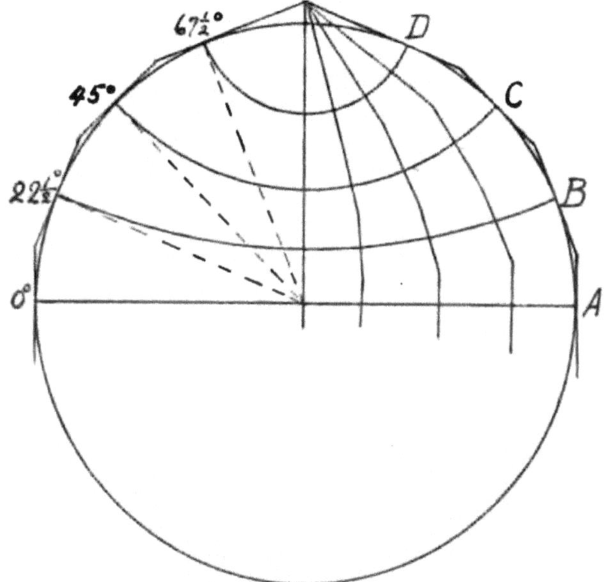

Fig. 20.—Construction of the polyconic projection.

near the line of tangency of the globe and the cone. If, now, instead of a single cone, a series of superimposed cones be used, each tangent to the globe at a different latitude, more such fairly accurate portions of the map may be obtained. The polyconic projection, in general, embodies this principle. Hassler (d. 1843), of the United States Coast and Geodetic Survey, devised this method. This is an excellent projection for representing large areas, such as continents. On such maps the meridians are not straight, but curve toward each other. The parallels are not quite concentric, but spread apart somewhat toward the margins of the map. The advantage of this map is that it shows very little distortion for the larger areas, except a little at the margins of the map. The same scale can be used for all parts of the map and in all directions, except at the periphery. It is reasonably accurate for a width of 40 degrees of latitude.

FIG. 21. — North America in polyconic projection.

For fixing correct form and relative areas the polyconic projection is the best, aside from the globe itself. North America, for example, should be pictured as shown in this projection, and not as in the Mercator. The simple conic projection is the easiest to draw where pupils have to make their own meridians and parallels.

Modified projections. — As a matter of fact, in actual cartography the projections are not made as above indicated. Tables have been computed for measuring off the parallels and meridians, and many such tables are greatly modified from the geometrical requirements of the projections in order to suit the exigencies of the shape of the page or chart, and some are juggled very arbitrarily indeed. There are many different ways of making the polyconic projection. As an instance of the scientific juggling, note the Mercator projection.

There are very many other projections, each with claims for general or special purposes. But the above are the ones most commonly seen in school maps. The teacher should be aware of the errors and limitations of maps, and also of the advantages and possibilities.

The data for maps. — A map presupposes a survey of some sort. The cartographer uses the data given him by explorers, sailors, travelers, and others, in the construction of his map. The correctness of the map evidently rests upon the accuracy of these eyewitnesses; on the exactness of their instruments and methods of measurement and computation of distance, time, elevation, latitude, longitude, etc.; on the thoroughness and extent of their exploration and investigation; on their knowledge of the natural conditions and resources; and on their general truthfulness and reliability. The human judgment is not infallible, hence maps are constantly undergoing modifications, revision, and refinement as previous mistakes are discovered, or new data are added. A glance at the earliest and latest map of North America well shows this progress.

Records of discoveries. — Explorers, like Stanley, Sven Hedin, or Peary, in traversing a new region, keep notes of their observations, and also estimate or measure distances, note compass bearings, determine latitude and longitude (location), and generally make sketch maps of their journeyings.

The earliest explorers simply follow the coasts or rivers of the newly discovered lands. The Hinterland, or the region farther inland, is then penetrated later, often in connection with commercial development.

In this way, the maps which were first largely blanks, are gradually filled in as the necessary data are collected.

Government surveys. — There are, however, more scientific and systematic surveys than these reconnaissance records of discoverers, explorers, and commercial agencies. Nearly all of the most enlightened governments have made very accurate surveys of their coastal lines and interiors. The United States Coast and Geodetic Survey is for such a purpose. This survey determines with refined instruments the latitude and longitude of the salient points; computes distances and areas mathematically from very accurately measured base-lines (usually segments of a meridian) by the method known as triangulation, in which even the earth's curvature is taken into account; elevations or contours are taken with delicate leveling instruments; the minor irregularities of the coast line are laid out by compass, and are measured with tape; and the depths of the navigable waters are sounded.

The United States Geological Survey is also an accurate survey to note, especially, the topography, mineral resources, hydrography, and other data. The country is surveyed in sections, called rectangles, over every mile of which surveyors and geologists actually travel.

Survey of public lands. — The United States Public Domain, that is, the old Northwest Territory, acquired as the result of the Revolutionary War, and other acquisitions since then, is all surveyed by the United States Land Office surveyors, preliminary to free disposal, or sale to settlers. The system in use was devised by General Rufus Putnam, of Revolutionary fame. The first step is to select, determine, and "run" a standard meridian by the solar compass, and a base-line or standard parallel at right angles thereto (Fig. 22). Then guide meridians and other standard parallels are run parallel to the first, at distances of twenty-four miles. The twenty-four mile squares are then subdivided into sixteen townships by means of minor meridians and parallels. Each township, six miles square, the political unit for some purposes, is further subdivided by means of north and south lines and east and west lines into thirty-six sections, which are one mile square (Fig. 23). These are again divided into

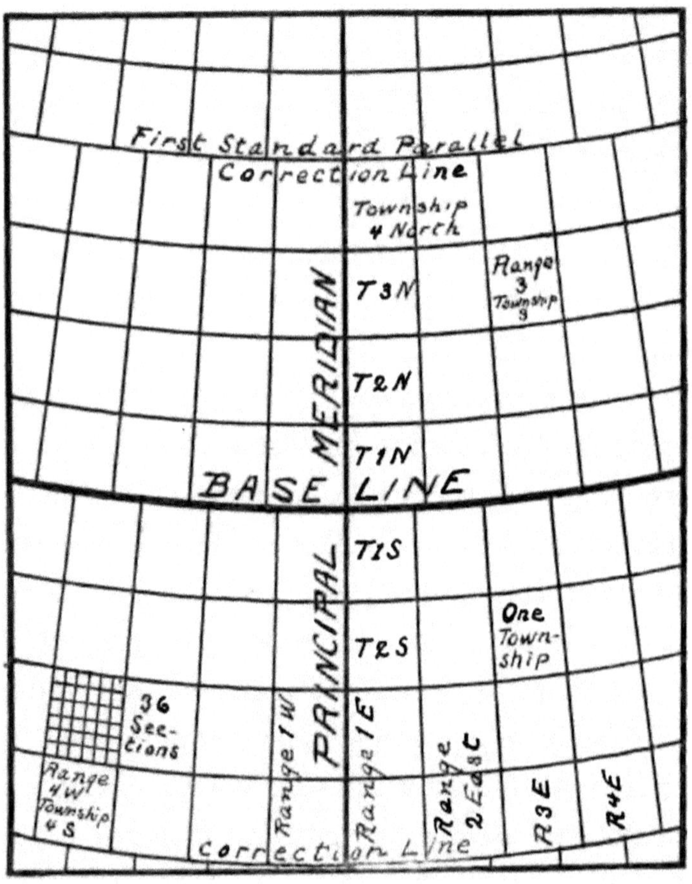

Fig. 22. — Diagram showing the use of meridians and parallels in the survey of the public lands of the United States. The larger rectangles are townships. The correction line is made necessary by the convergence of the meridians. Diagram shows method of naming and numbering.

quarter sections. This is as far as the government survey goes. Any further subdivision is made by local officials.

A section comprises one square mile, or 640 acres.

An average farm in the Middle West is a quarter section, 160 acres (Fig. 24).

6	5	4	3	2	1
7	8	9	10	11	12
18	17	16	15	14	13
19	20	21	22	23	24
30	29	28	27	26	25
31	32	33	34	35	36

Fig. 23.—A township divided into sections. Method of numbering.

All the intersections of these lines are appropriately marked by permanent "monuments," or located by reference to fixed objects.

Since meridians approach each other toward the poles, the sections at the northern edge of a twenty-four mile square are narrower, east and west, than those at the southern edge, and the difference would be considerable when

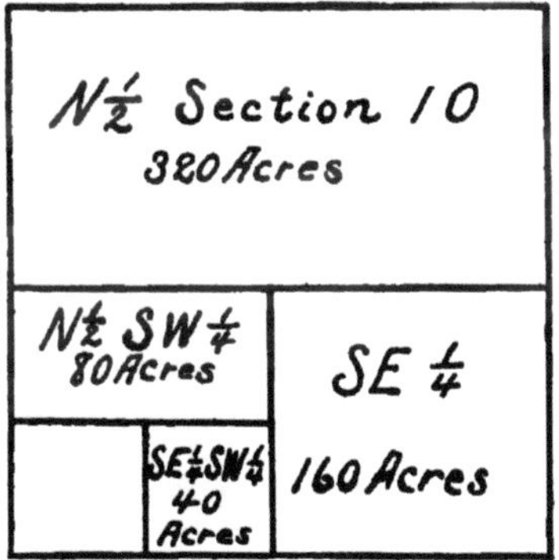

Fig. 24.—Showing subdivision of a section.

sections several hundred miles apart are compared, if nothing were done to prevent this. To correct for this convergence of the meridians, a new start is made at every fourth parallel, by again measuring off guide meridians every twenty-four miles east and west from a standard meridian. Such a parallel is known as a correction-line. The meridians on opposite sides do not correspond, except at the principal meridian.

City surveys for streets and lots are based upon the original United States Land Survey, but the surveys are made with much more care than for rural regions, owing to the value of real estate, and the danger of buildings not being on property lines.

Surveying is an ancient art. — Babylonian records show that land surveys were made there 4000 years ago. And in the ancient empire of the Nile, owing to the periodical obliteration of boundary marks by the flooding of the river, it was found necessary to appoint geometers, or surveyors, to relocate private claims. The Romans had a government land survey. But it is only in modern times that surveying has become an exact science.

Maps made from surveys. — Sometimes the surveyor himself draws the map from his own measurements and records. At other times the data of a land survey are turned over to cartographers to compile into a map.

The cartographer decides upon and constructs his projection of meridians and parallels, and then by records of latitude and longitude puts in the salient features, and

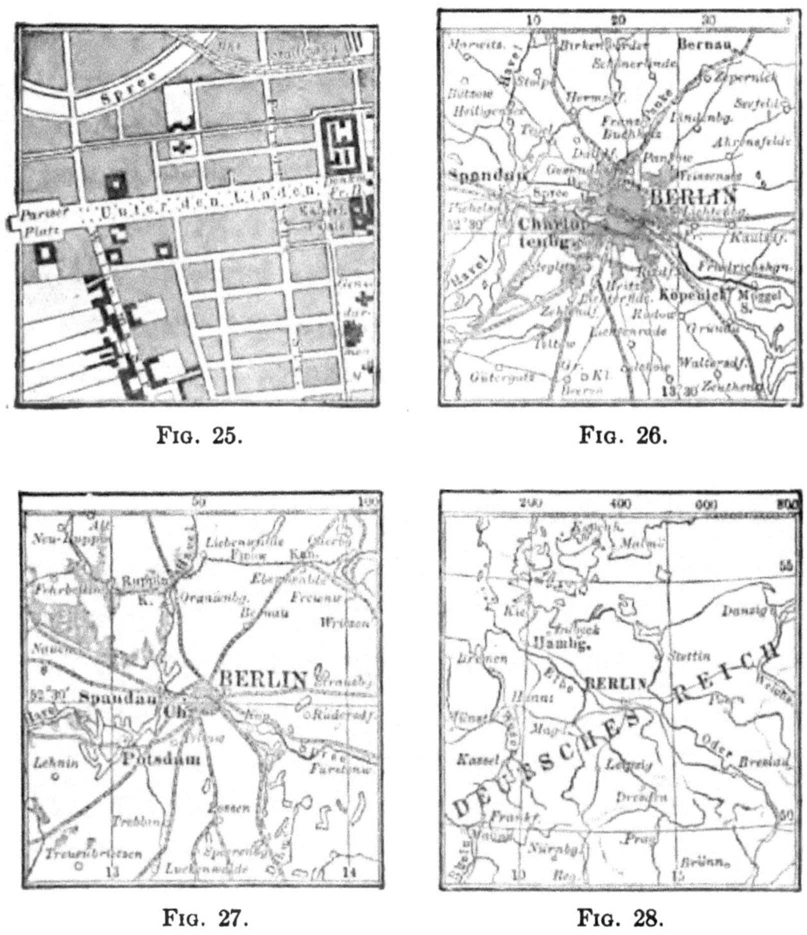

FIG. 25.

FIG. 26.

FIG. 27.

FIG. 28.

Berlin and vicinity on a scale of $\frac{1}{25,000}$, $\frac{1}{1,000,000}$, $\frac{1}{2,500,000}$, and $\frac{1}{20,000,000}$ respectively.

after that by scale of miles and data of directions fills in the minor details.

Scale of maps. — In maps on the scale of an inch to the mile every creek and farmhouse can be shown. In town maps the scale is often 20 inches to the mile. In maps of $\frac{1}{200,000}$ (the ratio to actual, natural dimensions), a common scale for wall maps of the smaller areas on large scale, only the larger irregularities of the coast, the larger streams, and the more important towns can be shown. A map of North America on this scale would have to be about 144 feet wide and 166 feet long. A map of this continent as usually shown in the school books, 8 by 10 inches, is on the scale of about 1 : 40,000,000. Compare Figs. 25, 26, 27, and 28.

Mechanical process of making a map. — The map is first drawn by hand. It may be reproduced by photography on a zinc plate which is then etched, and from this an engraving is made. The map is sometimes made from a copper plate etching. Colored maps are usually printed with lithographic stone or lithographic zinc plates, some with many colors necessitating the same number of printings. The cost of making a map in an ordinary school atlas may run from fifty to a hundred dollars. Cartography has developed from its earlier crude processes to a highly specialized science and a beautiful art.

CHAPTER XVII

GEOGRAPHICAL NAMES

'Tis good to muse on nations passed away
Forever from the land we call our own;
Nations as proud and mighty in their day,
Who deemed that everlasting was their throne. — SANDS.

Significance. — Many names on the map are full of significance if their etymology and origin are known. It adds interest and pleasure to the dull study of place geography to discover such meanings. It should be the aim of the teacher to explain, when possible and when profitable, the names of countries, cities, rivers, mountains, etc. Such meanings may add interesting geographical facts, or historical or other important associations, the knowledge of which would enliven and enrich the study, and often would tend to keep the facts in remembrance.

The etymology of many geographical names may be found in any complete dictionary. Isaac Taylor's *Names and their Histories* is an excellent reference for the names of Great Britain and Europe, and *Bul. 197, United States Geological Survey, The Origin of Certain Place Names in the United States*, by Gannett, for this country.

Geographical names often go back into antiquity far beyond the era of historic record. In fact, for some historic and ethnographic studies the geographic names of a region are the only clew. Thus it has been said that geographic names are fossil history.

It must be remembered that many of these names have suffered much change, by mispronunciation, misspelling, mistranslation, by a gradual change of meaning of roots, by abbreviation, or by mere degradation; also that the etymology of many such names cannot be determined with positiveness, and that there is much difference of opinion among authorities regarding derivations. In spite of this element of doubt, which is especially important in considering the prehistoric names, fairly good assurance may be felt about the etymology and significance of geographical names in general, particularly concerning the names in the newer countries, where the historic or physiographic reasons for the name are still quite apparent.

The first geographical names were probably those of landmarks, such as rivers, mountains, etc., and were used by primitive man in his wanderings. They were usually nouns, simply signifying the feature, such as *don* (river), *loch* (lake), *ben* (peak), sometimes, as to-day, coupled with an adjective prefix or suffix. It is remarkable how persistent these old names are, particularly those of rivers and mountains, lasting to the present day. Thus

Celtic roots persist in various parts of Europe from which the Celts passed away in prehistoric days. This race was probably one of the first, impelled by love of adventure and conquest, or crowding at home, to emerge from Asia. Celtic names occur all over southern and central Europe. The Celts had several root words for running water,—*avon*, *dur*, *wysg*, and *don* being modern Celtic-Welsh forms. These are believed to occur in the names of many European streams, as the Ofanto in Italy, the Inn in Germany, the Rhine (*ren-avon*, swift water), the Seine (*sen-avon*, slow river), the Garonne, and several Avons in England. The root *wysg* occurs in the Welsh word meaning stream, in the English Esk, Usk, Ouse, Oxford, and even in the Thames (*tam eisis*, broad river); and in the continental Aix, Weser, Wisbach, and others. The root *dur* is found in the Doura in Spain.

In the same way the extent of the incursion of each wave of migration, the Greek, the Roman, Teutonic, Slavonic, and Saracen may be seen in the names of the map of Europe.

When a conquering race came into a land previously peopled they retained many of the names given to physical features by the aborigines, as may be seen by the great retention of Indian names in the New World.

The later names in the older countries are those of cities and states. The first races of Europe had no settled habitation, or definite tribal boundaries. It is this class of names that are especially full of historic meaning. The various racial invasions, for example those into England, as also the different periods of settlement in America, are thus well marked by superimposed sets of names.

Names in Great Britain.—1. *Celtic.*—The remnants of the Celts are represented in the British Isles by the Irish, the Welsh, and the Highland Scotch. At one time they extended over all England. The ancient Britons, whom Cæsar partly conquered, 55 B.C., were Celtic. Their names are found in England and Scotland. The numerous Avons as stream names are examples. It is redundancy to speak of the *River* Avon. Other Celtic names appear for river (see above).

Dun (*don*) is the word for a hill, usually fortified. This is a common name on the map of Great Britain, as Dundee, Dumfries, the Downs (dunes, hills); and London (*llyn*, a pool, and *dun*, hill-fort), which dates back more than two thousand years.

2. *The Romans* left their impress on the English map in the various Chesters (*castrum*, a fortified camp),—Chester, Chichester, Dorchester, Winchester, Leicester, Worcester, etc.

3. *Saxon.*—The geography of the next invaders, the Saxons, is indicated by many place names ending in *tun* (*ton*), a farm inclosure, or village; and names end-

ing in *ham*, home, farm village, as Aelfredston, Bilston, Darloston, Boston, Norton (Northtown), Easton, Sutton (Southtown), Weston, Merton (town by the sea); Walsingham, Cheltenham, Oldham, West Ham, etc. The termination *burgh* (*burg*, *borough*, *bury*), a fortified town, is also Saxon and appears in Salisbury, Peterborough, Shrewsbury, Bury St. Edmunds, Glastonbury, Canterbury, Bury. It is evident that some of these places were named after people, as in the case of Jonesville or Smithtown to-day.

4. When the *Danes* came they brought with them the names *by*, a town, and *thorpe*, a village, which we see attached to several English towns, — Appleby, Whitby, Derby (by the water), Rugby (Rockville), Althorp and Winthorp.

5. *Norse*. — The English and Scottish coast is dotted with towns ending in *ness*, nose, headland, as Skegness, Sheerness in England, and Inverness and Caithness in Scotland. The Naze, Oxfordness, and Dungeness are still used as names for capes. These names were given by the plundering Norsemen or Vik-ings (from *vik*, a creek, inlet, or bay on the Scandinavian coast). From *vik* are derived the many towns ending in *wick* or *wich*, as Wick, Berwick, Norwich, Ipswich, Sandwich (Sandy Creek), Greenwich, all towns on the coast or on rivers near the mouth, except a few like Warwick, which is inland. The English word yard is *garth* in Norse, in

which it means an inclosed or fortified place. From this come Fishguard and Applegarth.

Thus is history written on the map.

The map names of America should be of particular interest to American pupils. The non-Indian names are of so recent origin, and historically so well established, that their meaning and form have changed but little, and their interpretation is therefore less liable to error.

1. *Indian.*—The Indian aborigines lived on both continents as numerous scattered tribes in more or less permanent sections or domains. The American race is usually ascribed to the Mongolian stock. The tribes have a common root language, but many dialects have developed in different regions. This is shown by a study of the names of various parts of North America. In the Northwest are the ugly-sounding Aleut names, like Alaska, Skagway, Yakutat, Kadiak, Sitka, Kutlik, etc. The western United States coast tribes had better sounding ones: Tacoma (the highest, near heaven), Wallula and Willamette (Wallamet, running water), Shasta (a tribe of Indians), Tuolumne. The Indians of the Basin, the Shoshone group, are represented by Shoshone, Winnemucca, Utah (the mountain), Idaho (gem of the mountains). The fierce Sioux tribes had names like Dakota (allies), Iowa (sleepy ones), Missouri (muddy water), Nebraska (shallow water), Kansas (wil-

lows), Omaha (up-stream), Topeka (a good place to dig potatoes), Oklahoma (home for all Indians). The Algonquin tribes of the Ohio Valley and the Upper Great Lakes gave us Minnesota (much or cloudy water), Minnehaha (laughing water), Michigan (big lake), Illinois (a tribe), Ohio (beautiful river), Wisconsin (rushing water), Chicago (skunk cabbage), Kalamazoo, Sheboygan, Erie (wild cat tribe), Allegheny (the fairest river), Kentucky (the prairies). The mighty Iroquois tribes of the Lower Great Lakes and the Hudson gave us Ontario (beautiful lake), Mohawk (muskrat), Genesee, Cayuga (long lake), Oswego (broad valley), Niagara (neck or strait; thundering water), Manhattan (of doubtful origin, some authorities giving it as "little island"; others, as "the place of drunkenness," referring to Verrazano's carousal with the Indians). The Indians of the Gulf region had the mellifluous, alliterative Tallahassee (old town), Chattanooga (eagle's nest), Alabama (the clearing), Mississippi (father of the waters), Natchez, Altamaha, Appalachicola, Okifinokee, and Appalachian (near the sea). The names of Mexico are largely Aztec, — Mexico (home of the god of war), Mazatlan, Tepic, Zacetecas, Popocatapetl, Tlaxcala, and Tehauntepec.

Many Indian names are translated literally, — Big Stone Lake, Spearfish, Red Cloud, Pipestone, Red Lodge, Medicine Lodge, etc. Also many through mispronunciation, mistranslation, or degradation have but slight resemblance to their originals in the Indian language. Thus Ouachita (buffalo country) has become Wichita.

The names of half the states are Indian, the majority of the rivers of the Mississippi System and the Eastern states, most of our lakes, and legions of counties, townships, and cities. These names will persist long after the Indian has ceased to exist as a separate tribal entity, and will be historic evidence of the once continental sway of the Red Man. Practically all these names had some significance, even to the Whites, at first, referring chiefly to physical features, but they are already being used generally without understanding. Nevertheless, they are still interesting on account of their alien origin, their alliterative or musical sound, and the piquancy of their forgotten meaning.

2. *Spanish.* — The succession of explorers and immigrants in America is plainly marked on the map. First came the Spaniards, who together with their spoliation of the Aztecs and other Indians combined a certain religious zeal and devotion attested by the many sacred names they bestowed on their discoveries and domains: San Salvador (so named by Columbus in gratitude for his deliverance from the dangers of his first voyage), San Juan Bautista (St. John the Baptist), St. Augustine, San Antonio, Corpus Christi (Body of

Christ), San Diego, Los Angeles (*La puebla de la Nuestra Señora la Reina de Los Angeles*, the city of Our Lady, the Queen of the Angels, was the lengthy original title), San José, Santa Maria, San Francisco, Sacramento (the sacrament). The name California was given after the name of a fabled isle of precious stones in a Spanish novel popular at that time. Many Spanish names refer to some physical characteristic of the place. The numerous Salinas speak of the salt deposits in that arid zone (Arizona). El Paso is The Pass (Ute Pass) between the Rockies of the United States and the Sierras of Mexico. The groves of cottonwoods (Alamedo, Alamo) and white oaks (Albuquerque), and the "fertile plain" (Las Vegas), were grateful oases in this land of drought. The Spanish name for mountain is Sierra (a saw), and thus we have Sierra Nevada (white). Colorado means red, and Rio, river (Rio Grande).

3. *French.*—The trail of the Frenchmen leads from the St. Lawrence to Lake Superior, and from there down the Mississippi to New Orleans. They got along more amicably with the Indians than did the English, and as lonely traders and still lonelier missionaries they paddled their birch canoes up the larger streams, and on the Great Lakes, and carried them over the portages, or around falls and rapids. They lived in the Big Woods in savage teepees, cut off from civilization by a thousand miles of wilderness.

The French, also, showed their piety in a religious nomenclature of places, of which St. Lawrence, St. Anthony Falls, Sault (falls) St. Marie, St. Paul, St. Louis, are examples. Detroit (a strait), Fond du Lac (end of the lake), and Prairie du Chien (prairie dog) are French. Unlike their Anglo-Saxon brethren the French did not give their own names to their discoveries. Their modesty has been rewarded by later generations naming in their honor many spots along the old French routes of discovery, — Champlain, Marquette, Duluth, Joilet, La Salle, Hennepin, Le Sueur, etc.

4. *English.* — Next came the English occupation with a great blanket of English names.

(*a*) Religious names.—The Puritans, who came to avoid religious persecution, and to live their lives in accordance with their beliefs, showed their fervor also in giving religious names,—Salem (Jerusalem), Providence, Concord. And of a later date are the many Bethels, Bethlehems, Jordans, Zions, Zion Cities, Lebanons, Canaans, Shilohs, Goshens, Carmels, Tabors, etc.

(*b*) Royal names. — The Puritans were always inclined to be rather independent and democratic; but their Cavalier cousins south of the Mason and Dixon Line were more friendly to the king and the nobility. In the North we find few names in honor of royalty or the nobles, but in the South we have Virginia (Queen Elizabeth), the Carolinas and Maryland (after Charles I and his queen), Georgia (George II), Charleston (Charles II), Jamestown (James I), Annapolis (wife of James I), Elizabeth City, Va., Georgetown, Baltimore, Delaware. Albany and New York (Duke of Albany, Duke of York, later James II) are examples in the North.

(*c*) European repetitions.—Isaac Taylor thinks that English names are uninteresting and prosaic, and do not generally show appreciation of natural beauty. Be that as it may, they must have been treasured in the hearts of the emigrants, who on coming to the new country still paid homage to the mother country by repeating them on the American map. So we have in New England and elsewhere the names of Plymouth, Boston, Bath, Portland, Exeter, Portsmouth, Dover, Manchester, Lynn, Cambridge, Gloucester, Worcester, Springfield, Northampton, Northfield, Norwich, New London, Danbury, New Haven, New Britain, Windsor, Reading, Chester, etc., all good old English place names. The names of some eighty English towns thus suffice for a thousand American places.

The same thing was done by the Dutch in New Netherlands, New Amsterdam, Amsterdam, Flushing, and Brooklyn; by the Swedes in New Sweden (Delaware); by the Germans in Hanover, Berlin, New Ulm, Frankfort, etc. All these borrowed or second-hand place names have no special fitness or significance, except that they reveal the cosmopolitan sources of our immigrants, and their *Heimweh* or love for the old home.

Curiosities in geographical nomenclature are the numerous names taken from classic history, even mythology. A one-time surveyor-general of the state of New York, an admirer of the Ancients, was responsible for the names of Troy, Utica, Syracuse, Rome, Ithaca, Palmyra, Corinth, Marcellus, Camillus, and Athens which appear on the map of the state. These names have been much repeated in other states, with others added. We have Cairo and Memphis reproduced on the Mississippi; Carthage, Hannibal, Cincinnati, and Alexandria. From mythology are taken Olympia and Phœnix; and we have the Eureka of Archimedes many times. Philadelphia may be added as a happy invention on the classic model.

5. *Native.* — But Americans have coined or invented a host of names for themselves, repeating the practice all over the world in all ages.

(*a*) Descriptive.—Just as in prehistoric times the Phœnicians named a rocky islet Tyre (Heb. *Tsor*, a rock), so in most recent times the most natural way of naming a place is by reference to some physiographic feature. Thus we have Little Falls, Portage, Lockport, Niagara Falls City, Atlantic City, Ocean Grove, Sulphur Springs, Lake City, El Paso, River Falls, Iron Mountain, Grand Rapids, Detroit, Terre Haute (High Ground), South Bend, Rockford, Salt Lake City, Death Valley, Butte (an abrupt peak), Little Rock, Hot Springs,

Montana (mountainous), Maine ("the mayn land"), Rhode Island (from a roode Eylandt, red island, in the Bay), Rocky Mountains, Bad Lands, etc.

Many names contain adjectives or phrases descriptive of the beauty of the place: Fairview, Belleview, Buena Vista (good view), Bellaire (good air), Greenfield, Evergreen, Point Pleasant, Eau Claire (clear water), etc.

Many rivers are named after the color of their waters, as Red, Green, White, and Black; and mountains have ever been thus called, as the Blue Mountains, the Green Mountains (hence Vermont), the White Mountains, the Black Hills, etc.

(*b*) Biological.—Another large class of American names are biological, indicating the kind of animals, trees, or other vegetation that once abounded in the vicinity, examples of which are Buffalo, Beaver Dam, Bear River, Big Horn Mountains, Snake River, Goose Lake, Pelican Rapids, Eagle City, Musselshell River, Eel River, Cape Cod, White Oaks, Albuquerque (white oaks), Cottonwood, Alamo (cottonwoods), Baton Rouge (red stick, cedar), Pine Bluff, etc.

(*c*) Industrial.—Some American cities are named after some natural resource, or the chief industry "that has made them famous": Farmingdale, Wheatland, Port Tobacco, Pomona (after the Goddess of Fruit), Olean, Oil City, Petrolia, Carbon, Carbondale, Minersville, Galena (lead ore), Leadville, Silver City, Golden, Gloversville, Mechanicsburg, Linoleumville, Emporium, — not all that might be asked for a name always, but perhaps good advertising.

(*d*) Biographical.—Another great class of cities in the United States have biographical names. Many are given in honor of presidents, governors, and other statesmen, army and naval leaders, or other great men dear to the hearts of the people; and some have been given in admiration of foreign heroes or leaders, some of whom have rendered this country service. It is said that more cities and towns (65) are named after Franklin than after any other man. If, however, counties and townships, not to mention streets, are considered, Washington easily leads (320). Hamilton, Adams, Jefferson, Madison, Jackson, Lincoln, Garfield, are great favorites. Lafayette, Steuben, Pulaski, Pitt, and other foreigners are honored.

Seas, bays, straits, capes, and islands are often named after their discoverers or explorers, as, Vancouver Island, the Strait of Juan de Fuca, and Puget Sound. This feature is especially noticeable in the more recent discoveries of Australia, Polynesia, and the polar regions.

The very name America came about in a similar way, though partially based on an error. Amerigo Vespucci, an Italian, made several voyages of exploration, following up and extending the work of Columbus, 1499–1503. He published the first printed account of the New World.

There was a German geographer, Waldseemüller by name, in France, who wrote a Latin book in 1507, in which he said, " And the fourth part of the world having been discovered by Amerigo or Americus, we may call it Amerige or America," thus overlooking the prior claims of Columbus. Dr. Penck suggests that the name America is not inappropriate, as the name Amerigo means grain (German, *Emerich*, *Emmer*).

To make some amends the country discovered as a result of Columbus' vision is poetically called Columbia, while we have the District of Columbia, and many places called Columbus or Columbia.

If one turns to the map of the polar and sub-polar regions he sees the names of the men who braved isolation, hardship, cold, starvation, and death in quest of the Northwest Passage, or the Polar Goal. Hudson's Bay reminds us of the pathetic story of the fate of this discoverer, cast adrift with his son in a small boat by his mutinous crew. After him, also, we have Hudson's Strait and the Hudson River. In the Arctic waters we find the names of Davis, Baffin, Ross, Frobisher, Behring, Franklin, Peary, and others.

(*e*) Proprietary.—Besides the many places named deservedly in honor of great men, there are in this country a host of cities and towns named after unhistoric personages, perhaps an early settler, a great landowner who owned the town site, a leading manufacturer, a financier, or perhaps only a politician. Every one is familiar with such names as Evansville, Stevenspoint, Harrisburg, Youngstown, Brownsville, Barnesville, Greenville, Pottstown, Smithtown, etc. It is these names that irritated Matthew Arnold, and our own Emerson, because of their prosaic character and monotonous repetition. But they represent a very natural method of naming a place, and one which has been practiced by all races. In England the many hams, tons, burgs, burys, fields, and bys are for the most part composed of these roots combined with family names. In Europe most places have existed beyond the memory of man, and such patronymics excite no question. Here, however, the commonplace character of Smith of Smithsville, or of Mr. Potts of Pottstown is still fresh in mind, and therefore less romantic.

(*f*) Frontier types.—As a contrast to the euphonious classic names are the appellations given by our pioneers, hunters, cowboys, miners, and lumberjacks, names less polite, yet decidedly expressive and appropriate at the time given. Thus, Stranger, Deadman's Creek, Three Devils, Bonanza, Jimtown, Roundup, Stampede, Gin Flat, Eight-mile, Hog Ranch, Billy Creek, etc. Some of these destined to grow into importance become ashamed before the world of their humble name and origin, and petition the legislatures to change their name to something more orthodox.

Application in teaching. — The mature student of geography finds in the meaning and origin of geographical names much of interest. While the teacher in the elementary school cannot apply such linguistic and historic studies directly, she may give the pupils now and then a translation, if profitable, and may to a certain extent make the children feel that names do represent history, race, and language; and that many of the names on the map are truly descriptive of geographical conditions. Tracing the meanings of names is one of the profitable and legitimate pastimes of geography.

CHAPTER XVIII

THE GEOGRAPHY OF INDUSTRY AND COMMERCE

A distinct phase of geography.—So much of geography deals with industrial occupations and trade that in the high school and college it is differentiated as a separate branch under the name of Commercial Geography. Even in the upper grammar grades a special emphasis is often placed on this phase of the subject. So far as intrinsic interest, human importance, and rational unity are concerned, it deserves such distinction. In the elementary school, it is, however, generally combined and blended with the other phases of the study.

Commercial study in the primary course.—Industrial geography has the pedagogical advantage of dealing with human needs and human occupations. It springs out of the necessities and activities of the home. It is enacted in every shop, and is represented by the traffic of the street and by the shipping of the harbor. The child necessarily has considerable appreciation, from observation and experience, of the industrial life of the community. Home geography extends this knowledge by a more thorough study of familiar, typical industries and teaches a few general relations, such as the sources of commodities, division of labor, raw material and finished goods, buyer and seller, exports and imports, etc.

In the "first round" of the world, in primary geography, these elementary notions are applied in a broad view of the conspicuous occupations of mankind in America and the rest of the world. Through this the pupil learns of modifications of methods employed in his own community, of entirely new industries, and something of the interdependence and interrelations of distant regions. He also begins to see that man's occupations are determined by natural conditions of climate, location, resources, etc.

The approach in the lower grades should be, preferably, from the human side. The industry should be considered more as an outcome of human interest or need, than as a causation by physical nature. The point of view should be, What do the people do for a living? rather than, What is the effect of nature on man's mode of life? The latter treatment may be reserved for the higher grades.

An industry should be studied somewhat intensively, and as concretely or graphically as possible. It should be an important, typical industry.

One and a half pages out of the four on New England, in Dodge's *Elementary Geography*, are devoted to commercial matters; and Tarr and McMurry's *New Geography*, First Book, gives ten out of the eleven pages on the same section. These data are given to show the varying importance attached to commercial geography in the lower grades.

An example: Study of a ranch. — In the following illustration taken from an elementary text, note the preponderance of the human element. Even the title sounds better to a child than "A Study of the Cattle Industry." This is, no doubt, a somewhat extreme example, but if all the primary geographies were as well adapted to the interests of children, the subject would find greater popularity.

A RANCH

There is a belt of high plateau land east of the Rocky Mountain foot-hills, stretching from Texas to North Dakota, which has very little rain, not enough to make grain growing profitable, and so it is devoted to grazing. Where the buffalo once fed in countless numbers now graze thousands of cattle. . . . No hay is equal to these grasses, dried where they stand, and waiting to be nibbled through the winter months.

. . . But sometimes the cattle are in immense herds, and feed upon great tracts of unfenced land, where it is necessary for men to watch and care for them. These herders are called cowboys.

The cowboys almost live in the saddle. They wear overalls of leather and wide-brimmed hats, carry large revolvers and use big spurs on their long boots. They endure rough fare, hard work, and all kinds of exposure to the weather. . . .

The cowboy learns to throw the lasso or rope with great skill, for he practices from boyhood. The rope is usually made of leather or grass and is about forty feet long, with a noose at one end, six feet or more in length. The coils of the rope are held in the left hand, and the noose is swung around the head with the right, and then forward and over the head or around the feet of the animal to be caught. . . .

Cowboys are skillful riders. . . .

In summer the cowboy rides all day among his cattle to see that they do not stray too far from good feed and water. Toward night he drives them to the bedding ground. . . . A few cowboys are on duty to watch them. Wild cattle are easily frightened at night; then they jump to their feet and start to run away. . . .

As different cattle look much alike, it is necessary for the owner to have his initials or some private mark on every animal in order to prove ownership. . . . These marks, or *brands*, are written on the hides of the living animals with a hot iron for a pen. . . .

The round-ups take place in the autumn and spring. The cowboys come together from long distances, each one knowing not only his own brand, but that of many neighbors. All the cattle in a certain section . . . are driven to one central place. . . . A man rides among them, and when he sees a cow or a steer with his own brand upon it, he runs it out of the herd to a second man who holds it.

A well-trained horse is a great help in doing this. Many of the best horses for ranch business are bred in Texas. . . . The Texas ponies are small, but tough, quick, and very intelligent. Some of them are docile and willing, but others are apt to "buck." When a horse bucks . . .

When the cattle are full-grown they are sent by rail to the stock-yards of Kansas City or Chicago, where they are turned into meat, which is shipped to all parts of the country. You owe the roast beef you have for dinner to the grass that grows on the far-off ranches and the labor of the hard-worked cowboys.

A more intensive study of commercial geography is made in upper grades. The degree of detail of treatment varies with the author, and with the times. In the books of several generations ago very little was said on this subject. The present is an intensely commercial age, and the business world is continually crying for a commercial education. This demand has been met more or less by some textbooks of geography.

Authors are not, by any means, agreed as to how far to go into the biology of commercial plants and animals, or the technique of culture and manufacture, or the details of commerce. For example, Frye gives about ten words to the subject of Irrigation; Dodge, 90; Redway and Hinman, about 100; King, 1300; Tarr and McMurry, 1700. This applies to advanced geography in each case. The variation is in part due to the different demands at different times, and partly to the author's judgment.

Type studies. — Some authors believe that the description of the cotton plant, for example, does not properly belong to geography, but to nature-study or botany; that the technical processes of a flour mill, or the details of a railroad business, are not geographical. It is probable, however, that such correlations of science, or trade technique, etc., will be generally regarded proper in the treatment of a limited number of type studies of industries, for the purpose of geographical unity.

The balance between physical and commercial geography and the other human phases of the subject varies also according to the author's training and predilections. Yet practically all recent writers give a large proportion to commercial geography. Thus for the New England states Frye's *Grammar School Geography* gives nearly two out of three pages to commercial geography; King's *Advanced Geography*, twelve out of fourteen; Dodge's *Advanced Geography*, six out of nine; Tarr and McMurry's *New Advanced Geography*, Second Book, eleven and a half out of sixteen.

In advanced geography much more can be done with the study of the relations of the industries, not only to each other, but also to the natural environment on which they depend; and certain laws can be shown to underlie the industrial and commercial activities of man. The causal treatment lends itself well to commercial geography. As a rule, the causal sequence — location, topography, climate, resource, industry — should be followed. This sequence is usually well marked, and pupils should learn to use it as a principle of study.

To appreciate these broad connections of commercial geography requires some maturity. The economic aspects of natural science and geography do not appeal greatly to younger minds, neither do the relations of things. But in the grammar grades the interest in such study is fairly well developed.

Commercial geography, to be appreciated as a unit, also requires a good general knowledge of the map of the earth, climates, and peoples, which is another reason for not pressing this subject in the lower grades.

Further, commercial geography is almost inextricably blended with history, sociology, and economics, of which the older pupils, even, have inadequate knowledge.

The relegation of commercial geography in this wider sense to the upper grades makes it possible to employ certain methods of instruction. In the first place, it may be studied more intensively. The great industries and commercial agencies may be studied as types in considerable detail (see Chapter XIX).

Such a study requires a text of the completer sort, or else the use of supplementary readers, reference work, or classroom development by the teacher. In this way a thorough description of the industry is given, providing not merely a few dry statistics, but some principles of industry in general, and stimulating the reason and the imagination.

Type study of lumbering. — The following is taken from a recent textbook for upper grades. The industry is taken up after the map study, topography, glacial effects, and climate have been considered as a setting.

LUMBERING

Extent of the forests. — In the days of the early settlers, most of New England was covered with forests, and one of the first products sent back to England was lumber. Now the woods have been cleared away from much of the land, but where it is too steep or too rocky for farming, large tracts of forest still remain.

For instance, there are large tracts of land in northern Maine, New Hampshire and Vermont, as well as in parts of the three Southern States (New England), that are still covered with timber. Standing on the summit of Mount Katahdin, one sees only a vast wilderness of trees in all directions. The nearest cultivated land is twenty-five miles to the east, while the unbroken forest stretches away much farther to the north and west.

Cutting of the timber. — Winter is the busy season for cutting timber in this wilderness, for the swamps, which are numerous, and in summer impassable, are then frozen. At that season, also, the snows have covered the bowlders and fallen trees, and made the surface level enough for sleds, loaded with logs, to be drawn through the woods.

Usually fifty or more men are necessary to a logging camp. With axes in hand, they go through the woods chopping down all the trees large and sound enough for good lumber. The limbs are then chopped off, and the logs are dragged by horses to the banks of the nearest stream.

Floating the logs to the mills. — When the snow melts in the spring, the cutting is over and another busy season begins. The ice on the river breaks up, the streams are swollen by the melting snows, and the logs are whirled off downstream in the swift current. Frequently, however, this flood of water is not sufficient to carry them. In such cases in order to provide more water, dams are placed across the streams, or at the outlet of lakes. When more water is needed, the dams are opened, and a flood is poured into the stream. In this way immense numbers of logs are floated, or "driven" downstream, forming what lumbermen call a "log drive."

The work of driving logs is a very exciting one. The logs often run on to rocks and shoals; and, as soon as one gets caught, others are held back by it. If the "jam" is not speedily removed the entire stream may become blocked. Such a condition is called a "log jam," and it is the business of the log drivers to prevent jams by freeing the logs that become thus lodged.

Some of the logs are stopped near waterfalls, far upstream where they are sawed into boards, lath, shingles, etc.; but most of them are carried to sawmills as far down the river as the current will take them.

Hardships of the lumberman's life. — During the season for cutting, the men go forth early in the morning and work until late in the evening, eating and sleeping in log cabins. Their beds are broad shelves of rough boards, covered with boughs from the spruce and balsam trees; and the camp is often so small that they must lie side by side, with scarcely room to turn. There is much exposure, too. The men may suffer seriously from the cold, for it is often necessary to work when the temperature is far below zero.

The work of preventing log jams brings even more exposure, for the workmen must frequently wade into the icy water, and ride upon the logs. One may often see a man carried along on a single log, clinging to it by means of the sharp spikes in his boots, balancing himself with a long pole. Now and then he must jump from log to log, as a squirrel springs from tree to tree. In this way the men are often wet from head to foot and may even be thrown into the water and drowned. So many hardships are connected with lumbering that a lumberman is said to become an old man after a few years of service.

This account is illustrated with appropriate cuts. Surely the pupil reading it must at least get a sympathetic appreciation of this industry.

Principles of commerce.—The simpler underlying principles of commerce should be taught. The specific examples should be analyzed to reveal them. The teacher should show how these principles recur again and again in other cases, till the pupil begins to look for them himself. In this way he will acquire a stock of working principles helpful not only in the continuation of the study, but also in appreciating and solving in later life the complex industrial and civic problems of modern society.

These principles, like all others in the elementary school geography, should not be taught in the abstract or in a general way, but should be derived naturally from the study of concrete, specific examples of industry and trade relations. Neither should they all be presented in one lesson. Months, even years, may be taken to develop them all, but in the upper grammar grades they should be organized and reviewed, and considered more in the abstract.

Among such principles should be the following: The needs of man, and how they are determined. The sources of man's resources, and how they depend on topography, climate, location, etc. Raw material and finished goods. Division of labor. Value of machinery. Effect of labor on cost. The law of supply and demand. How markets are determined. Routes of commerce in relation to topography. The means of transportation and their relative cost. The telegraph and other means of communication. The importance of good harbors. What constitutes a good harbor. The geographic causes of the location of cities. What decides the location of an industry. The laws of international trade. The tariff. Other governmental control in commerce. See also Chapter XX.

Statistics. — Commercial geography necessarily deals with statistics of amounts of resources, values of manufactures, railway mileage, and the like. It would be folly to require the pupil to retain these any great length of time, even if they could be memorized. No doubt there are a very few statistics of population, distance, etc., worth remembering. But for the most part it is neither wise nor profitable to memorize them. Statistics are presented to give some comparative ideas of the quantitative importance of the things to which they refer. They are mere stepping-stones, once used, to be forgotten, though the general notion they were to teach it may be necessary to retain.

Statistics serve to show the relative values of our resources, manufactures, means of transportation, etc. They show whether our industries and commerce are progressing or declining. They serve to show our standing in comparison with other countries.

It should be remembered that textbook statistics are often woefully behind the times. To be of any value, their date should be considered. The teacher should try to get the later returns from other sources, census returns, government trade reports, yearly almanacs of newspapers, etc., if the statistics in the textbook are antiquated.

General review of commercial relations. — In practically all modern advanced geographies, and in some of the elementary texts, there are, after the study of the United States, or after the survey of the world, chapters often called General Review, or Comparative Review, which deal with a summary of the commercial data of the United States, and a comparison with other countries to show relative strength and the trend of international trade.

Such a review serves not only as an organizing summary, but through the comparison of country with country further facts of relative commercial strength, and principles of commerce, commercial routes, and means of communication are brought out.

Observational basis of commercial geography. — As in other fields, observation and personal experience count for a great deal in the study of commercial geography. The subject should be made as practical as possible, taken out of the pedantry of the textbook, basing it wherever possible upon the real observations of the pupil. The local artisans, the factories, the traffic on the street, the shipping in the harbor, all can be used to render the subject real. Individual observations should be encouraged, preliminary direct studies assigned, and occasionally safe and feasible visits made to factories and other industrial plants.

A collection of commercial specimens is of great use. Foodstuffs, fabrics, building material, etc., in the raw and finished state, or showing stages of manufacture, are useful. It is not necessary to make a large collection. A few of the great staples to serve as types are sufficient.

Pictures of all stages of industry and of trade are extremely desirable. Many excellent pictures may be obtained as advertising from commercial houses. There are a few school charts of the industries, but these are of foreign make, and are apt to show out-of-date methods. Some showing the primitive hand processes are good, however. Current popular journals contain a great wealth of up-to-date matter and pictures on many phases of our industrial life.

Commercial maps. — It is an excellent plan for teachers to make rough sketch maps on the blackboard, or, better, on heavy paper, of the distribution of commercial products, trade routes, and the like. The pupils also should be required to draw commercial maps, generally on the printed outlines. One kind of map always appeals to the native instincts of children, the pictorial or realistic map, showing the distribution of commercial features by means of pictures or actual specimens pasted or fastened on the map. A mineral chart or agricultural chart could thus be used to enlist the activities of each pupil in the class in the construction of a common map. It is a good exercise.

Statistical diagrams. — The vast amounts of some resources, products, or manufactures, etc., are so inconceivable and meaningless that it is necessary to use some method to interpret them other than mere statistics. The usual device in many books of rectangles or squares of proportionate areas to represent the different quantities is an excellent one, since it appeals to the eye and the reason better than numbers. The secondary device of using pictures of the things themselves represented, in proportionate sizes, appeals still more to the children. The circle with proportionate divisions is another good statistical device.

Tabulation is helpful to the learner. If properly tabulated on the board or on charts, interesting relations which would not be seen otherwise may be shown. The articles of commerce may thus be classified, the relation between raw and finished goods shown, the source and markets indicated, etc. Pupils should be taught to make such tabulations themselves in order to better organize their knowledge.

Raw Material	Source	Finished Product	Market
Wheat	Mississippi Valley	Flour	Europe
		Bran	China
		Cereal goods	Africa

Supplementary literature. — There are many good supplementary readers pertaining to commercial products, manufacturing processes, and trade. The classic F. G. Carpenter series of Geographical Readers, Chamberlain's series of *How We Are Fed, Clothed, Sheltered,* and *How We Travel;* F. O. Carpenter's *Foods and their Uses;* Rocheleau's *Geography of Commerce,* — are all for the elementary school. The older pupils should be encouraged to write short papers on what they have read on assigned topics. Current magazines, also, may be used to good advantage.

"**Research**" **by pupils.** — A very practical bit of "research" by pupils is to visit shops, factories, warehouses, docks, etc., to note the commodities there, and by questioning the people in charge, or from the tags and labels, learn of their source or destination.

A class in New York City wrote letters to the big steamship companies, asking them to send the names of ten leading imports and ten leading exports handled by their companies, and then tabulated and had printed the results of their inquiry.

Commercial news in newspapers. — Another good way of rendering this study vital is to read the daily papers for crop reports, commerce notes, shipping reports, etc. To read the following in the paper is much more interesting and real than to learn these facts from the musty statistics of some textbook.

NEWS OF SHIPS AND PORTS

NEW YORK, Mar. 1, 1912.—The New York and Porto Rico Line's steamship San Juan arrived yesterday afternoon at the East Central pier, Atlantic dock, from Mayaguez, Ponce and San Juan. She brought 54 passengers and a cargo of oranges, nuts, cigars, tobacco, bay rum, pineapples, grapefruit, cocoanuts and sundries.

The Booth Line's steamship Benedict arrived yesterday at Pier 4, Martin's stores, from Manaos, Itacoatiara, Para and Barbados. She brought 4720 cases of rubber and 20,000 hectos of Brazil nuts. Rubber is going up again and the Benedict's cargo is valued at over $2,250,000.

The Joint Service steamship Indrawade arrived yesterday at Funch, Edye & Co.'s pier, Bush's stores, from Yokohama, Yokkaichi, Moji, Shanghai, Singapore, Allepy, Cochin and Gibraltar, via Boston. She brought a cargo of copper, porcelains, toys, paper, carpet wools, straw braid, beans, bristles, wood oil, sago, gums, pearl shells, gambier, gutta, rubber, coir, matting and general merchandise, including sixty-six cases of discarded queues from Hongkong.

The Booth Line's steamship Clement sailed yesterday from Pier 4, Martin's stores, for Barbados, Para and Manaos. She takes out a few passengers and a full general cargo, consisting largely of flour, foodstuffs, provisions and lumber.

CHAPTER XIX

INTENSIVE STUDY OF GEOGRAPHY

In teaching geography one is confronted with a dilemma, — the necessity of giving a good view of the earth as a whole, and the importance of selecting and emphasizing the most vital topics for thorough study. The two problems are in a measure incompatible. The attempt to study a vast multitude of facts in a general course in geography necessarily leads to superficiality. On the other hand, singling out the most essential topics for more complete study teaches the geography of the earth in spots only, leaving too much a blank.

The difficulty is usually solved by providing a general, avowedly superficial, course, covering the whole globe, for beginners, after they have finished home geography; and for the upper grades a more thorough, detailed study of the same field, in which, however, certain great topics are singled out for a still more intensive treatment. (See Type Study, page 241.)

By thus rapidly traversing the world twice, continent by continent, country by country, the pupil receives a fair general notion of the relations of the world as a whole.

Emphasis on geographical facts should be discriminating.—The facts of geography are not all equally important, and should not be taught alike. Discrimination should be used. Some topics should receive much more attention than others. The geography of Japan is vitally important to the Japanese, but not to American children. To the latter the geography of America is most essential. To American pupils the geography of England is more important than that of Austria, for evident historic and economic reasons. Climatic features are more important than earthquakes. The less vital topics may be judiciously slighted to save time for thorough study of the more essential.

Therefore the lion's share of the time is given to our own continent and the United States. It is absolutely necessary to do this for pedagogical, patriotic, historic, and economic reasons.

When the pupils have first studied their own country, which they can understand the best, they have a standard of comparison, or a basis of interpretation, for the study of foreign parts.

Within the study of the United States itself judgment must be used in the selection of the essential and the nonessential.

The textbook as guide.—To a great extent this selection is made for the teacher by the author of the textbook, or by the syllabus, or course of study. Still much remains for the teacher to decide.. Also some of the textbooks do not keep the best balance of the subject.

Geographical units. — Happily the older method of studying the country state by state after the same monotonous plan, and with much repetition about physical features and industries, and the like, is giving way to the more rational treatment by sections embracing groups of states comprising either physiographical regions, or commercial units, or both (see page 248). The North Atlantic states constitute such a well-defined, natural unit. By the map study each state gets sufficient individual attention. The description is then given for the group as a whole. The study would then take up these topics common to all of them: the irregular coast and its influence on the people, the mountainous character of the section, glaciation, scenic aspects, the lumber industry, the truck farms, the big cities, the water power, and the manufacturing industries (cotton, leather, etc.). The Appalachian portion provides mountain studies, coal and iron mines, oil and gas wells, great manufacturing cities. In the South Atlantic section are the balmy climate, cotton, semitropical fruits, the negroes. And so on across the continent, each region has its characteristic features, natural and human.

It is these characteristic topics for the different sections that deserve especial attention. Each important topic should be thoroughly studied in the region where it is most developed and most typical. Thus studied intensively, it will serve as a basis for the understanding of similar conditions elsewhere. There it may be referred to but lightly because already understood.

Thus the study of lumbering in Maine will serve perfectly for the same industry in Michigan, Wisconsin, Minnesota, and Canada. The study of glacial soil and the effects of the glacier in New England prepares for this feature in other regions. The study of a metropolis like Boston or New York gives a picture repeated in every other large city of the United States.

Type study. — This leads to the discussion of type study. A type is a topic that stands for a group or a class, a standard of comparison, and an interpreter of other similar facts. Type study in geography means the selection of representative topics or features of the subject for especial emphasis or detailed study, for the purpose of using them as illustrations of their class.

The confusing wealth of subject matter in geography requires reduction into a scope possible to compass in the assigned course. This requires elimination, selection, grouping, and condensation. By careful discrimination much of the less essential may be entirely cast out, or judiciously slighted. The method of type study permits the presentation of many facts under comparatively few larger representatives.

This method has long been in use in other subjects, especially literature, history, and science. Guyot and Smith were probably the first in this country to employ the method in elementary geography in 1866. The King Geographies also have many excellent types, and others of more recent date, notably the textbooks of Tarr and Frank McMurry. Charles McMurry has in his *Special Methods in Geography* made the principle clear and shown its application in geography. The examples quoted on pages 75 and 149 are types.

Examples of type study. — All kinds of geographical topics lend themselves to the type method: a river (Mississippi), a mountain system (Appalachian), the prairies, the seacoast, the Great Lakes, a mine (coal, iron), agriculture (wheat, cotton), the cattle industry, manufacturing (flour, lumber, shoes, fabrics), commerce (a railroad), a city. The following, taken from a recent textbook, well illustrates the intensiveness, the detail, the causal treatment, and correlation of the method:

IRRIGATION

. . . There are a few other, smaller sections (Cal.) where the rainfall is sufficient for agriculture; but the only way in which farming is possible in most parts of the West is by means of irrigation.

The influence of irrigation is well illustrated in the region near Denver, which lies in the midst of an arid plain. This plain is crossed, however, by the South Fork of the Platte River, from which a ditch, as large as a canal, is led out upon the plain. The river has a rapid fall, but just enough slope has been given the ditch to allow the water to flow. Thus the ditch soon runs on a higher level than the river, and the land between it and the river is lower than the ditch.

Water from the ditch may then be led out over these fields to irrigate them. For this purpose ditches branch off from the main canal, and each of these is divided and subdivided to supply farms along its course. When a field needs water, one of the smaller ditches is tapped and the field is flooded; or else the water is led into furrows a few feet apart. The method followed depends upon the kind of crop that is under cultivation. As there is danger that the supply of water may not last through the summer, reservoirs are built to store the water of the spring freshets, and when needed this is allowed to flow into the ditches.

Of course such an arrangement is expensive, and each farmer must pay for his water at a certain rate, as each tenant of a house in a city pays for his water or gas. That a farmer can afford to pay for water, however, is well shown in this case; for on the upper side of the ditch, which cannot be reached by the water, the land is only fit for grazing, while on the lower side there are rich fields of grain, vegetables, and alfalfa. The latter, like clover and hay, is fed to stock. It is one of the most important crops in the arid regions, where there is much demand for fodder for cattle, hogs, sheep, and horses.

Without irrigation, crops could not be grown in this vicinity. It would then be necessary to bring farm products from Kansas, Nebraska, and other states, a distance of several hundred miles. It is evident, therefore, that irrigation must have had a great influence on the settlement of the West.

(Then follows a sketch of the Rocky Mountain states and Southwest, with the crops raised by means of irrigation, and the development of the important cities in these sections.)

The value of irrigation is well shown here (Southern California). Before irrigation was introduced into Southern California, this region could support very few people. Now, in Los Angeles and vicinity, there is a population of over two hundred thousand.

The description of these few places serves to show the importance of irrigation in the West. It is not to be understood, however, that these are the only noted irrigated sections, for there are many others. Most of the largest and best known are along the large rivers. For example, irrigation is extensive along the Yellowstone and Missouri rivers and their tributaries in Montana; along the Snake River and its tributaries in Idaho; along the Yakima and other streams tributary to the Columbia River in Washington, Oregon, and Idaho; along the Gila and Salt rivers in Arizona; along the Rio Grande and Pecos rivers in New Mexico; and along the Sacramento, San Joaquin, and other rivers in California. . . .

The irrigation of Arizona deserves especial mention, partly because of the extensive irrigation works that the government has constructed there, and partly because of the climate. One of the greatest irrigation works undertaken is the Roosevelt dam in the Salt River, which will supply water for a large area near Phœnix. The climate near this city and Tucson is such that even semitropical fruits are produced. Here are raised oranges, lemons, grapefruit, figs, olives, pomegranates, and even dates. . . .

So important is irrigation that it is introduced wherever possible, and every year new irrigation systems are being built, some at great expense. Since much of this arid region is public land, the United States government is aiding in this work. There is, in fact, a special department of the government in charge of it, and every year millions of dollars are being spent in this way.

Enormous dams are built, forming lakes in the mountain valleys, and these are filled in the spring when the snow melts. Then, in summer, when the crops need water, it is let out of the reservoirs into the irrigation canals. In this way the amount of farm land in the arid West is being greatly increased. This is one of the most important works in which our government is engaged.

The account is illustrated with appropriate cuts.

Advantages. — Type study is simply a very intensive study of a topic in many relations. Its purely geographical, its scenic, biological, economic, historic, literary, and other aspects are all considered, not as so many separate studies, but all woven together to form a composite picture, that presents a fuller, richer, and better understood unity than the study of any one aspect could afford.

It is assumed that the topic will be taught properly with concrete illustrations, elaboration and explanation. By such correlation, all-round study, illustration, and use of supplementary reading, the subject is given freshness, vividness, and reality, and loses somewhat its dry, unreal, textbook character. It affords a welcome relief from the monotony of superficiality by a chance for a bit of thoroughness.

Another advantage of the type study method is that it permits the application of the sequential or causal order of study. Instead of the lesson being simply a list of facts to be memorized, it becomes a thoughtful study, a logical development with an organic unity. The many-sided correlation with science and history not only makes this causal study effective, but throws out many suggestions that arouse the imagination, and force the mind to take a broader outlook on the subject.

Modifications of the type.—In teaching by this method it must be remembered that the types chosen must be real types, selected with care, so that they may present as many as possible of the characteristics of their class. The study, however, should include some comparison with others of the class to show that modifications are possible. Thus when the wheat industry of the Mississippi Valley is studied, reference might be made to the variation of harvesting as practiced in the fields of Washington and California; and to the harvesting, threshing, and milling as still carried on by primitive peoples.

The chief objection to the type method is that it is too slow, and that only a few types can be studied thus intensively. It is, in ordinary schools, futile to teach only through types. There is always need of general geography to fill in the gaps left by the type method. In fact, the types require the more general, diffusive course as a background or setting.

In the type study method there may, also, be some danger of overcorrelating and dragging in things that are not germane to the subject. Type study is too slow to permit much digression. Overcorrelation may render the subject so elaborate that the pupil may "not see the forest for the trees." If it be remembered that correlation is not an end, but a means, of building a unified whole of the topic, this danger is averted. The subject should not be so elaborate that the pupil cannot analyze it.

Types in the lower grades. — Type studies, or topical studies, of the simpler kind may be made in the lower grades. But, in general, this method requires a general knowledge of the world as a whole, of history, and of nature-study; the ability to read reference books and supplementary readers easily and intelligently; and the power to reason and discriminate, — conditions not found in the lower grades.

While some of the more modern textbooks in geography aim largely to supplant the supplementary reader by the almost complete type treatment, there are still many briefer texts where this method must be supplied by the teacher, with the aid of wide reading on her own part, and the extensive use of supplementary readers by the pupils. In this case the type method affords the independent teacher an excellent opportunity of breaking away from " the bondage of the text," and, as it were, of making with her pupils her own textbook through reference work.

The Topical Method. — Much that has been said about the type method applies to what is called the Topical Method. Type study is topical study, but the types are selected primarily with the idea that they are representatives and stand for a class.

But that is not necessarily a consideration in the topical method. Any worthy feature of geography, several of the same class, even, may be used in the topical study. The main consideration here is to secure an interesting and intensive treatment, broader relations, more rational and less memoriter study. It was one of the first attempts to get the pupils and teachers more free from the order of the textbook. It is particularly good for reviews. The lessons are usually assigned and developed according to a topical analysis or outline. The textbook and supplementary references are used as the basis for the preparation of the lesson.

The type study method as a principle. — The type method is one step in advance of the topical method, a more careful discrimination in the selection of topics so as to have them representative. It demands a reduction in the number of topics. The type method is more of a working principle in geography, in the light of which, or by means of which, further studies are interpreted.

Regional Geography. — Another method of thorough or intensive study, in the upper grades especially, is the method of Regional Geography. This means the intimate study of the interrelation of man and nature

The first regional study is home geography. — The home community and vicinity, both civic and natural, are studied here. The relation of man to nature is brought out, and the whole constitutes a well-rounded geographical unit.

A geographical unit is a region that presents a general uniformity of topography, climate, vegetation, natural resources, occupations, or industries. If the human aspects are left out of consideration, it is a physiographic unit or region; but if the life and works of man are emphasized, it is an economic or industrial unit. In the same way we may have racial or ethnographic units and political units (states).

In regional geography the political boundaries are necessarily often crossed, and parts of different political units included, which in this method is of minor consequence.

Thus the commercial and industrial center or unit of New York City includes the Jersey towns across the Bay — Jersey City, Bayonne, Hoboken, Newark, etc., and the towns of Yonkers, New Rochelle, etc. in New York State. All these towns have the same community interest as Greater New York. Their growth and business depend directly on New York City, and to a very large extent their inhabitants work in the Greater City by day and only sleep in these suburbs by night. It is therefore fitting to study this large population center together as one.

Again Pittsburg stands for an industrial center of a different type. This city is surrounded by a cluster of towns, all, like Pittsburg, handling coal and iron, smelting ore, rolling steel, and casting machinery. Their location was largely determined by nature, as was certainly their business growth. To work out this relation to the topography and mineral resources of the immediate vicinity, and to the farther ore fields of the Superior region, and to the various markets, makes an interesting, instructive study.

An international industrial unit. — Similarly the European Pittsburg, the region of Lille, Nancy, Liege, and Essen, where the three countries of France, Belgium, and Germany fit together, is another industrial unit which disregards political boundaries.

The Alps lie in five different countries, but to get the best idea of this interesting system of mountains, — their formation, character, scenery, and influence on the industries of man, — they should be studied as a unit, not cut up and studied in parts in the different countries to which they belong. The Alps are a physiographic unit.

Our own Appalachian System may be studied in a similar fashion. The Mississippi Valley, the Great Basin, the Great Western Plains, the Prairies, the Russian Steppes, the Desert of Sahara, and the Tropical Forests of Brazil are other physiographic regions.

The advantages in regional study are, first, that of handling a whole unit and treating it with satisfying comprehensiveness; second, that of being able to apply the causal method in working out the twofold aspect of Earth and Man; third, that it is time-saving and concentrating, as there are fewer great geographical units than political; fourth, that it is an excellent method for review and organization; fifth, that many of these geographical units are at the same time types.

Adapted for upper grades. — With the exception of home geography, regional geography is not adapted to the lower grades. It requires a fair knowledge of the world as a whole and of the map of the nations. For upper grades the regional treatment would be very good for a review. It would present a new and pleasing point of view, and a new method of approach. Many new and significant relations would be discovered which escaped notice in the usual systematic study of country by country, according to the political map. The study of the Great Plains, page 75, is a regional study.

Comparative Geography. — The term was introduced by Ritter, but was applied by him more to a categoric comparison of similar features in different lands, as the rivers of Europe with those of Asia, their mountains, etc., for the purpose of deriving general principles.

Intensive comparison. — A later meaning of the expression sometimes called Intensive Comparison is closely related to the Causal Method. It requires a reflective comparison of different parts of the world to form certain generalizations and principles. Thus, Of what importance is the ocean? What is the relation of rivers to man? What is the climatic effect of elevation? are questions requiring mature, comparative consideration.

Review by comparison.—But there is another sense in which the expression, the Comparative Method, or Comparative Geography, is used. It means the frequent reference to previously studied types or lessons, such as home geography, physiographic and industrial types, even type continents, during the study of new lessons. It is virtually making use of the apperceptive basis wherever a new study is made. The purpose of such comparison is first to give a better understanding of the new topic; to bring out interesting similarities or differences that help, through association, to fix the fact; to weave together or organize widely separated lessons, and ultimately the whole subject, into a whole; and incidentally, though of no slight importance, to review the old facts to refresh the memory. Therefore it is sometimes called the method of Review by Comparison.

Illustration.—The study of Europe presupposes a study of the North American Continent. The general features of topography, climate, industry, etc., should be recalled to aid in the understanding of the new continent: Compare the two continents as to area; as to irregularity of coasts. What is the chief coastal industry of New England? Why? Would the same be true of Europe? Why? In what latitude are the British Isles? Compare with that of Labrador. What do the isotherms of England indicate? Let us look for the cause of this climate. In what wind belt is Labrador? Do the winds blow from the sea there? What kind of winds blow over England? When sea breezes blow on the land on the Pacific Coast how do they affect the temperature? Are these winds moist or dry? How is the moisture of these winds condensed in western United States? Now, what should be the effect of the Atlantic winds on England? Etc. In this way the study requires thought, and becomes much more interesting and effective than the ordinary memoriter process of learning the text.

CHAPTER XX

PRINCIPLES OF GEOGRAPHY

Correlation in geography. — Repeated reference has been made in the foregoing pages to the unpedagogical and wasteful method of learning geographical facts in isolation or without reference to their relations to each other. Various ways have been suggested to bring about the desirable association of fact and fact. Among them are the causal relation series, group classification, types, and the comparative method. These are all systematic organizing processes to reduce the heterogeneous mass of geographical matter to order and unity, not merely for the sake of the science, but rather for the sake of the learner, as a help to the understanding and to assist the memory.

Generalizations of geography.—There is still another way of organizing the facts of geography, and that is by reducing them to definitions and abstract principles. In arithmetic there are a thousand and one problems, yet these fall under relatively few rules for solving, and under few captions. It is so in geography. The definitions and principles may, also, as in arithmetic, be used in solving further geographical problems.

These definitions and principles were, in the geography of our grandfathers, usually stated dogmatically at the beginning of the book, and applied deductively to the rest. The fault of this plan was that the pupils had no real concept of these fundamentals, and therefore the deductions were vague, unreal, or entirely impossible. This naturally brought a revolt, and there came into vogue a series of texts that developed these abstractions from the pupil's own experience in home geography. These were called the Inductive Geographies, or Natural Method of Geography.

The geographies of to-day, in general, follow this plan. The facts of physical geography, including climate and human occupations, are treated inductively, and then applied to the following descriptive geography.

Concepts *vs.* words. — Care must be exercised that these definitions and laws of geography have a meaning to the pupil, or they may be simply parroted after rote study. By drawing these concepts from the pupil's own environment and experience, requiring him to express his generalizations in his own language, by assisting him with field studies, experiments, pictures, and other concrete demonstration, by rendering them interesting and clearer by oral description and supplementary reading, these basic definitions and principles may be given a real meaning. If the pupil can in his mind's eye see a mountain, a river, a spring, a quarry, a grain field, the lumber woods, the prairie, the factory, the bustle of a big city, — he has the concept, whether he can give the definition or not. And if we could be sure that he had this concept, it would not matter very much about the formal definition. In a similar manner larger concepts of physiographical regions, climatic relations, or even whole continents may be developed. Good concepts of definitions serve to tie together a multitude of geographical facts into bundles of sorted knowledge.

Principles of geography are the natural laws according to which physical and human agencies in geography act. Rivers illustrate a great, though simple, principle; namely, that water flows downhill. From numberless outdoor observations, perhaps repeated in classroom experiments, the pupil generalizes that water flows down a slope. Simple as it is, this is an important principle in geography. From several experiments and other observations he learns the principle that cold air displaces warm air and that this is the primary cause of winds. He learns from observation and reading that mines are chiefly located in mountain regions, because of the fracture, faulting, and erosion of the strata, thus exposing the mineral resources. In the same way he learns the principle that we export our surplus, and import what we need when we do not produce enough.

From concrete cases, then, the abstract law or principle is generalized. Unfortunately teachers often, and many texts, do not push the pupils beyond the premise on to the conclusion. That is, all the necessary facts for the generalization are presented, but the matter is not clinched by the derivation of the principle embodied. Even in the primary grades, and increasingly more so in the upper grades, numerous simpler principles may be developed. This practice would stimulate the pupils to think, and would do much to raise the subject in intellectual merit.

Of course, these abstract concepts cannot be grasped all at once by the pupils. It may be necessary to wait till the second, third, or even later occurrence of the principle; but a time will come when the principle has been sufficiently illustrated to be inferred. In this way, often, past lessons are reviewed and associated. These definitions and principles, like the facts of the map, climate, industry, and the like, are a part of the subject matter of geography, and should not be neglected. Like the facts referred to, they require drill and review to fix them.

But these generalizations are not an end in themselves, interesting as they may be; they rather serve as working rules, or a means for the interpretation of further studies and the harmonizing of previous lessons.

The principles of geography are the philosophy of the science. — They are often to be found only between the lines. The teacher, certainly, should know something of this philosophy, and should teach according to and toward it; so that ultimately the pupils will see something of it. The principles that thus underlie geography knit the whole subject together, and serve to organize it into a science.

Below are the chief concepts and principles of geography, aside from simple definitions of the ordinary geographical features, that pupils of the eighth grade should possess as a result of their course.[1]

Important Facts and Principles of Geography

Mathematical

The Sun holds the earth in its orbit, gives light and heat, and makes life possible on the earth. Affects the tides.

Rotation causes day and night, rising and setting of sun, moon, and stars, causes difference of time between places of different longitudes — 15 degrees of longitude makes a difference of one hour.

Revolution (with inclination and parallelism of axis) determines seasons, the year, zones of light.

Latitude and Longitude are used to locate places. Latitude and longitude are used in surveys (boundaries, etc.). Longitude is based upon the prime meridian (Greenwich).

[1] The student should find illustrations of each of these principles as he reads them.

Physical Geography

Topography. — 1. *Coasts.* — Depressed part of surface is sea bottom; the elevated, continents. These relations are unstable, coasts rising or being submerged (drowned), affecting the form of seacoast. Rising coasts are straight or smooth in outline; sinking coasts are irregular. The former afford poor harborage; the latter, good harbors, and stimulate sea commerce and fisheries.

2. *Plains.* — Two types, coastal and interior. The strata of plains are usually not much folded or uplifted. Plains have the largest rivers. Plains are not deeply eroded by rivers, hence good communication, stimulating settlement and commerce, also encouraging invasion. Agriculture and herding, and, where forests, lumbering, are the chief industries. Plains have the densest population. Many and large cities are found here. Manufacturing and commerce thrive.

3. *Plateaus.* — Are broad, uplifted (high), yet not greatly folded strata. They determine the drainage of the continents. Are much dissected by rivers, hence communication is bad. Temperature is lowered by plateaus. Plateau industries — farming, grazing, lumbering, manufacturing (water power). Population is sparse, owing to difficulty of travel and commerce. Plateau peoples are apt to become isolated, and backward in civilization.

4. *Mountains.* — Are folded, often broken, highly lifted strata, generally much eroded (therefore contents exposed, and hence quarries and mines). Temperature decreases gradually from base to summit. Mountains running north and south affect especially the distribution of rainfall. Cause condensation and rainfall on their windward side; cut off rain from their lee. Their perennial snow, glaciers, and rain supply the many rivers that rise here. Mountain regions have sparse population. Mountains are difficult to travel over. They act as barriers to animal and plant life, to migration of nations, to trade and customs, are often political boundaries. Mountain industries — herding, lumbering, manufacturing (water power), mining, quarrying. Mountains are used for recreation largely on account of their scenic aspect.

Ocean (Seas, Lakes). — In depressions on the earth. Divide the lands. Compel navigation. Stimulate marine commerce. Water, the cheapest means of transportation. Modify extremes of temperature. Source of rain (evaporation). Tides caused by attraction of moon and sun. Ocean currents (chiefly drift by prevailing winds) equalize temperature of the ocean water; slightly affect navigation. Waves both erode and make coasts and islands. Impede navigation. The conquest of the ocean is coördinate with history and civilization. Many great ports and commercial centers on coasts.

Fisheries (including sealing, whaling, etc.) an ocean industry.

Weathering. — Solvent water and chemically acting elements in the air, expanding ice in pores of rock, acids of plants and animals, and gravity are the agents. Result — sculpturing of land forms (scenery), decayed rock, soil. The kind and character of the soil depend upon the kind of rock from which it was formed (sandstone forms sand; granite forms sand, clay, etc.). Soil is the basis for agriculture, the greatest human industry, the basis for human life. Other industries — glass making (sand), brick making (clay) — depend on products of weathering.

Streams. — Rain, the source of streams. Their course determined by the slope of the land. Running water erodes. Streams carry sediment. This is deposited in part (largest particles first) or all when the velocity of the water is partially or completely checked. Result — bars, deltas, flood plain. Streams undercut on the outer curve (swiftest current) and deposit on the inner curve of a bend (slow current), resulting in meandering. Deltas form in quiet lakes, bays, or seas; estuaries where the sediment is removed by the waves and currents (tidal).

Navigable rivers occur more in plains than in plateaus (slower). Such rivers stimulate exploration, settlement, commerce. Water power and manufacturing are found at falls, rapids, and on swift streams, chiefly in highlands. Here manufacturing cities may develop. By modern transmission of water power by electricity such power may be utilized hundreds of miles from its source, in places more accessible and convenient for commerce. Great river plains are the seat of greatest populations and highest civilizations. Here agriculture and related commerce flourish. Rivers are used for commercial navigation, and their valleys for wagon roads and railroads, and canals (easy grades). Rivers are difficult to cross, requiring ferries, bridges, tunnels. Rivers are often natural boundaries.

Glaciers. — Result from the perennial accumulation of snow on mountains. This snow changes to ice by pressure, thawing, and freezing. The mass of ice moves down the slopes like a plastic body, "flows," but does not slide. A glacier advances lower to a point where it melts as fast as it advances. Here is the "foot." The melting glaciers feed streams and rivers. Glaciers erode and grind the strata over which they move, making glacial débris or glacial soil. This they carry to the foot and deposit there as a moraine. Glacial soils are generally deep and fertile, but sometimes too thin, sandy, or rocky for agriculture (New England). Glaciers dam up rivers, causing lakes and waterfalls. Glacial scenery — falls, lakes, hilly topography. Economic consequences — generally beneficial to agriculture and water power (manufacturing), but the hills interfere with travel.

Climate. — 1. *Heat belts.*—The spherical earth receives the parallel rays of the sun at varying angles, most vertically near the equator, more slantingly near the poles. The heating effect of the rays decreases as they fall more slantingly. Therefore cold at the poles, hot at the equator. The earth is traversed east and west by isotherms. Certain isotherms, *e.g.* 70 and 30 degrees, mark off irregular bands called heat belts, usually five, though by subdivision more. Land absorbs and radiates heat more quickly than does water. On account of this the isotherms and heat belts are deflected over the land toward the equator in the winter, toward the poles in summer. All isotherms and heat belts migrate north and south with the apparent shifting of the sun, according to the season. Animal and plant life is distributed in east and west zones, adapted to the temperature. Man must adapt his life to the heat belts—clothing, habits, industry (agriculture). The highest civilizations are found in the temperate regions where the spur of climate is not so great as in the frigid, and where the climate is not so enervating, nor so generous with subsistence as in the tropics.

2. *Winds.*—Cause—convection and unequal barometric pressure. The convection is usually due to unequal heating of the sun's rays (varying angle) as in case

of trades and antitrades; or to unequal absorption and radiation of heat by land and water in different seasons (monsoons), or night and day (land and sea breezes, local). Air moves from the colder to the warmer region. Cold air is heavier, and displaces, pushes up, the warm air. Trade winds blow toward the equator at the surface of earth, and are deflected toward the west by the earth's rotation. These currents rise at the heat equator (belt of calms). Cooling in the higher altitude, they turn north and south, gradually descending as the antitrades. The antitrades are turned toward the east by rotation of the earth. The antitrades settle to the ground in about 30 degrees north and south latitude, here forming another calm belt (horse latitudes), and, because warming up are drying currents, form deserts. The westerlies may be considered as the antitrades continuing in the same general direction but on the surface of the earth. Most of the great nations of the world lie in this belt. Unequal atmospheric pressures tend to equalize, the air flowing from a region of higher to one of lower pressure. Air blowing from a "high" toward a "low" from north and south is deflected by the earth's rotation, just as the trades and antitrades, tending to set up an eddying motion — cyclone.

3. *Rain.* — Source — the sea, by evaporation. Air absorbs vapor to the saturation point. The saturation

point increases with the temperature. The warmer the air, the more water vapor it can hold. Air at the saturation point, when chilled, has some of its vapor condensed in proportion to the amount of chilling. The vapor in air is condensed as the air rises to colder altitudes by convection, or is forced up cold mountain sides. Clouds are the result of the condensation of vapor. They consist of minute drops of water (mist). The wind carries the clouds. The distribution and amount of rain varies with the prevailing winds, altitude, latitude, distance from sea. Rainfall is abundant in the belt of calms, owing to great evaporation, and the ascent of the vapor till condensed by the cold. Rainfall is greatest on the windward side of mountains. Mountains running north and south seriously affect the distribution of the rainfall. It is greatest on the eastern side of mountains in the trade wind belt; on the western side, in the westerlies. Rainfall conditions change at the borders of wind belts, since a place (*e.g.* southern California) may first be in the trade wind belt (summer), then in the westerlies (winter), as the heat belts shift with the seasons; thus wet and dry seasons result. When winds descend they warm up, their moisture capacity or saturation point is raised, and they become drying winds; hence in such regions are deserts or semideserts. The same is true of the trades as they blow from colder to warmer regions, and where they have been blowing over the land instead of the sea deserts may result (Arabia, Sahara). The rainfall conditions in the western half of the United States are determined by the westerlies and the trend, location, and height of the western mountains. The eastern half of the United States gets its rain from the Gulf and the Atlantic through the agency of the cyclones. The south and east winds of a cyclone bring vapor. This is condensed because the winds go from the south to the north, because they meet the cold winds from the north, and because they rise to cooler heights at the low pressure center, and rain follows. This precipitation takes place chiefly in the eastern half of the cyclone. Cyclones drift with the westerlies toward the east. Hence storms migrate eastward. Places over which a cyclone passes experience a regular sequence of weather changes. These facts are the basis for weather predictions. Rain is an important factor in determining the amount and kinds of vegetation. Forests require the most rainfall, over twenty inches; grasses next, then desert plants. Agriculture must be adapted to rainfall conditions. Cereals, especially wheat, do not thrive in too moist a climate (over fifty inches), but may be grown with fifteen inches. Agriculture is possible in semi-arid and desert regions by means of irrigation. Unequal distribution of rain determines the north and south belts of vegetation types, especially marked in North and South America. Jungles, forests, llanos, pampas, prairies, steppes, deserts, are types of vegetation resulting from varying rainfall. Forests do not cause rain, but conserve and retard the run-off. Therefore forest reserves. Rainfall supplies streams, springs, wells. Rainfall affects navigation, water power.

Commercial Geography

Commerce. — Man's industry depends upon his needs. These depend upon climate, topography, natural resources. His needs increase with his civilization. Savages have few needs beyond bare necessaries for existence, and these are supplied generally by nature direct, or without much effort. Civilized man needs food, clothing, shelter; but also conveniences and luxuries beyond what is needed for bare existence. Civilized man is provident, specializes in industry, has division of labor, — this resulting in exchange, trade. Diversity of climate, topography, natural resources, and racial characteristics stimulate trade. The law of supply and demand governs exchange. Countries sell their surplus as exports, and buy imports which they cannot produce at all or not as cheaply as other regions. Nature furnishes raw materials for man to convert into finished goods or products. Commerce is the exchange of raw and finished materials, and is carried on by the industry of transportation. Industry and commerce both require labor and capital, and are stimulated by peace and stable government. Great commercial nations maintain great navies on the theory that they guarantee peace and are a protection to commerce. Colonial possessions foster trade with the mother country. Trend of commerce is affected by government regulations, tariffs, etc.

Animal industries. — 1. *Hunting and fishing*, the earliest human industries. They require the wilderness for hunting grounds. Supply a precarious existence.

2. *Fur Trade.* — This is closely connected with the last. Flourishes in cold temperate, and sub-polar countries. With advance of settlement game and fur animals vanish.

3. *Herding.* — Requires extensive lands for pasturage. Hence practiced in open plains, prairies, steppes, but also on nonagricultural lands on mountain slopes. The herding of cattle, horses, sheep, etc., began far back in the history of civilization, the pastoral period, and was a great step in advance. Represents a provident method of food and clothing supply. Generally herding peoples are nomadic. Connected with herding is the meat industry (ranching, killing, packing, shipping, selling — done with much division of labor in widely different regions). The wool and leather industries also are connected with the last. In general, poultry, swine, cattle, sheep, horses, are raised in small numbers everywhere

on small farms, but herding of great herds is done on the frontier, — the foothills, the semiarid plains, etc.

Agriculture. — More people are occupied in this than in any other industry. Culturally, agriculture corresponds to the stage of the domestication of animals. it shows forethought, provision for the future. Wild stocks of plants are improved by cultivation, and by selective breeding. Agriculture is strictly limited by topography, soil conditions, and climate. By irrigation, unfavorable rainfall conditions are modified, making agriculture possible. Crops must be adapted to natural conditions. Crops are chiefly distributed in east and west belts according to temperature; in north and south belts (North and South America) according to rainfall. The chemical nature (fertility) of the soil affects vegetation. Quartz sand (New England) has too little; alkali land (West) too much soluble matter. Rocky or very hilly land is unsuitable for farming. The great level plains of the world are the chief seat of agriculture. Forests must first be felled to permit farming. The treeless prairies are especially suited for agriculture. Agriculture is vastly facilitated by the use of improved machinery (invention). Modern science has greatly improved the methods of farming, and the productivity of the crops. By importation (United States Department of Agriculture) new plants, adapted to various soil and climatic conditions, are introduced, and the possibilities of farming increased. In newer lands farming is generally on a large scale, with few crops. In older settled regions there are smaller farms and more diversified farming. Near cities there is truck farming. In new countries agriculture is usually the first industry, later manufacturing develops, and may even displace the former (New England).

Lumbering. — At first always based upon natural forests; later upon planted forests (forestry). Forests grow where there is twenty inches of rain a year and it is not too cold. The tree-line on cold mountains and in polar countries marks temperature limit of trees. Conifers thrive in colder regions; hardwoods, in warmer. Lumbering is usually carried on at the frontier and on mountains. Methods vary with climate and topography. In the north lumbering is usually conducted in winter. Logs are floated down streams with spring floods. Destruction of forests reduces lumber supply, also permits too great erosion and floods. Forest reserves are for purpose of checking these evils. Forests regulate the supply of water in streams. Architecture and making of furniture are affected by forests.

Mineral industry. — Depends upon mineral content of the earth. Methods vary with the mineral and its mode of occurrence. Many mines are in mountains because the folded strata are eroded and the contents exposed. But mining can be conducted on plains (coal fields of Ohio, etc.). Mining is often the only object of settlement of a country; may be transient. More permanent ore deposits develop manufacturing towns. Coal and iron the most important mineral resources. No nation can aspire to commercial supremacy without these. Close connection exists between the coal and iron industries — smelting requires coal; coal is necessary to run machinery. Where coal and iron are found together great manufacturing centers arise. Stone and clay are important as building materials. Architecture is affected by the materials of construction, — iron, stone, brick, etc.

Manufacturing. — Depends upon the stage of civilization, the needs, inventiveness, and industry of the people, and upon the nature and abundance of the raw materials, and the availability of power (wind, water, coal, electricity). May be conducted in nonagricultural lands, as mountains and seashore, but also thrives in agricultural regions of later development. Must have means of transportation, — sea, rivers, railroads. Must have markets, domestic and foreign. Agricultural raw materials: grain, corn, cotton, sugar, meat, wool, hides, etc. Raw materials from forests: lumber, bark, pulp, sap. Raw materials from mines: stone, clay, cement, phosphate, coal, metals, minerals. The cost of finished product depends upon price of raw material, labor, capital invested, taxes, duties, power, transportation,

Transportation.—Kinds: man, beast of burden, wagon, rail, boat; these in the order of expense, the cheapest last. Routes: overland, tunnels, rivers, sea, canal. Perishable goods shipped by fastest means and shortest routes. Heavy commodities by water, or slow freight. Topography and water ways determine routes. Commerce seeks the shortest and cheapest routes. Valley grades of rivers, mountain passes and valleys, level plains, are easiest for overland commerce.

Location of cities. — Generally in the beginning some physical feature or physical condition determined the choice, though it was often affected by historic or economic conditions, or even mere whim and chance. Favorable locations: on good harbors, in center of region rich in resources, near productive country that is accessible by good routes of commerce, at railroad centers, at the mouths or confluences of rivers, at the natural breaks in navigation (falls, rapids, shoal water), at water power (falls and rapids), at coal fields (power), favorable climatic region.

CHAPTER XXI

CORRELATION

The principle of correlation applied in geography. — There was a period, the first part of the nineteenth century, when geography first reached its standing as a distinct science, when it was limited strictly to geographical facts in the narrower sense, and consisted chiefly of definitions, locations of places, mathematical geography, and a few facts about the topography, climate, and industries of the various countries.

The product was a categorical statement of the geographic features from the static standpoint. There was very little, if any, reference to their significance, their causes, or consequences, or their other relationships; or of the bearing of geography on other subjects; or of these on geography. Naturally such geographies were uninteresting.

They were merely lists of geographical facts, arranged in a more or less systematic and logical order. The easiest way to learn such books was by committing them to memory, which was then avowedly the most "pedagogical" method, and various devices were used to aid the memory in accomplishing the task.

Unfortunately this method is not quite extinct. It is a very common practice in the classroom, and some textbooks do not suggest or permit a better way.

But the Herbart-Ziller principle of correlation, that neither facts, lessons, nor whole subjects should be treated as separate entities, but should rather be studied in connection with other facts, lessons, or subjects, and woven into a larger, richer fabric, a larger truth — has been applied also to geography.

By correlation is not meant an arbitrary, forced, unnatural association of facts or subjects, but bringing together that which is naturally, logically, and even necessarily related, for the purpose of presenting the facts thus correlated in a new aspect, to approach the subject from a new point of view; to explain a fact by means of that which is correlated; or to get a new light or a new truth by reflecting on the correlation presented.

If the study of geography is to be truly rational, not memoriter merely, previous, related lessons or facts should be used as stepping-stones in the study of any new lesson. It is unpedagogical not to consider, to correlate, this fundamental knowledge.

Examples. — The study of the climate of a land, for instance, should be worked out by applying principles of topography, wind, and temperature learned in previous lessons. The shifting of the heat belts is explained by the lesson on the seasons. The industrial (mining) section around Lake Superior should be brought into relation with the previous study of the Great Lakes Waterway, and the Pittsburg (coal and iron) region. This last example of correlation would teach such commercial principles as the dependence of section on section, the great advantage of natural routes of traffic, the cheapness of water transportation, and other general truths. The commercial supremacy of New York City in the New World must be based on its harbor, central location, rich interior, the construction of the Erie Canal along a route prepared by nature, and the modern railroad facilities. This case of correlation shows the additional facts of historic development, the value of the work of previous generations, and the controlling influence of nature.

Correlations of geography. — An almost constant correlation of the experiences and knowledge of home geography should be practiced throughout the course as a measure of the foreign geography, or a means for understanding it. This is using home geography as a principle of study.

In a similar way geography should be correlated with natural science, mathematics, history, and literature. These are brought in only " to lend a hand " in explaining purely geographical facts; to make them more interesting by showing that they have a wider application than just in geography; or to bring out general ideas not possible by the solitary study of geography.

Geography is the study of the Earth and Man as related to each other. There are two view-points in this subject, the one looking toward the phenomena of nature, the other at the lives of men. The Earth is the inanimate sphere with its modifying natural forces, its vegetation and animal life. The Man element deals with man not only as a creature with animal needs, but with intelligence in adapting himself to natural conditions, even to the extent of modifying some of them; with his economic, social, governmental, and even spiritual problems. In this sense, geography is an all-inclusive, complex science, dealing, in a measure, *and in its specific way*, with the facts of astronomy, geology, meteorology, botany, zoölogy, ethnology, anthropology, economics, sociology, history, civics, and even art, literature, and religion.

Geography a unity. — Geography is far from being a jumble or patchwork of all these subjects. " Geography is not the dumping ground for all subjects or sciences for which there is no other place." (Kiepert.) " Geography should be a closed unity." (F. Lampe.) " Geography is a unity, with a well-defined essence of its own. Complexity is no reproach. The same is true of history, language, economics, and biology." (William Davis.) Botany deals with the geographic distribution of plants, yet does not presume to teach geography as such. Likewise when geography includes historical references or sketches, laws of physics, or descriptions of plants of different climates, it is not attempting to teach history, physics, or botany. The object is to give, perhaps, an historical perspective, to trace the historical development of a geographical topic; to use the facts of geography to explain the conditions of an historic fact. By such correlation geography is enlivened and enriched. But geography is not the only subject benefited, for the benefits from correlation are mutual.

The first correlation of geography is with nature-study. — In fact, in the beginning, in the primary grades, geography is not separated from nature-study, but is taught under that name. Such topics as weathering, soil, rocks, minerals, brook, erosion, forms of water, rain, snow, clouds, wind, sky, sun, hills, valley, and other familiar topics appear in nature courses, yet are strictly geographical in their nature. The principles of plant and animal life, and the facts about specific plants and animals, *e.g.* cultivated plants, trees, and domesticated animals, are likewise available in geography.

It is not, usually, till the fourth year of school that nature-study and geography come to the parting of the ways. Even then they should not entirely lose sight of each other, but whenever it is to their mutual advantage should bridge the gap by correlation. In many well-organized school courses these two subjects are so planned as to permit this correlation. In fact, nature-study should be the handmaid of geography throughout the elementary school course, as natural science is the auxiliary of the science of geography in higher institutions.

The lesson on corn, wheat, or the cotton plant in nature-study cannot but help the geographical study of the industry based on the plant. The pupil who has followed the cycle of the trees and herbs through the seasons is better able to understand the references in geography to the climatic effects on vegetation. If he has cultivated a garden, or raised a potted plant in nature-study, he is better able to appreciate in geography the great industry of agriculture.

Nature-study can do much to supplement geography, or to take from geography the more biological features less germane to the latter subject. Some geographers do not believe in including the biological description of the animals and plants of geography, nor even the industrial processes of production and manufacture. It is all the more necessary, therefore, to have nature-study coöperating with geography, so that in the latter subject it may be assumed that the natural science phase of things geographical has been taught, or that the barest reference to this suffices. This assumption is by no means well founded, so many authors of geography boldly include considerable nature-study, necessary for the proper development of the subject.

Physics and geography. — This is, for example, well shown by the correlation of physics. It is perfectly legitimate to begin the beautiful causal series of climate study with simple experiments in evaporation, condensation, convection of air, and the principle of the barometer. For it is an utter impossibility to give a real conception of rain, clouds, and winds without these explanatory principles from physics. But it would not be proper, in the geography lesson, to discuss the application of physical laws to other than purely geographical matters. It would have been better, of course, if the necessary physics lessons had been taught in nature-study or elementary science beforehand, and then simply applied in geography.

Arithmetic, also, is correlated with geography in drawing to scale, comparison of areas, estimating distances, statistics, latitude and longitude, difference of time, and circular measure. Not enough consideration is given to the proper correlation of these two subjects, since we try to teach children the use of the scale before they have had the necessary fractions, and refer to degrees of latitude and longitude, and to linear measurements before they have had denominate numbers. This leads to confusion and parroting. But when pupils have the basic arithmetical knowledge, they should be required to apply it in appropriate places in geography.

History and geography are inseparable, just as geography and science are inseparable. History, perhaps, has more need of geography than this subject has of history. Without a geographical arena, it would be vague, unreal, unsatisfying, and abstract. History is mundane, happening in definite localities, and is to a large extent actually determined by the geographical factors of these regions. The battle of Thermopylæ, Hannibal's invasion of Italy, Columbus' discovery, the history of the "Tight Little Isle," the history of abolition in New England and of slave-holding in the South, the settlement of the Mississippi Valley, would all have been different, or would, perhaps, not have occurred at all if the geographical stage of these events had been different. A knowledge of the topographic, climatic, racial, industrial, and other geographic conditions of history enable one to appreciate it all the more.

On the other hand, in the study of geography, the allusion to famous incidents or historic progress in the regions studied make them more real and interesting, and serve to emphasize the human element, without which geography would be only geology or physical geography. Geographical features should be studied in the light of history in order to give perspective, to trace origin, or development, in which step by step the combined effects of man and nature may be seen shaping their progress. The very names on the map are foolish or meaningless unless we know their origin. Many of them enshrine the memory of great events; Babylon, Jerusalem, Rome, Constantinople, Orleans, Waterloo, Sedan, Plymouth, are names that wrap in themselves much history, and to pass over them in geography without a reference to this history is like *Hamlet* with Hamlet left out.

American geography must be studied in the light of European history, especially English, if we wish to understand it fully. The events of early settlement, the nature of the colonists, the various nationalities developing the continent, the languages, civic institutions, and spiritual ideals can only be appreciated fully by considering the historic factors determining them. One of the aims of geography is to develop patriotism. This cannot be done by simply bragging about the vastness of our country, its limitless natural resources, and the majesty and beauty of its scenery, but requires some knowledge of the trend of history, the way in which the weal and the woe of the inhabitants have been affected by their phy[illegible] environment, and how they labored to adjust [illegible]s to this environment, or heroically made for themselves a new one by strength of arm and intellect.

In Europe, particularly in Germany, history and geography are taught in much more intimate union than in this country. In fact, there geography is commonly taught by the history teacher. In America, if the departmental system prevails, it is more frequently taught by the science teacher. There geography has not quite reached the status of a major subject, but is still treated as a secondary one, bearing especially upon history. This is no doubt due to the intense national spirit pervading the whole system of education. History and geography are made to bring out the greatness of the Fatherland, and to teach an intelligent patriotism.

There is room for this ideal in the United States. The children of to-day will be the leaders of the nation thirty years hence. The future citizen should know the geography and history of his country. Pliny said long ago, " It is a shameful thing to live in one's native land and know it not." Geography teaches the present environment, natural and human; history teaches the past. We must adapt ourselves to our present environment by the light of the experience of the past.

Before the nineteenth century, geographies, outside of the astronomical portion, were chiefly histories. Not much was known about the real geographical facts, and so to make the books full and interesting a great deal of historical matter, though for the most part unrelated to geography, was brought in. Then came the revolt of geography and the establishment of its independence as a science. Then followed the period of dull geographies, consisting chiefly of gazetteer-like lists of bald facts. Ritter (died 1859), primarily a historian, brought back history into geography, but this time to show the true interaction and interrelation of the subjects.

In the higher science of general geography to-day, there is much of world history, and of the philosophy of history. The elementary geographies, however, have not kept up with this movement, and only in late years do we find refreshing signs of this humanizing tendency.

Correlation with Literature. — There is another way of putting life and interest into geography, and that is by correlation with literature. There is no good reason why the language of school geography should be dull and pedantic. But whatever the reason, few textbooks in geography "read like a story."

The teacher can correct this fault in part by supplementing with outside reading from standard authors. Good descriptions of scenery and places and narratives of geographic or historic incidents are as necessary as maps, pictures, and specimens to bring the real subject, the earth and its inhabitants, before the eye, and to create a liking for the study. Some of this literature may be used by the teacher as inspiration and suggestion for oral descriptions. Some of it may be read in class, and some may be given to the children to read at home. In Chapter XXV will be found suggestions for suitable reading.

More correlation with literature would help to correct the neglect of the æsthetic element in geography. The teacher, so taken up with the necessary drill on the "dry bones" of geography, is apt to forget or to slight the brighter side of the subject. This is short-sighted, since interest and pleasure in study reduce the effort of both pupil and teacher. By pointing out the beauties of the local landscape, by showing pictures of scenery of other places, and by oral description or by reading good descriptions, this æsthetic appreciation of the earth could be cultivated.

The desire to enjoy scenery is a chief reason for travel, and this travel instinct may be aroused and utilized in the pupils by presenting the picturesque and the majestic in geography. What a pity to give a child no further notion of the grandeur of a mountain than he gets from a definition like, "Mountains are much higher than hills," or, "Mountains are folds in the earth's crust." Contrast the effect of the following account from Bayard Taylor's description of The Austrian Alps, in *Views Afoot:*

to the hero worship of the children, and may have an uplifting effect on their character.

Poetry in geography. — Finally, there is a place for poetry in geography; not the foolish doggerel intended as mnemonic aid for learning the names of places, but real poetry that expresses the elevated emotions and thoughts aroused by the beauty of scenery, or the awe of reflection on the majesty of the forces of nature, or the spiritual interpretation of earthly phenomena, or the lesson that may be drawn from them and applied to human life. The poets of all lands and all ages have felt the charm and grandeur of the earth, and have helped others also so to feel. There are many æsthetic subjects in geography whose effect would be heightened by reading in class an appropriate poetical selection. In Europe this is done, — even singing is thus correlated.

CHAPTER XXII

THE EVOLUTION OF GEOGRAPHICAL KNOWLEDGE

The beginnings of geography are unrecorded, for geography is older than history. No doubt primitive tribes were familiar with their own locality, but with none far beyond that. Geography, however, includes, as a science, knowledge of distant, foreign regions. In this sense, the evolution of geography is coördinate with the spread of civilization.

Ancient geography. — The geographical wisdom of the earliest civilizations, that of the Chaldeans, Hebrews, and Egyptians, was limited to the region between the Persian Gulf and the desert of Egypt. These people were not inclined to travel, or to international trade. Their geography is recorded in their sacred books, for example in Genesis. They made a beginning in astronomical geography; the pyramids had, in part, at least, an astronomical function, and tablets with maps have been found in the ruins of Babylon.

The Phœnicians, a Semitic race, driven by the Jews to the Mediterranean Coast, took refuge on islands and promontories (Tyre and Sidon), and learned the art of navigation. These restless people were great wanderers and merchants. They were the middlemen between the Western barbarians and the Asiatic civilization. They crept along the Mediterranean coast beyond the Pillars of Hercules (Gibraltar) and even, says tradition, to the Tin Islands (Britain). Yet extensive as was their journeying, we have it recorded only in tradition.

The Homeric poems are an illustration of such tradition. Aside from a rather limited amount of true

FIG. 29.—The world as known in time of Homer, 900 B.C.

geography, Homer's epic contains much of fancy and of myth with which the less known parts of the earth were pictured. This geographical fiction of Homer probably had more weight in after times than the true geography.

Homer imagined, as did also the Babylonians, that the earth was flat, round like a shield, and with a river, the Oceanus, flowing all around it. These notions prevailed for many centuries.

The Greeks, in their expansion of empire, added to the known lands, especially in the east, as far as the

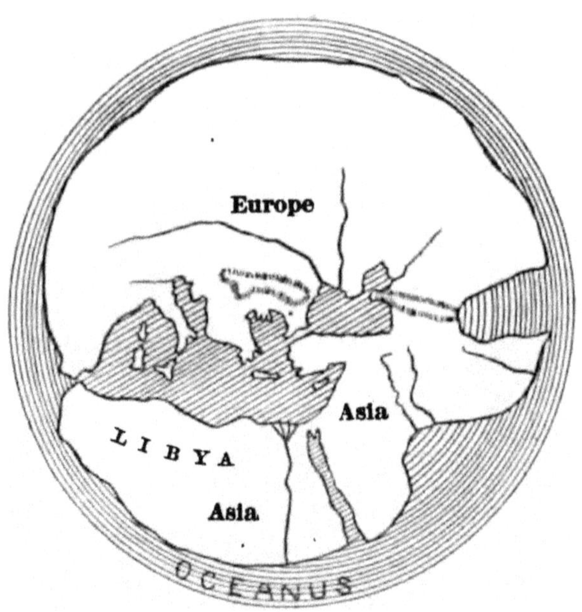

FIG. 30. — The world as known by Hecatæus, 500 B.C.

Indus. Authentic writers of this period, such as Herodotus, 450 B.C., gave good descriptions of the world as then known. The Greek map included all the European Mediterranean countries, the Black Sea region, Asia Minor and western India, and northern Africa. Grecian astronomers held advanced ideas. They believed the earth spherical, and Eratosthenes of Alexandria,

240 B. C., by means of a shadow-stick, the gnomen, calculated the circumference of the earth as 245,000 stadia. The exact modern equivalent of a stadium is in dispute, and we do not know how accurate this estimate was, but the error was not great, as one stadium was approximately equivalent to ten miles.

The Greeks followed the steps of the Phœnicians in the Mediterranean and Asiatic commerce. For the benefit of the merchants *peripli*, or guidebooks of the coasts, were prepared. The oldest Greek map known is that of Hecatæus, 500 B.C.

Roman geography. — Next followed the rise and expansion of the Roman Empire. While the Romans

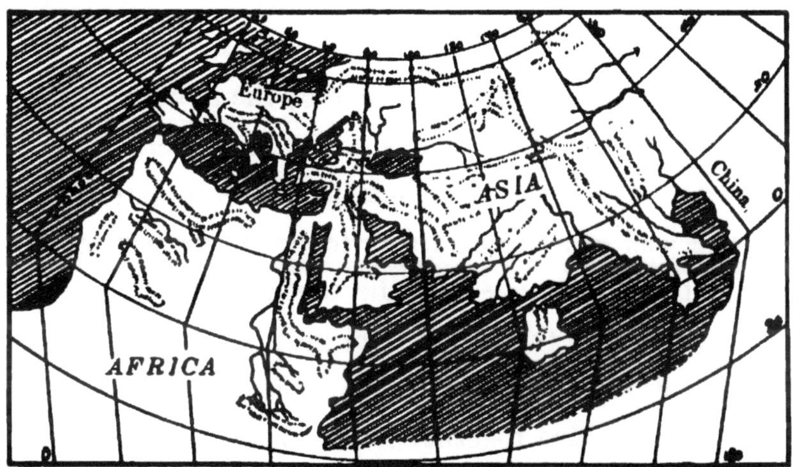

Fig. 31.—Map showing Ptolemy's knowledge and theory of the world, about 150 A.D.

did not increase the bounds of the Greek geography, except toward the north and west, they developed the knowledge of the interiors. Hitherto explorations had been littoral, except in Asia Minor. But the Romans explored the Hinterland, built splendid highways for military and commercial purposes, subdued and policed the semisavage tribes of western Europe, and by their stable government did much to foster trade and the growth of towns. Trade between the West and the East was extensive. In fact, commerce was the main impulse of the Roman expansion. Excellent road maps and coast *peripli* were prepared.

The geographical knowledge of the Ancients is summed up in the works of two great writers, Strabo, 20 B.C., and Ptolemy, 150 A.D. (See next chapter.)

The Middle Ages were, for geography, as for most learning, the "Dark Ages," all the more so for the repeated destruction of the map of Europe by the almost constant warfare between the various tribes that were destined later to crystallize into nations. The population of Europe was in a state of flux for centuries. The Germanic barbarians overran the south of Europe. The fierce vikings of the North were invading and colonizing western Europe. The nations of France and England were being welded together from various tribes. A new force in the Western world were the invaders from Asia. The Moors took possession of Asia Minor, northern Africa, and Spain. The savage Mongols from the plains and plateaus of northern and central Asia pushed their empire through Russia to the banks of the Danube. All this incursion and ravaging must have utterly confused the geography of Europe, at least so far as the political map is concerned.

Monastic geography. — This was preëminently a period of religious zeal, both for the Christian and the Saracen peoples. The learning of the former was at this time strictly ecclesiastic, and the wisdom of the Ancients was despised and forgotten. Geography was colored and modified to suit religious views. The Homeric flat, circular earth and surrounding ocean were revived. Distant lands and the "Sea of Darkness," the Atlantic, and the torrid zone were invested with frightful monsters and natural terrors that for many centuries deterred the most adventurous explorers.

The Saracens, on the other hand, had absorbed much of the classical learning of Byzantium and Alexandria, and strove in the universities in Spain to maintain it. These schools were the chief centers of thought in the Dark Ages. Their geography was essentially that of Strabo and Ptolemy. The Arabs were the chief navigators of the Mediterranean and Indian seas at this period, and there were among them great travelers and geographers, but owing to the Saracen language in which they wrote their geographical descriptions, these had not great weight in Europe.

The crusades spread geographical knowledge. — In

another way, though indirectly, the Saracens aided geographical knowledge. The Holy Land was in their possession. In the twelfth and thirteenth centuries, especially, a religious fervor seized Europe, and many crusades went to Palestine, sometimes to be met with resistance by the Saracens, and again to be met on more friendly terms. At any rate, these crusades did much to revive an interest in foreign lands, and to promote commercial intercourse between the West and the East.

Marco Polo. — In connection with the pilgrimages and crusades there was considerable travel by monks, curious travelers, and merchants. The most romantic of these medieval travels was that of Marco Polo toward the end of the thirteenth century. As above stated, the Mongols or Tartars had overrun eastern Europe. Western rulers sought to form alliances with the powerful Mongol Khans or kings, and sent embassies to their semibarbaric court in far-off Cathay (China). On one of these embassies went Marco Polo, then a young man under twenty, a native of Venice. To the impressionable youth the journey overland through Central Asia, and his long years of favor and honor at the Chinese court, must have been exceedingly novel and interesting. After long years he returned to his native city to relate and publish a remarkable story of travel and adventure which fired the imagination of all Europe.

The Isles of Spices. — The East had always held men

in thrall. They knew that Asia was of vast extent, and stories of Cathay and Cipango (Japan), and the Spice Islands (the East Indies) had long floated about. More tangible were the luxuries that indirectly and through many lands, overland and by sea, came from the Orient. Silks and cotton, gems and gold, from India; perfumes and spices from the Islands of the East; medicines and dye-stuffs from Arabia, were eagerly sought by Western traders. The spices, alone, at this time made the nations strive for a monopoly in the trade. Salt is so highly esteemed that races risk their lives to secure it. Almost equally great was the demand for the spices of the East. We who have the modern variety of palatable, mixed dietary can hardly imagine how important was the need of spices for the people of those days when salt meat and salt fish were the staple articles of food and needed something to render them appetizing. The popular spices of this period were nutmeg, cloves, pepper, cinnamon, and ginger. Camphor, spikenard, myrrh, and musk were the aromatics most in demand.

Oriental trade routes. — The Chinese had long been in communication with the tropical Archipelagoes, and the cargoes they brought from there, together with their own silks, etc., they sold to the Arab traders who made regular sailings, according to the monsoons, to Singapore. These Arabs controlled the marine trade of the Indian Ocean, Persian Gulf, and the Red Sea. Tropical prod-

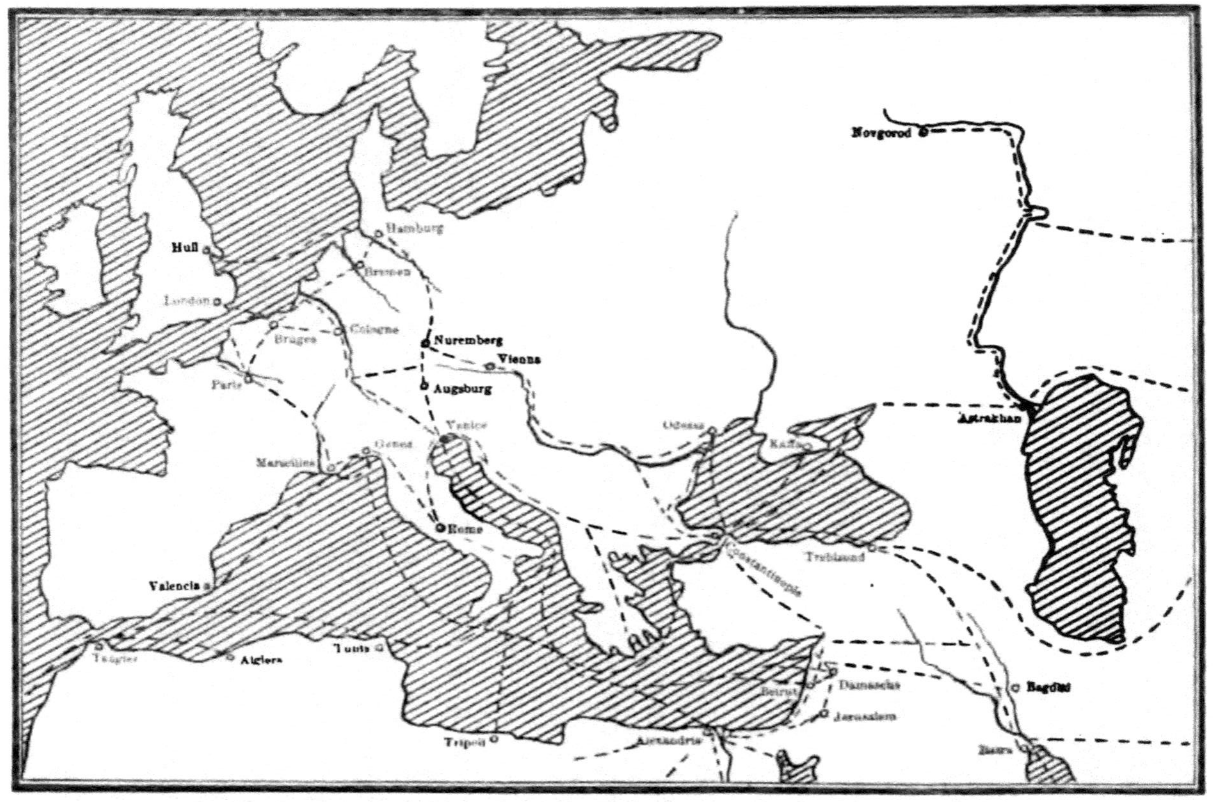

FIG. 32. — Ancient and medieval trade routes over land and sea.

ucts also came from Ethiopia (Nubia) and the oases of the desert, via Alexandria and the Phœnician and Syrian ports (Tyre, Beirut). The Phœnicians, and then, in turn, the Greeks, Genoese, and Venetians, had the monopoly of the Mediterranean commerce, distributing the Oriental goods from the eastern ports all along the coast. The further distribution then proceeded up the chief rivers and overland into the interior.

There was an extensive overland trade from Asia. From China caravans used to travel through Mongolia and Turkestan, around both ends of the Caspian Sea to the Black Sea, where the goods were then shipped by water for the south of Europe. A land route from India ran through Mesopotamia, and then divided at Damascus, one branch leading to the Mediterranean ports, and the other to Constantinople. From the latter city one route of commerce ran across the Balkan Peninsula to the Danube, Germany, and the North Sea. Another route from Constantinople crossed Macedonia, and followed the Adriatic up to Venice. Italy was traversed by a trade route along its western side, which connected Rome and Genoa, and then led around to Marseilles, up the Rhone, across France to Britain. Venice was also connected with this last route, and also with the route from Constantinople to the Hanseatic towns of the northwest.

***Italian* trade monopolies.** — The Italian cities, especially Genoa and Venice, by "cut-throat" competition, secured and held the monopoly of the Oriental trade from the twelfth to the fifteenth centuries. Genoa had the monopoly of the northerly routes to the Black Sea and Constantinople; and Venice, the southern routes to Palestine and Alexandria. Both cities became very wealthy and powerful.

The westward route to the Indies. — Italy and the Levant having the monopoly of the eastern trade over the direct routes, the western nations began to seek another route to this field of riches. This became all the more necessary after the Turks captured Constantinople (1453) and Alexandria, thus closing the eastern route of commerce.

Portuguese discoveries. — About the beginning of the fifteenth century Portugal, under the scientific and pious Prince Henry, called The Navigator, was the first thus to seek a new way to the Indies. It was natural that Henry should think that the way might lead through the Atlantic. He saw the possibility of rounding Africa. The old maps always showed a river (the ancient Oceanus), or an ocean south of that continent, and the medieval maps represented it much smaller than it really is. Thus encouraged, Henry proceeded to do what no one else had done before, namely, to develop the art of oceanic navigation. True, the Norsemen had crossed the North Atlantic in their long ships from island to island; and Greek and Arab sailors had learned to sail boldly across the Indian Ocean, taking advantage of the periodic monsoons. But the open sea, especially the Atlantic, had always had its real or imaginary terrors for western sailors, and men did not trust themselves to sail beyond the horizon. The old legends and old maps told of human and animal monsters. The torrid zone, it was believed, could not be crossed on account of the fiery heat, while far out beyond the horizon one would come to the edge of the earth. Henry taught Europe the groundlessness of these fears. He built larger sea-going vessels, perfected the mariner's compass, which not long before had been introduced, probably from China, by pivoting it in a box; he improved the astrolabe, for determining latitude; he built an astronomical observatory; founded a school of navigators; and employed the best cartographers of Europe.

Circumnavigation of Africa. — Under the urging of Henry, Portuguese sailors pushed, year after year, farther down the coast of Africa. Excellent pilot charts, *portolanos*, were made of the newly discovered coasts, and in the end, 1497, the circumnavigation of Africa was accomplished by Vasco da Gama, and the new route to the Spice Islands established, but not until after the death of the Sailor Prince and Columbus' bold venture. The African coasts were exploited by the Portuguese; gold, ivory, and slaves were brought thence.

Portuguese colonies were planted in Africa, Ceylon, India, and the East Indies, and soon this western nation had taken away from the Italian and Egyptian cities the Oriental trade they so long enjoyed.

The Norsemen. — In the tenth and eleventh centuries the Norsemen scoured the northern seas in their stanch viking ships, pillaging, conquering, and colonizing at various points on the coasts of western Europe. Some ventured out into the colder waters of the North Atlantic and discovered Iceland, Greenland, and even North America. Colonies were established in these regions. But nothing came of these achievements at the time. No other nations seem to have heard of the discoveries of the Norsemen. Even their own people forgot them, except as they are recorded in the legendary sagas.

Columbus. — The story of the discovery of America is familiar. Columbus evidently did not fear the mythical monsters believed in by so many of his day, and he accepted the theory of the sphericity of the earth, a knowledge of which had been revived by the Moors, and by the Greeks who fled from the Turks at the sacking of Constantinople and Alexandria. Columbus held the Ptolemaic idea of the smallness of the earth, especially as to the shortness of the distance to the Indies by way of the Atlantic westward. The maps of Toscanelli and Behaim showed China only four thousand miles west of

Europe. He was therefore all the more ready to try to sail east by going west. His object was not to discover a new continent, but to find a new route to the East Indies, India, and China. He was never disillusioned of the notion that he had really discovered these regions,

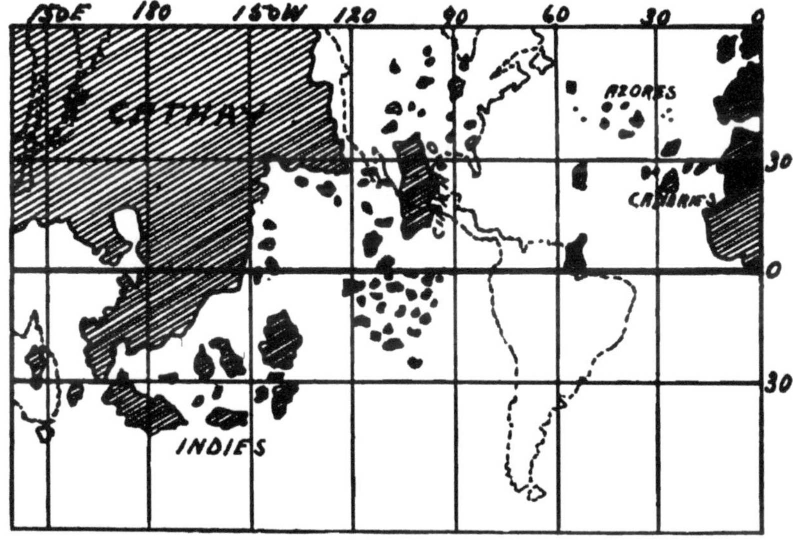

FIG. 33. — Map showing the geographical ideas of Behaim, Toscanelli, Columbus, and others about 1492. Note the nearness of Asia to Europe. Japan is placed in the longitude of North America. The dotted lines indicate the actual positions of China, Japan, Australia, and America.

and the names, American *Indians* and the West *Indies*, stand to-day as a monument of this error. Columbus, however, set an example which was soon emulated by others. The fifteenth century gave the Old World a New World, and vastly enlarged its geographial conception.

Magellan. — The first circumnavigation of the earth

was accomplished by the great voyage of Magellan's ships, 1519–1522. This gave a practical proof of the earth's sphericity, also of the fact that Eurasia was smaller and the earth larger than had been believed. Incidentally the voyage also clinched the fact that America was a distinct continent.

The Discoveries Period. — The century and a quarter beginning with the year 1400 is known as the Discoveries Period. The broadening of geographical knowledge, and the stimulus to the imagination must have done much toward bringing on the Renaissance. By 1550 practically all the continental shores of the world were known, with the exception of those of Australia and the polar lands.

Motives of exploration. — It is interesting to pause to consider the motives that have led men to brave the dangers of unknown regions. For the most part they were commercial — for gain. The Phœnician peddlers traveled the Mediterranean countries for gain, and earned an unenviable reputation for sharp bargaining. The Greeks and Romans conquered empires in order to exploit them commercially. Semibarbarian Teutons, Norsemen, Vandals, and Huns erupted from their native countries for plunder. Migration and colonization are usually the result of necessity, the need of more productive fields than the home country affords, or perhaps overpopulation.

The trader sometimes preceded the discoverer, at least soon followed in his track. The quest for the East was mainly for commerce. The item of spice alone was responsible for great overland journeys through Asia, for the exploration of the Indian Ocean, for the circumnavigation of Africa, and the discovery of America.

That there were other motives cannot be denied. Alexander and the Cæsars, no doubt, loved power and conquest. The Saracens were imbued with a fiery religious frenzy when they swept through Asia and Africa, giving their vanquished foes the choice of Islam or the sword. The Christians of Europe, during the Middle Ages, pressed as pilgrims and crusaders through the troubled and dangerous chaos of countries, actuated by religious zeal. And some, like Herodotus, Strabo, and Marco Polo, traveled because they were curious, and liked to travel.

With the seventeenth century, however, a new motive for exploration developed, which does not mean, though, that other motives did not continue as in the past. The new motive was that of scientific research, the desire to discover for the sake of the discovery. For this purpose the great nations have maintained geographical societies, which encouraged such exploration, and governments have frequently sent out scientific expeditions.

Captain James Cook. Australia. — Prince Henry is credited with such uncommercial motives, though his merchant sailors did not share them. With Captain James Cook's voyages, 1770–1776, scientific exploration really began. In 1542 the Spanish, in search for the Spice Islands, discovered Australia, but its insular character was not known for two hundred years. For a long time it was thought to be the fabled Southern Continent around the South Pole, hence the name Australia (*auster*, south). The Dutch, who in the sixteenth century displaced the Portuguese in the Indian waters, had explored the south and west coast. It was left for Captain Cook to complete the coastal survey. He also discovered New Zealand, and many other islands of the Pacific. He was slain by the Hawaiians, 1776.

Africa. — The opening up of the Dark Continent was the work of the nineteenth century. The explorations of Mungo Park, Livingstone, and Stanley in Africa were also scientific. The tropical heat, the dense forests, and tropical diseases called for a heroism and perseverance of the highest order in these pioneers.

The polar regions have always had a peculiar fascination for mankind. The hardy Norsemen were the first to discover the Arctic lands of Iceland, Greenland, and Labrador. After the successful exploits of the Portuguese and Spaniards during the Discoveries Period, France, England, and Holland emulated their example, trying to find new routes to India. The Northwest Passage to India was attempted by each of these nations, resulting only in defeat, so far as their primary purpose was concerned, yet adding to the geography of the Arctic seas.

During the eighteenth and nineteenth centuries the scientific motive prevailed in the exploration of polar regions. Some of the saddest and finest stories of heroic endeavor have been written in these frozen seas.

The destiny of the Russian Empire led to the east, through the frozen tundras, and the fertile plains of Siberia to the Pacific. It was the Russian commander Behring, 1728, who proved the separation of Asia from North America, by sailing through the strait that now bears his name. In 1879 Nordenskiold successfully sailed the Northeast Passage, around Europe and Asia; while Collinson, in 1850–1855, and Amundsen, in 1903–1906, worked their ships through the tortuous shoals of the Northwest Passage, long sought for, and long abandoned as a possible commercial route.

The early years of the twentieth century saw the settlement of the question of the Poles. Peary, 1909, found the North Pole in the midst of the Arctic Ocean; and Amundsen, 1911, the South Pole on a glacier-covered plateau of the Antarctic Continent.

" The final achievement of the Pole will not give us another pound of whalebone, nor will it open up any new route of navigation; it will simply add to useless knowledge. . . . Most knowledge is at first profitless for food and shelter, but it is exhilarating to the soul just the same." (*The Independent.*)

Further exploration. — The general map of the globe is complete. Yet there still remains work for the geographer. Much of the interior of continents still requires exploration. Vast areas need careful surveying. Problems of geology, climate, plant and animal life, and ethnographical questions are still to be solved. And man and his ways, and the beauty of the natural scenery, will always appeal to the geo-historian.

CHAPTER XXIII

THE HISTORY OF THE SCIENCE OF GEOGRAPHY, AND THE HISTORY OF ITS PEDAGOGY

Geography as a science. — We have seen how the knowledge of the extent and appearance of the world increased with the migration of races, with conquest, commercial expansion, and religious crusades, and through scientific exploration. The new facts thus acquired by the world were recorded from time to time in the books as geography.

The orderly, logical account of the knowledge of the extent, appearance, and life conditions of the earth; and of the habits of its forms of life, particularly its peoples, is the science of geography. It attempts to bring out the relations that exist between the various geographical factors or features, and, as far as possible, tries to find out underlying principles. Geography as a science has necessarily lagged behind discovery.

The data of geography.—It is the duty of the scientific geographer to scrutinize, weigh, and harmonize the accounts of travelers, the data of commerce, and the more scientific records of explorers, surveyors, and scientists. It is not an easy matter to thus compile a science correct in all respects. Insufficient data, inaccurate observations, accounts colored by partisanship or bias, pure fiction and superstition, have always entered into the science of geography, and these errors of the human judgment have not yet been all eradicated.

Mathematical geography is the oldest branch of the science of geography. The Chaldeans, Chinese, Hindoos, Jews, and Egyptians made the first contributions, giving us geometry, the idea of a spherical earth, circular measure, the calendar, knowledge of the eclipses, and the first measurements of the earth.

Herodotus. — The Greeks were the first to write scientific descriptions of the earth in general. Herodotus, 450 B.C., summarized the existing knowledge of his own and foreign lands, and the earth in general. Eratosthenes, 240 B.C., wrote a comprehensive geography, and made the first mathematical measurement of the earth.

Strabo. — The Romans were too busy developing their conquered territories commercially to allow the writing of geography. They had maps and accounts of their newly acquired possessions which were set up at the time of the celebration of their victories. But they did not write any systematic geography. This was left for two Greeks of the Empire to do.

Strabo, 20 B.C., wrote a great work on the geography of his time. It was a philosophical, scientific, systematic treatise, divided into mathematical, physical, and political branches, thus setting a standard that has been followed to this day. He appreciated the effect of the environment on the people, but used geography as an · to history. He has been called the Father of ography.

Ptolemy. — But the most influential figure in ancient geography was Claudius Ptolomæus (Ptolemy), a Greek, of Alexandria, 150 A.D. He believed in a spherical earth, but made it the center of the universe, an idea that was destined to prevail for 1500 years. He wrote a great work on mathematical geography, and in the famous library at Alexandria he made a critical study of the geographical data acquired up to that time, and prepared his great map of the world. He used meridians and parallels, fixing the prime meridian at the Canary Islands, then the farthest west, where it was kept till the eighteenth century. He estimated, but with error, the latitude and longitude of places, and placed them upon the map. He overestimated the extent of Eurasia, assuming it to be from west to east larger by more than 75 degrees than it really is, thus leaving the distance west from Europe to China too small.

Ancient school geography. — As far as school instruction in geography is concerned, the ancients have but little to show. Geography hardly existed as a separate science, but was blended with history, astronomy, and geometry, in which there was probably some reference to descriptive and mathematical geography. Socrates is said to have used a map in teaching his disciples, and the Romans set up in public places tablets of maps descriptive of their conquests.

During the Middle Ages geography as a science followed the general decline of learning. The best geography of the ancients, Strabo's and Ptolemy's, was neglected, and inferior data were accepted, even the mythology of Homer being revived. The errors of Ptolemy were preserved because they fitted well with the Christian cosmography. The monks copied and made excerpts from inferior works. Their maps, *mappe-mundi*, were marvels of inaccuracy, legendary lore, and superstition, representing a strictly ecclesiastical interpretation of the world. Jerusalem was generally placed at the center of the map. The road maps were somewhat better, but chiefly intended for pilgrims, and comprised mainly a list of "holy places."

The Renaissance saw the voyages of the Portuguese and the Spaniards. A new spirit came into all science, including geography. Pretentious, systematic "Cosmographies" were written. One of these, 1507, by the German Waldseemüller, fixed upon the New World the name "America." The German geographers were especially active. Cartography was developed to a high degree by Gerhard Krämer (Latin, Mercator), 1512–1594, who invented various projections, the so-called Mercator's Projection being the most famous. Behaim, also, constructed his first globe in 1492. This does not show the new world, to be discovered that same year.

Copernicus. — In this period physics and astronomy were greatly advanced. Copernicus, 1543, revolutionized previous astronomical notions (Ptolemaic system) of a geocentric universe, by substituting the present heliocentric theory. This, with the new Discoveries of Lands, caused the loosening of the grip of the classic geography on the minds of men.

Pedagogy of geography in the Middle Ages. — During the Middle Ages geography was still largely a part of astronomy, history, geometry, or even religion, and was taught in connection with them. The chief pedagogical improvement was in the use of maps and globes, though none were yet used in elementary schools.

Philosophic geography. — With the modern period came a number of geniuses who dealt with the philosophy of the earth and its place in the universe. Varenius, of Amsterdam, 1622–1650, wrote the first general physical geography, in a very modern way, using the causal relation and the comparative method. It was for a century the standard of general geography, and was translated by the great Newton for students in English universities. Varenius was the founder of physical geography. Newton (d. 1727) himself contributed to the science of geography the law of gravity and orbital motion. Kant (d. 1804) and Laplace (d. 1827) proposed the nebular hypothesis of the origin of the earth. Anthropogeography, the place of man on the earth, his relation to his environment, was first considered fully by Herder, in his *Philosophy of History*, 1785.

Beginnings of modern methods of instruction. — During this period of discovery and commercial expansion there was more need for geography, and a beginning was made with instruction in this subject in the elementary schools. By 1600 some textbooks of geography had been written for German schools. Comenius (d. 1671) urged this study upon the schools, emphasizing home geography as the beginning, geography of one's native country, and the use of pictures (Orbis Pictus).

Rousseau. — It was in the next century, however, that the pedagogy of geography received serious consideration. This was a period of revolt against formalism and bookishness in education. The school of educators represented by Rousseau (d. 1778) demanded naturalness in education, and emphasized the humanities. Rousseau spoke against the emphasis usually placed on mathematical geography. He said the children of his day could glibly locate foreign places, but could not find the way from their home city to the next town. "Why begin with celestial and terrestrial globes, and maps? Why these symbols? Why not begin with the earth itself, the home locality, so that pupils may know what they are studying about?" said Rousseau. He gave a great impetus to the learning of home geography by observation, and helped to adapt the study to beginners.

Francke. — Under the direction of Francke (d. 1727) in Germany, geography assumed a firm place in the curriculum of the higher school as a distinct subject. The textbooks then in use were of the question and answer form, and atlases were separate.

Basedow (d. 1790) wrote the first illustrated textbook of geography, beginning with home geography. He also used current events, imaginary journeys, and supplementary reading, and correlated with nature-study, — all decidedly modern.

Herder, above mentioned, as superintendent of schools, lent his influence in establishing the young subject, in promoting home geography, and giving it a human tendency.

The eighteenth century must be considered as most revolutionary and progressive in the matter of the pedagogy of geography.

Pestalozzi (d. 1827) did not carry his theories of child psychology and concrete instruction into practice in geography. He did not use maps, and his method of instruction in geography was very formal. He taught, for example, alphabetic lists of place names before anything was learned about them. Geography is, however, indebted to him for his insistence on adapting instruction to the child, the observational method, and the synthetic order of study, which he applied to education in general, and especially for the inspiration of his disciples, who carried out his ideas in geography better than he himself could or did.

Correlation of geography with natural science. — The eighteenth century had been rich in discovery and exploration. The geographers of the nineteenth century had to collect and sift the new material and to correlate the new geography with the new sciences of botany, zoölogy, meteorology, and geology, which were rapidly developing. Hugh Murray (d. 1846) in England, and Conrad Malte-Brun (d. 1826) in France, were leaders in this new movement in scientific geography.

Modern geography, as a science, was founded by Karl Ritter (d. 1859). He was a scientific geographer and historian, and a great teacher. He, more than any one else before, realized the intimate relation between man and nature, and made this the means of uniting into an organic unity what had up to this time been largely a mass of unrelated facts. This idea he expressed in numerous works, particularly in his *Geography in Relation to the Nature and History of Man.*

He emphasized the necessity of using physical geography as the basis of political geography and history.

He coined the expression "comparative geography," meaning a comparison of the physical features of one country with similar features in another, therefrom deriving some common principles. He not only wrote works on the science of geography, but labored with his contemporaries to adopt his ideas and to make of geography a cultural and disciplinary study, which to this time it had scarcely been. He taught the Pestalozzian doctrine of beginning the subject with the child's natural environment. He urged home geography. He insisted on map drawing. No other man has had such an influence in shaping geographical science and geographical instruction. His ideals still hold good to-day.

Humboldt. — Another great influence in geography at this period was that of Humboldt (d. 1859), a great naturalist and explorer, and author of *Cosmos*. While Ritter was led to geography through history, Humboldt came to it through natural science, and his works naturally reflect this interest. He emphasized the physical side of geography. He made altitude studies, and invented profiles and isotherms, and developed the subject of plant geography.

Ratzel. — Among the Ritter school, Ratzel (d. 1904), author of *Anthropogeography*, was (after Ritter) the greatest. He emphasized the human, the historic, and also the æsthetic side of geography. Through his vivid, interesting, and appealing description of the earth he raised the subject of geography to the æsthetic plane.

The "New Geography." — With the new development of the sciences in the nineteenth century, particularly in geology and biology, since the days of Darwin and Huxley, 1870, there has been a tendency to swing away from the humanistic treatment of geography as represented by Ritter, Peschel, Ratzel, and Guyot, toward the physical side. The Ritter school treated the subject of physical geography scenically and statically, as if the earth's topography did not change, and mountains were everlasting. The "new geography," however, treats geography dynamically. The *forces* of the earth receive more attention, and their effects are noted. The new geography looks backward for explanations of the present features, and forward to ultimate conditions. The causal treatment marks the subject to-day. In short, it is evolutionary in character. The Ritter school considered the earth adapted to man, the teleological view; the modern school considers man's life, like that of other creatures, plants, and animals, as a response to, or determined by, physical nature. The tendency is thus to magnify physical nature, and to minimize man. This tendency is shown, perhaps, more in the United States than elsewhere. William M. Davis is the chief representative.

Regional geography. — One consequence, a good one,

of viewing more fully the physical side of the earth, is the present-day tendency to drop the old systematic treatment of geography by countries and states, or at least to supplement it by studying the earth by physiographic regions, or industrial units, which is really an application of the comparative method in the higher sense.

Modern specialization. — Geography has become so broad a science that one mind is scarcely able to treat it adequately in all departments. Hence there is a growing tendency to specialize in one branch or another. One of the newer branches is commercial geography, emphasized especially in this country and in England. The rise of this subject has been brought about by the tremendous material development of the world in the last fifty years. Its introduction in the schools is in response to a demand from the business world.

Two tendencies in geography. — Ever since geography began to be written two tendencies or two schools existed, usually side by side, sometimes one predominating, sometimes the other. They are the humanistic and physical interpretations of geography. The character of the instruction in the elementary schools usually reflected the two tendencies, though always lagging behind.

Geography in the curriculum. — Geography is to-day a highly accredited subject, with a large allowance of time in the curriculum in all enlightened countries. In England and America it stands on its own footing and should really be correlated far more than it is with history and nature-study. In Germany and France geography is still in the shadow of history, being very closely woven together with that subject, especially in the study of the Fatherland.

Home and general geography are taught in the elementary grades; physical and commercial geography, in the higher school and university.

In Europe there are chairs of political geography in the universities, and it is taught in secondary schools. This branch, most unfortunately, is below par in this country, receiving scarcely any attention above the elementary school.

CHAPTER XXIV

SOME AMERICAN TEXTBOOKS OF GEOGRAPHY

The first geographies used in this country were "made in England." The character of these early textbooks may be judged from *Geography Made Familiar and Easy*, by J. Newberry, 1748, London. This or a similar title was a favorite form at the time. Geography was still pleading for a place among the studies. Hence these early books generally contained in their preface "arguments to recommend the study of a science so useful and entertaining." Newberry's geography, like many others up to 1850, was of the question and answer type, a method followed first by the German Hübner in his geographies, and probably borrowed from church pedagogy. In fact, some of these textbooks were entitled "Geographical Catechism." As the main object of the textbooks of this period was to teach names and locations — "sailor's geography," the catechism method was an orderly and expeditious, if not interesting, method of memorizing. Says the author of another primer of geography, J. Johnston, London, 1787, "Children have better memories than judgment: the latter should be improved by the former," and he claims

MADE EASY.

BEING A SHORT, BUT COMPREHENSIVE

System

OF THAT VERY USEFUL AND AGREEABLE SCIENCE.

EXHIBITING

In an easy and concise View, the Figures, Motions, Distances, and Magnitudes of the heavenly Bodies: — A general description of the Earth considered as a Planet; with its grand Divisions into Land and Water, Continents, Oceans, Islands, &c. — The Situation, Boundaries and Extent of the several Empires, Kingdoms, and States, together with an Account of their Climate, Soil, Productions and commerce: — The Number, Genius, and general Character of the Inhabitants: — Their Religion, Government and History: — The Latitude, Longitude, Distances, and Bearings of the principal Places from Philadelphia and London, and a Number of useful Geographical Tables.

Illustrated with two correct and elegant MAPS, one of the World, and the other of the United States, together with a Number of newly constructed Maps, adapted to the Capacities and Understanding of Children.

Calculated particularly for the Use and Improvement of SCHOOLS in the United States.

By JEDIDIAH MORSE, A. B.

"There is not a SON or a DAUGHTER of Adam, but has some "concern in both GEOGRAPHY and ASTRONOMY." — DR. WATTS.

"Among those Studies which are usually recommended to young "People, there can be few that might be improved to better Uses "than Geography." — *Essays on various Subjects.*

NEW HAVEN:

Printed by MEIGS, BOWEN and DANA, in Chapel-Street.

PLATE 1. — Reprint of title page of Morse's *Geography Made Easy*, 1774. With permission, from the G. A. Plimpton collection.

that his *Geography for Children* is an easy method. "Even young ladies, in two months' time may be in-

AN

ASTRONOMICAL

AND

GEOGRAPHICAL

CATECHISM.

FOR THE USE OF CHILDREN.

By CALEB BINGHAM, *A. M.*

THE SECOND EDITION.

PUBLISHED ACCORDING TO ACT OF CONGRESS.

"The Earth, the Heavens——are fraught with Inſtruction."

BOSTON:
Printed and ſold by *S. HALL*, No. 53, Cornhill.

Sold alſo by the Author, No. 44, Cornhill.
1796.

PLATE 2.—Title page of a small geographical pamphlet. With permission, from the G. A. Plimpton collection.

structed in the rudiments of geography, and be able to give pertinent answers to a question."

Unpedagogical treatment. — Aside from names and locations, Newberry's book consisted of general definitions, some mathematical geography (largely globe exercises), and a very slender description of countries. The book started out with general definitions and mathematical geography, and then followed with a deductive application, a method wholly unsuited to beginners.

The book, like many others of its time, was of the "vest pocket" size, an interesting commentary on the amount of geography required in those days. The book had no pictures and no maps, except a frontispiece of the world in hemispheres. It was the custom then to use a separate atlas with the textbooks.

Morse, the Father of American Geography. — The first really American geography was written by the Rev. Jedidiah Morse, New Haven, 1774. It was called *Geography Made Easy.* Morse is called the Father of American Geography, and it is to his credit that he emphasized the value of geography as a patriotic study for Americans, and a preparation for good citizenship.

Morse's book does not differ from the previous English texts, except in a better application to American geography. It has no pictures, only one map of the world, and one of North America. These are plain, copper plate cuts. The political part is better than the rest, containing some history, and descriptions of customs to enliven its dull monotony. In spite of its limitations this

[13]

1. ♈ Aries, the ram, in March	7 ♎ Libra, balance, Sept.
2. ♉ Taurus, the bull, April	8. ♏ Scorpio, scorpion, Oct.
3. ♊ Gemini, the twins, May	9 ♐ Sagitarius, archer, Nov.
4. ♋ Cancer, the crab, June	10 ♑ Capricorn, goat, Dec.
5. ♌ Leo, the lion, July	11 ♒ Aquarius, water bearer, Jan
6. ♍ Virgo, virgin, August	12 ♓ Pisces, fishes, Feb.

Q. 41. Why are these constellations called by such animals' names?

A Those who divided the starry heavens into constellations, must call them by some name, to know and distinguish them by; and the several clusters thus laid off, probably bear some resemblance to the animals on Earth whose names they wear.

Q. 42. What do you mean by the Sun entering the 12 signs?

A. When the Sun is said, for instance, to enter Aries, the meaning is that he then comes between the Earth, and the first degree of that sign

The names and order of the twelve signs, may be easily remembered by the following verses of Dr Watts

The *Ram*, the *Bull*, the heavenly *Twins*,
And next the *Crab* the *Lion* shines,
The *Virgin* and the *Scales*
The *Scorpion*, *Archer*, and *He Goat*;
The *Man that bears the water pot*,
And *fish* with glittering tails.

Q. 43. What is the *Ecliptic*?

A The Ecliptic, so called from eclipses happening under it, is that circle, supposed in the middle of the Zodiac, which crosses the Equator at an angle of 23° 30', and is the path the Sun describes, and never quits, while he passes through the twelve signs, as above described.

Q. 44. What causes an *eclipse* of the Sun?

A. An eclipse of the Sun can never happen, but at the change of the Moon; and as the Moon continually wheels round the Earth left about, and completes her revolution in her month; so it will sometimes happen, that in passing from the east to the west of the Sun, she must come betwixt him and the Earth, and hide a part, and sometimes, though very seldom, the whole of his disk from us.

Q. 45 How can the Moon come between us and the Sun? Are they not both at an equal distance from us?

A. The distance of the Moon from the Earth, is 240,000 miles;

Plate 3.—Sample page of Patillo's *A Geographical Catechism*, 1796, Halifax, N. C.

itants, but by numerous emigrations from New-England. The people of the northern counties are mostly from New-England. Though the English language is generally spoken through the state; yet in some parts it is greatly corrupted by the Dutch. In some instances they yet have schools and public worship conducted in the Dutch language, but the custom is going out of use, and soon no language will be spoken, but the English. The emigrants from New-England, it may be supposed, retain the customs and manners of those states. Long island was also settled from England or New-England; but the other parts of the state differ considerably in character from New-England. Beside the Dutch, many Germans are settled on the Mohawk; on the Hudson are Scotch settlers. In the city of New-York are found many Germans and Scotch. In New-Rochelle, and on Staten's island, many French emigrants are settled. All those people in some degree retain the customs, manners, and opinions of the countries, whence they came. The inhabitants in 1800 were 586,050, of whom 20,613 were slaves. The militia, in 1808, were 92,564.

Climate.—The northern part of the state resembles Vermont; but is more mild, owing to the great lakes in the vicinity. West of the Alleghany mountains the seasons are temperate. On the lower part of the Hudson and the sound, the weather is very changeable.

Towns.—New-York is the capital of the state, situated on the southwest point of Manhattan island, and contains 82,000 inhabitants. The houses in general are of brick, with tiled roofs. Federal hall is the most superb building in the city; it is occupied by the legislature, and judicial courts. The state prison is a noble pile of buildings, which does honour to the humanity and wisdom of the government, by whom it was erected. It is 307 feet in length, 3 stories high; the lower story is 10 feet high, the other two 13 and a half each. The walls are thick, and of hard stone; the grates are of iron bars, steeled, and hardened. There are in the city 26 houses for public worship, 3 Dutch churches, 4 presbyterian, 2 associated, reformed Scotch churches, 1 associated Scotch church, 5 episcopal churches, 2 German Lutherans, and Calvinists, 3 methodists, 2 baptists, and for Moravians, Roman catholics, French protestants, and Jews, one each. The hospital of New-York is a spacious building; beside its oth-

PLATE 4.—Sample page from Parrish's *A New System of Geography*, 1810, Newburyport, Mass.

book enjoyed a tremendous popularity, passed through twenty-five editions, and was still in use in 1865.

Revolt. — The gazetteers and catechisms finally brought on a revolt among teachers. They were criticized as too uninteresting, unpedagogical, unconnected, and too great a burden on the memory.

In 1822 William Woodbridge published at Hartford his *Rudiments of Geography* "on the new plan of comparing facts and arranging them in classes and reducing them to general principles." These principles were first stated, and next applied in a description of continents as wholes, and finally in a description of the states. This avoided repetition: "The countries of the torrid zone produced fruits and vegetables. Therefore from the map the child can see what is raised in Hindoostan or Guinea." The treatment is thus analytic-deductive. At the end of the book is a fair "general view" of physical features, manufacturing, commerce, and peoples. Evidently the author wished the pupil to exercise judgment as well as memory, and saw the value of comparison. He believed in pictures, though the woodcuts of the text are very crude and few.

In many respects Woodbridge, who had a keen interest in geography, and belonged to several European geographical societies, was ahead of his times, at least in America. And yet his book is, for the most part, dull. It is based chiefly on map study (atlas) and the descriptive text is very meager. From this time on map study became very prominent.

Primary geography. — Thus far no attempt had been made to adapt the subject to child psychology. But by 1830 the influence of Pestalozzi and his school began to influence American education. The influence of Ritter in emphasizing the human element was also noticeable.

One of the earliest books to attempt an adaptation to the beginner was Goodrich's *System of School Geography*, 1836, Hartford, inspired by the monumental work of Malte-Brun in France. This little book begins with home geography, and then proceeds synthetically — inductively. The language, too, is simplified, and adapted to young readers, and there are numerous pictures. The mathematical geography is made very simple. The descriptive part makes historical connections, and leans towards the æsthetic treatment. In these respects the book is pedagogically planned. But the map work is still chiefly locational, and at this period pupils were required to learn not only the states and their capitals, but the counties of each state and their shire towns. The book shows an advance in map study, in that, after a study of the separate states of a section, the section is reviewed as a group — a slight recognition of physiographic regions. Home geography, however, had not come to stay, because teachers were not prepared for it and did not understand its value.

GEOGRAPHY:

OR,

A DESCRIPTION OF THE

WORLD.

IN THREE PARTS.

PART I.—GEOGRAPHICAL ORTHOGRAPHY,
DIVIDED AND ACCENTED.

PART II.—A GRAMMAR OF GEOGRAPHY,
TO BE COMMITTED TO MEMORY

PART III.—A DESCRIPTION OF THE EARTH,
Manners and Customs of the Inhabitants, Manufactures, Commerce, Government, Natural and Artificial Curiosities, &c.—To be read in Classes.

ACCOMPANIED WITH AN ATLAS.

To which is added,

An Easy Method of constructing Maps, illustrated by Plates.

FOR THE USE OF SCHOOLS AND ACADEMIES.

BY DANIEL ADAMS, A. M.
Author of the Scholar's Arithmetic, &c.

Fourth Edition.

BOSTON:
PRINTED AND PUBLISHED BY LINCOLN & EDMANDS,
No. 53 Cornhill.
1819.

PLATE 5.

About this time geography became graded into two, or sometimes three, books. Maps were now placed in the textbooks, instead of in a separate atlas. In general, the primary books were a blessed relief, when compared to the dull stuff that preceded.

It is not to be expected that protests against these new-fangled methods, "this puerile language," were not heard. In Jacob Willett's *New and Improved School Geography*, 1826, we read: "It has not been deemed expedient to sprinkle this book with pictures, from a conviction that they serve to divert the attention of the pupil rather than to inform his mind or improve his taste." And so he goes back to the catechism style, without illustrations.

Geographies of the mid-nineteenth century. — In 1844, in New York, Sidney Morse, son of Jedidiah, Father of American Geography, published *A System of Geography* of the conventional formal sort. The chief merit of the book is the more logical and sensible map study.

Morse advises teachers to drill first on the introductory pages of definitions and principles; next to go through the whole book, drilling on the maps; and then to go back and take up the descriptive text, — a German custom, and certainly systematic and orderly, whatever might be said of its interest and connectedness.

The maps in this book were large, hence the book had

the usual atlas form. These maps were "the first made by the lithographic process" in colors, but this was

xli PREFACE.

which the compiler introduces here as equally applicable to the use of his own :—

"The proper mode of using this little book to advantage, will, it is apprehended, be, to let the pupil commit the whole of the facts to memory, at the rate, perhaps of one, two or three a day, according to his age and capacity; taking care at the end of each section, to make him repeat the whole of what he has before learnt."

"In connexion with this labor, he may be usefully employed in examing the maps ; and in answering, in writing, the questions that are formed from them. If he read over also a part of the vocabulary each day, comparing the words with the places on some maps of a larger scale than could be bound up with this grammar, it may be affirmed, that half an hour only spent in this manner every day, will render any youth familiar with geography in the course of a few months.

"He may then be called on to answer, without hesitation, the questions which are framed from and correspond with the facts stated in the grammar ; and if he be required to do this in writing, it will be the means of improving him in the art of composition, while it grounds him in all the fundamental principles of Geography.

"That part which relates to the use of the globes, and which contains every fundamental problem, may be learnt at any time that the preceptor shall see fit The questions founded on this part will be found a useful and agreeable exercise."

PLATE 6.—From the preface of Jacob Willett's *New and Improved School Geography*, Poughkeepsie, 1826, showing approval of the memoriter method of studying.

nothing much as far as artistic appearance was concerned, for they were poorly printed, and the colors were not well selected. Some of the earlier books had used different colors for the boundaries, but in this book the states were colored throughout.

At this period spherical, orthographic, and conic maps were employed, but Mercator's projection was not in general use. The illustrations of this period were very much improved. There were more numerous, more artistic woodcuts. They were also better related to the text than formerly. In some, as in Cornell's geography, they were truly beautiful.

The middle decades of the nineteenth century were a period of very formal geography. There was much drilling on maps, on unnecessary and unimportant details, chiefly as to mere location, without much logical sequence. Map drawing was much insisted on, in fact, became a fetish. The pupils at any rate must have had the map well impressed on their memory. In Morse's book and others, such as Monteith's, Cornell's, Smith's, Colton's, there was much classifying and systematizing of the descriptive matter, so much so that it was chopped up into paragraphs without apparent connection or continuity. This made it easy to memorize, which seems still to have been considered the chief pedagogical principle in geography; but the vital and interesting relations between the facts of geography were lost. Reflection and judgment were discouraged, and memorizing was at a premium.

The books of the period differed among themselves mainly as to scope and emphasis on one topic or another. One made a hobby of mathematical geography, another of historical correlation, another of home geography, another of map study.

Ritter's influence in recognizing physical geography as related to human life was felt now in this country, and all texts were admitting that physical geography should be the basis of political, and therefore devoted space to it, but in a way so unconnected that it showed the real significance of this branch of geography had not yet been appreciated. None of them really apply the causal principle.

Guyot. — In 1849 there began a rejuvenation of geography teaching when Guyot came from Switzerland to this country to lecture to teachers on the teaching of geography. He was a disciple of Ritter, and had adopted the new primary methods of Pestalozzi. He broke away from the choppy, systematic, categoric treatment, and put life and unity into the subject. In collaboration with Mrs. Mary Howe Smith, of the then famous Oswego Normal School, he wrote a series of three graded geographies, from 1866–1874, each of a distinct scope and order of treatment and designed for particular grades. The primary geography was not merely an abridgment of the higher, as had been so generally the case with the older "series."

14 MAINE.

The sea breezes render the air moist along the coast. The soil is generally fertile. The climate is favorable to the growth of grass.

The northern portions are yet covered with forests; the southern parts, toward the sea shore, present many flourishing towns and villages. The state abounds in lakes and streams, but they are not well suited to navigation. It has an extensive sea coast, and many fine harbors, favorable to commercial pursuits. The people have therefore, generally, neglected agriculture and manufactures, and devoted themselves to commerce.

Many of the inhabitants of Maine are engaged in cutting down the forest trees, and converting them into lumber, which is shipped to the West Indies, and various parts of the United States, and exchanged for flour, sugar, cash, and other articles which the people have need of. This business, which is called the lumber trade, constitutes one of the leading occupations of the inhabitants. The following cut represents men cutting down the trees in the background; in the foreground is a saw-mill, sawing the logs into boards; also a vessel, loading with lumber to carry it away.

The people of Maine occasionally ship cargoes of ice to New Orleans and the West Indies. During the winter, the extreme cold in this state creates large masses of ice in the rivers; a ship is easily supplied with a cargo of it, and in the sultry climate of the West Indies, nothing can be more grateful.

The ice is exchanged for sugar, molasses, spirits, and other pro-

---

What renders the air moist along the coast? What of the soil? What is the climate favorable to?

What is the situation of the northern portions of the state? What do the southern portions present? In what does Maine abound? Describe its sea coast and harbors. What have the people neglected? To what have they devoted themselves principally? What are many of them engaged in? What constitutes one of the leading occupations of the inhabitants of Maine? What does the picture represent?

What has the enterprise of the people led them occasionally to do? What can you tell me of their sending cargoes of ice to the West Indies? What is commerce?

Plate 7. — Sample page of S. G. Goodrich's *A System of School Geog-*

Guyot's *Introduction to Geography* is a beautiful, interesting reader in geography. It takes the child about his home locality first, then on journeys farther and farther from home. Physical, scenic, commercial, and historic units or types are chosen for these journeys. These travels are finally unified and summarized so as to present a picture of the whole country. A marked feature is that maps are not used before, but after, a region has been thus traveled over with picture and text. The map work also is definite, and limited to essentials. Before the Guyot books came out only political maps had been used in textbooks. He introduced a color-physical map by combining it with the political.

In Guyot's *Intermediate and Grammar School Geographies* the arrangement was analytical-deductive. Here physical geography was really brought to bear on the political. The map study was cut down to reasonable limits by a better selection, and was more than simply locative, being used for the development of topography, climate, etc., as well. Mercator's projection was used in some of the physical maps. For the first time separate color-physical maps were used in addition to the political.

Guyot and Smith were firm believers in map drawing, as were practically all authors and teachers of the time. They, however, made the mistake of recommending complicated construction diagrams, the formulæ for which the pupils had to memorize, for the drawing of the continents, etc. Map drawing at this period became very elaborate and time-wasting. With the seventies came a reduction in memoriter work, both in text and in map study; a better balance of the different branches; the

NIAGARA FALLS.

At its efflux from lake Erie, Niagara River, three quarters of a mile wide, and from 40 to 60 feet deep, flows

with a current of 7 miles an hour. As it proceeds, the river widens, and embosoms Grand and Navy islands, which terminate in beautiful points a mile and a half above the falls. Below the islands are rapids, which extend a mile, to the precipice, in which space the river descends 57 feet. At the precipice it is three fourths of a mile wide. Here Goat Island divides the river into two channels, and the channel between Goat Island and the eastern or American shore is also divided by a small island. Over the precipice the river falls perpendicularly about 160 feet. Much the greater part of the water passes in the channel between Goat Island and the Canada shore, and this fall is called, from its shape, the Horse-shoe fall. Between Goat Island and the small island in the eastern channel, the stream is only 8 or 10 yards wide, forming a beautiful cascade. Between this small island and the American shore the sheet of water is broad, and the descent greater by a few feet than at the Horse-shoe fall, but the stream is comparatively shallow. The best single view of the falls is from Table Rock, on the Canada shore, and the best view of the rapids is from Goat Island, which is ingeniously connected by a bridge with the eastern shore.

CHIEF TOWNS.

New York, the first commercial city in America, is admirably situated for trade, at the mouth of the Hudson, on a spacious bay, which forms one of the finest harbours in the world. About two thirds of the foreign goods consumed in the U. States are imported here, and the revenue to the U. S. from duties on them has been in some years $20,000,000. Regular lines of packets connect New-York with the principal ports in the Southern States, West Indies, and S. America, and with London, Liverpool, and Havre.

The city has suffered much from fires; and at the great fire in 1835, more than 600 stores, with their contents, valued at $20,000,000, and covering 30 acres of ground, were consumed in a single night.

The city is supplied with water from Croton River, in the northern part of Westchester county, by an aqueduct 41 miles long, completed in 1842, at an expense of 12,000,000 dollars.

Albany, the capital, on the west bank of the Hudson, a few miles below the mouth of the Mohawk, at the terminating point of the Erie and Champlain Canals, and of several railroads, is an old, wealthy, trading town.

Among the other towns are,

West Point, the seat of the Military Academy of the United States—on H—n river, in the Highlands;

Newburg, the depôt of a fine grazing country—on the H—n, a little above West Point;

Poughkeepsie, the depôt of a rich agricultural and manufacturing district—in D—s county, on H—n river;

Hudson, a trading town, with several ships in the whale fishery—on H—n river, in C—a county;

Troy, the seat of an active trade, and numerous factories—on the H—n, at the head of sloop navigation;

Schenectady, an ancient Dutch town, the seat of Union College—on M—k river;

Utica, the great central thoroughfare of the state—in O—a county, on M—k river;

Syracuse and Salina, noted for extensive salt-works—on Onondaga lake and E—e canal;

Auburn, the seat of one of the state-prisons—on O—o lake, at its outlet;

Rochester, famous for the largest flour-mills in the world—on G—e river, near its mouth;

Lockport, where the Erie Canal descends by five double locks from the level of lake Erie, and furnishes an immense water power—70 miles west of R—r;

Lockport, on Erie Canal.

Buffalo, the commercial emporium of the vast country on the upper lakes—on E—e lake, near its outlet;

Oswego, the principal commercial port of lake Ontario—at the mouth of O—o river;

Sackett's Harbour, the naval station of the United States on lake Ontario during the last war with Great Britain—near the mouth of B—k river;

Plattsburg, famous for the naval battle of September 11th, 1814, in which the American fleet, under M'Donough, captured a British fleet of superior force—on lake C—n, at the mouth of the S—c.

PLATE 8.—Sample page of Sydney Morse's *A System of Geography*.

relegation of mathematical geography until after the home geography; finer cartography; a better application of physical geography; the recognition of commercial geography; and the addition of state supplements. Representative texts of this period are those of Colton, Swinton, and Harpers. The latter made a special effort to emphasize the commercial side.

The "new" geography emphasizes the physical. — In the nineties a number of textbooks appeared, such as Frye's, Redway and Hinman's, and Morton's, which began to show the effect of instruction in physical geography and geology in the high schools, normal schools, and colleges. Maury, Hinman, Redway, Davis, Shaler, and others had been teaching the teachers of elementary and high schools the modern, dynamic, and evolutionary physiography which had made great strides during the two previous decades. Physical geography had also been introduced into the normal schools. Therefore the time was ripe for the new books above mentioned. Their chief merit is in the adaptation of physical geography to the elementary school, and in a better application of the causal relation principle. Topographic forms and the forces that made them, the waters of the earth, meteorology, and the adaptation of animal and vegetable life to the physical environment are the chief points in which advance is shown. The commercial phase continues to show progress.

Woodcuts give way to photographic processes, increasing the veracity of the illustrations. The maps are more perfect. A new kind of map now added is the photo-relief map.

But in the descriptive or political part these books are not much better than their predecessors, consisting of the usual laconic, statistical, enumerative paragraphs in the usual unconnected order. That which should be the most fascinating part of geography is dull and uninteresting. The lack in this respect was partially made up by supplementary readers, some excellent ones now appearing, as the famous F. G. Carpenter's Series, and the Readers by King.

The recent geography returns to the human side. — Since 1900 the other element in geography is again emphasized as it should be. The human side had been neglected in the enthusiasm for the new physical geography, but was now again recognized. In the textbooks of King, Dodge, and of Tarr and McMurry we find this juster balance between man and nature, and, what is more important, the interrelation is worked out much better. The interests of the child are again considered. The human element in geography will always hold the first place in the interests of children. We find therefore in the primary geographies of the present day a greater emphasis on human life and human occupations, and through them an approach to the physical environment.

LESSON XLII.

Important Places in New York.—What is the chief city in New York? Ascending the Hudson from New York, what place do we find on the west bank, near the Jersey line? What place is next above it on the same bank? For what is West Point noted? *For being the site of the United States Military Academy.* What places lie on the west bank of the Hudson between West Point and Albany? What places on the east bank between Poughkeepsie and Albany? What places on the Hudson above Troy?

How is Lewiston situated? Lockport? Keeseville? Amsterdam? Kingston? Owego? O'vid? Havana? Flushing? What place at the northern extremity of Seneca Lake? At its southern extremity? In what direction is Corning from Jamestown? What place on the Delaware, near the junction of New York, New Jersey, and Pennsylvania? How is Saratoga situated? For what is it noted? *For its mineral springs, which have made it a favorite summer resort.*

Important Places in New Jersey.—What is the chief city of New Jersey? *N . . . . k.* In what direction is Newark from New York? What place on Raritan Bay is a railroad terminus? What other place on this bay? What is the most northerly place in New Jersey situated on the ocean? For what is Long Branch noted? *It is a favorite watering-place.*

How is Dover situated? Elizabeth? Atlantic City? Millville? Salem? Princeton? Morristown? Name the places on the Delaware below Trenton. In what direction is Rahway from Newark? Paterson from Newark? Paterson from Trenton?

Important Places in Pennsylvania.—What is the chief city in Pennsylvania? *P.* What place about six miles north of Philadelphia? *G.* What place on the Delaware below Philadelphia? What places on the Delaware above it? Name the places on the Monongahela. What place west of Philadelphia, and connected with it by railroad?

How is Carbondale situated? Scranton? Pottsville? Allentown? Great Bend? Mauch Chunk (*mawk-chunk'*)? Columbia? Gettysburg? Beaver? In what direction is Doylestown from Philadelphia? What place on the Delaware, opposite Burlington, N.J.? What place on the Susquehanna, opposite Wilkesbarre? For what is Wyo'ming memorable? *For the massacre of its people during the Revolution by a party of British and Indians.*

Plate 9.—**From S. S. Cornell's *Grammar School Geography*, illustrating the detailed and nonessential character of map study about 1850.**

In the advanced geographies the causal order is used more directly, and still the industrial and social life of man is made prominent, as it should be.

Another excellent feature of these recent books is the application of such pedagogical principles as correlation with science and history; the method of comparative review; and the use of topical or type study, permitting a more connected and unified presentation.

Supplementary literature. — There are now a great many excellent supplementary readers, — some of them little monographs, from the child's standpoint, of various countries; general descriptive readers; readers of scenic description; information readers on the industries; nature readers; and readers in physical geography. They all help to enrich the subject, to weave it together, or to bring out its æsthetic aspect.

Beauty of present texts. — Modern books possess, in addition, the advantage of the improvements possible by the high perfection of present-day typography, photography, including the color-processes, and cartography, which gives them an artistic finish never dreamed of by the Father of American Geography.

As textbooks, both from the pedagogical standpoint, and that of the art of book-making, the American textbook in geography stands at the head.

CHAPTER XXV

LIST OF GEOGRAPHICAL BOOKS

METHOD

Davis, Geographical Essays, Ginn & Co.

Frye, Child and Nature, Ginn & Co.

Frye, Manual of Geography, Ginn & Co.

Geike, The Teaching of Geography, Macmillan Co.

King, Methods and Aids in Teaching Geography, Lee & Shepard.

McMurry, Special Method in Geography, Macmillan Co.

Redway, Teachers' Manual of Geography, D. C. Heath & Co.

Redway, The New Basis of Geography, Macmillan Co.

Trotter, Lessons in the New Geography, D. C. Heath & Co.

Archer, Lewis, and Chapman, The Teaching of Geography, Black.

The Journal of Geography.

Mill, Guide to Geographical Books and Appliances, Phillips & Son.

PRIMARY GEOGRAPHY

Home geography.

Tarr & McMurry, Home Geography, Macmillan Co.

McMurry, Excursions and Lessons in Home Geography, Macmillan Co.

Long, Home Geography, American Book Co.

King, Home and School, Lee & Shepard.

Straubenmüller, Home Geography, Ginn & Co.

Fairbanks, Home Geography for Primary Grades, Whitaker & Ray.

Dunton, First Lessons in Geography, Silver, Burdett & Co.

Longman's Pictorial Reader in Geography, Longmans, Green, & Co.

Earth and sky.

Payne, Geographical Nature-Study, American Book Co.

Nichols, Underfoot, Lothrop.

Nichols, Overhead, Lothrop.

Pratt, Storyland of Stars, Educational Publishing Co.

Boyle, Calendar Stories, Flanagan Co.

Races.

Deming, Indian Child Life, Stokes.

Holbrook, Hiawatha Primer, Houghton, Mifflin & Co.

Peary (Mrs.), The Snow Baby, Stokes.

Smith, Eskimo Stories, Rand, McNally & Co.

Andrews, Ten Boys of Long Ago, Ginn & Co.

Andrews, Seven Little Sisters, Ginn & Co.

Industries.

Dopp, The Tree-Dwellers, Rand, McNally & Co.

Dopp, The Early Cave-Men, Rand, McNally & Co.

Dopp, The Later Cave-Men, Rand, McNally & Co.

Dopp, The Tent-Dwellers, Rand, McNally & Co.

Dutton, Hunting and Fishing, American Book Co.

Dutton, In Field and Pasture, American Book Co.

Descriptive Geography — Travel.

King, This Country of Ours, Lee & Shepard.

King, The Land We Live In, Lee & Shepard.

Chance, Little Folks in Many Lands, Ginn & Co.

Riggs, Stories of Lands of Sunshine, University Publishing Co.

Carroll, Around the World, Ginn & Co.

Winslow, The Earth and Its People, D. C. Heath & Co.

Our Little Cousins Series, 30 vols., by different authors, Page & Co.

Little Journeys Series, a number of volumes, by different authors, Flanagan Co.

Textbooks, General Geography.

Tarr & McMurry, New Geography, Book I, Macmillan Co.

Frye, Elements of Geography, Ginn & Co.

King, Elementary Geography, Scribners.

Dodge, Elementary Geography, Rand, McNally & Co.

Rabenort, Geography, American Book Co.

ADVANCED GEOGRAPHY

Textbooks, General Geography.

Tarr & McMurry, New Geography, Book II, Macmillan Co.

King, Advanced Geography, Scribners.

Dodge, Advanced Geography, Rand, McNally & Co.

Redway & Hinman, Natural Advanced Geography, American Book Co.

Rabenort, Geography, American Book Co.

Frye, Grammar School Geography, Ginn & Co.

Descriptive Geography.

Monroe & Buckbee, Our Country and Its People, Harper & Bros.

McMurry, Type Studies from United States Geography, Macmillan Co.

McMurry, Larger Types from American Geography, Macmillan Co.

Fairbanks, The Western United States, D. C. Heath & Co.

Our Country Series, Mason & Co.

Carpenter, Geographical Readers, one volume on each continent, American Book Co.

Chamberlain, The Continents and Their People, Macmillan Co.

Herbertson, Descriptive Geography, Black. North America, South America, Europe, British Empire, Asia, Africa.

Winslow, Geography Readers, D. C. Heath & Co. Distant Countries, Europe, Our American Neighbors, The United States.

Peeps at Many Lands (with color plates, by various authors), Black. The World, Belgium, Corsica, England, France, Scotland, Germany, Greece, Holland, Ireland, Italy, Norway, Switzerland, Wales, Turkey, Canada, West Indies, Burma, Siam, India, Palestine, China, Korea, Japan, Egypt, Morocco, S. Africa, Iceland, New Zealand, South Seas.

Lyde, Man in Many Lands (illustrated with color plates), Black.

Tomlinson, The British Isles, Houghton, Mifflin & Co.

Commercial Geography.

Keller & Bishop, Commercial and Industrial Geography, Ginn & Co.

Rocheleau, Geography of Commerce and Industry, Educational Publishing Co.

Herbertson, Man and his Work, Black.

Protheroe, The Dominion of Man, Methuen & Co.

Allen, Stories of Industry, Ginn & Co.

Carpenter, F. G., Geographical Readers, American Book Co.
How the World is Fed.
How the World is Housed.

Chamberlain, Home and the World Series, Macmillan Co.
How we are Clothed.
How we are Fed.

How we are Sheltered.
How we Travel.

Carpenter, F. O., Foods and Their Uses, Scribners.

Rocheleau, Great American Industries, Flanagan Co.

Mowry, American Inventions and Inventors, Silver, Burdett & Co.

Warman, The Story of the Railroad, Appleton.

Shinn, The Story of the Mine, Appleton.

Laut, The Story of the Trapper, Appleton.

Physical Geography.

Dodge, Reader in Physical Geography, Longmans, Green, & Co.

Barnard, Talks About the Weather, Funk and Wagnalls Co.

Harrington, About the Weather, Appleton.

Giberne, Ocean of Air, Carter Bros.

Holden, Earth and Sky (Young Folks' Library), Hall & Locke.

Rogers, Earth and Sky, Doubleday, Page & Co.

Shaler, The Story of Our Continent, Ginn & Co.

Shaler, First Book in Geology, D. C. Heath & Co.

Fairbanks, Rocks and Minerals, Educational Publishing Co.

Ball, Starland, Ginn & Co.

Miscellaneous.

Dorling, All About Ships, Cassell.

Ingersoll, The Book of the Ocean, The Century Co.

Oles, The Life Savers, Dutton & Co.

Scott, Romance of Exploration, Seely & Co.

Williams, The Romance of Exploration, Lippincott.

Jenks, Boy's Book of Exploration, Doubleday, Page & Co.

Towle, Marco Polo, Lothrop, Lee & Shepard.

Starr, Strange Peoples, D. C. Heath & Co.

BOOKS ON SUBJECT MATTER FOR THE TEACHER

Many of these books may also be used for reference work by pupils in the upper grades.

Atlases.

Century Atlas of the World, Vol. 12, of the Century Dictionary and Cyclopedia, The Century Co.
Citizens' Atlas of the World, Bartholomew Co., Edinburgh.
Philip's Systematic Atlas, Philip & Son, London.
Longman's School Atlas, Longmans, Green, & Co.

General Geography.

Mill, International Geography, Appleton.
Russell, North America, Appleton.
Mackinder, Britain and the British Seas.
Stanford, Compendium of Geography, 12 vols., Stanford.
The National Geographic Magazine.

Physical Geography.

Tarr, Physical Geography, Macmillan Co.
Redway, Elementary Physical Geography, Scribners.
Fairbanks, Practical Physiography, Allyn & Bacon.
Davis, Physical Geography, Ginn & Co.
Gilbert & Brigham, Introduction to Physical Geography, Appleton.
Dryer, Lessons in Physical Geography, American Book Co.
Dryer, High School Geography, American Book Co.
Salisbury, Barrows, and Tower, Elements of Geography, Holt & Co.
Mill, Realm of Nature, Scribners.
Salisbury, Physiography, Holt & Co.
Huxley, Physiography, Appleton.
Ritter, Comparative Geography, American Book Co.
Reclus, The Earth, Harper & Bros.

Guyot, The Earth and Man, Scribners.
Shaler, Aspects of the Earth, Scribners.
Shaler, Land and Sea, Scribners.
Shaler, Man and the Earth, Fox, Duffield, & Co.
Bullen, Our Heritage, The Sea, Smith, Eldert, & Co.
Tarr, Physical Geography of New York State, Macmillan Co.
Powell, étc., Physiography of the United States, American Book Co.
Russell, The Glaciers of North America, Ginn & Co.
Russell, The Rivers of North America, Putnam.
Bowman, Forest Physiography, Wiley & Sons.
Norton, Elements of Geology, Ginn & Co.

Geology.

Tarr, Elementary Geology, Macmillan Co.
Brigham, First Book in Geology, Appleton.
Chamberlain & Salisbury, Geology, 3 vols., Holt & Co.
Heilprin, The Earth and its Story, Silver, Burdett & Co.
Ball, The Cause of the Ice Age, Appleton.
Gee, Short Stories in Nature Knowledge, Macmillan Co.
Crosby, Common Minerals. D. C. Heath & Co.

Miscellaneous.

Johnson, Mathematical Geography, American Book Co.
Ball, Story of the Heavens, Cassell.
Young, Elementary Astronomy, Ginn & Co.
Keane, Ethnology, Cambridge University Press.
Ratzel, History of Mankind, 3 vols., Macmillan Co.
Taylor, Names and their History, Rivington, Percival, & Co.
Jacobs, Story of Geographical Discovery, Appleton.
Keane, Evolution of Geography, Stanford.

Geographical Influence.

Brigham, Geographical Influence in American History, Ginn & Co.

Semple, American History and its Geographic Conditions, Houghton, Mifflin & Co.

Semple, Influence of the Geographical Environment, Holt & Co.

Brigham, From Trail to Railroad, Ginn & Co.

Marsh, The Earth as Modified by Human Action, Scribners.

Freeman, The Geographic History of Europe, Longmans, Green, & Co.

Commercial Geography.

Gregory, Keller, & Bishop, Physical and Commercial Geography, Ginn & Co.

Redway, Commercial Geography, Scribners.

Brigham, Commercial Geography, Ginn & Co.

Robinson, Commercial Geography, Rand, McNally & Co.

Gannett, Garrison & Houston, Commercial Geography, American Book Co.

Trotter, Geography of Commerce, Macmillan Co.

Lyde, Man and His Markets, Macmillan Co.

Patton, Natural Resources of the United States.

Freeman and Chandler, Commercial Products of the United States, Ginn & Co.

Willets, Workers of the Nation, 2 vols., Dodd, Mead & Co.

Martin, The Story of a Piece of Coal, Appleton.

Nicolls, The Story of American Coals, Lippincott.

Greene, Coal and Coal Mines, Houghton, Mifflin Co.

Channing & Lansing, The Story of the Great Lakes, Macmillan Co.

Curwood, The Great Lakes, Putnam.

Van Hise, The Conservation of the Natural Resources of the United States, Macmillan Co.

Price, The Land We Live In, Small, Maynard & Co.

Johnson, Elements of Transportation, Appleton.

Descriptive Geography — Travel.

Stoddard Illustrated Lectures, 10 vols., Balch Bros. Grand Cañon, Yellowstone, Mexico, California, Norway, Switzerland, Greece, Austria, Italy, Turkey, France, Germany, Spain, Holland, Belgium, England, Russia, India, Palestine, China, Japan, Egypt.

Holmes, Illustrated Lectures, McClure & Co. England, France, Germany, Greece, Spain, Italy, Switzerland, Russia, Norway, Sweden, Denmark, Morocco, Egypt, China, Corea, Japan, Philippines, Hawaii.

Singleton, Series; Dodd, Mead, & Co. Historic Landmarks of America, Paris, Russia, Venice, Switzerland, Great Rivers of the World, Japan.

Johnson, Travel Series, Macmillan. Among English Hedgerows, The Land of the Heather, The Isle of the Shamrock, Along French Byways, Highways and Byways of the Mississippi Valley, Highways and Byways of the Great Lakes, Highways and Byways of the South, Highways and Byways of the Rocky Mountains, Highways and Byways of the Pacific Coast, New England and Its Neighbors, Picturesque St. Lawrence, Picturesque Hudson.

Our European Neighbors (illustrated, by various authors), Putnam. France, Denmark, Germany, Holland, Russia, Switzerland, Spain, Italy, Turkey.

Our Asiatic Neighbors (illustrated, by various authors), Putnam. India, Japan, China.

Travel Series, beautiful color plates, Black.

Ball, Sussex, England.

McCormick, The Alps.

Mempes, Paris.

Baedeker, Guide Books of nearly all Countries of the World, Scribners.

Wey, Rome, Winston Co.
Norman, All the Russias, Scribners.
Great Streets of the World (by various authors), Scribners.
Taylor, Views Afoot, McKay.
Singleton, Guide to Great Cities, Northwestern Europe, Baker, Taylor & Co.
Mackinder, The Rhine, Dodd, Mead & Co.
Peixotto, By Italian Seas, Scribners.
Marshall, Cathedral Cities of France, Dodd, Mead & Co.
Wilson, In Scripture Lands, Scribners.
Elmendorf, A Camera Crusade (Palestine), Scribners.
Goodrich, Africa To-day, McClurg & Co.
Penfield, Present Day Egypt, The Century Co.
Johnston, The Nile Quest, Stokes Co.
Stanley, In Darkest Africa, 2 vols., Scribners.
Carpenter, South America, Wilson.
Bingham, Across South America, Houghton, Mifflin & Co.
Domville-Fife, The Great States of South America, Bell & Sons.
Ober, Camps in the Caribbees, Lee & Shepard.
Ober, Our West Indian Neighbors, Potter & Co.
Carson, Mexico, Macmillan Co.
Shaler, The United States, 3 vols., Appleton.
Austin, The Land of Little Rain, Houghton, Mifflin & Co.
Lummis, Strange Corners of our Country, The Century Co.
Peixotto, Romantic California, Scribners.
Bacon, The Hudson River, Putnam.
Chambers, The Mississippi River and Its Wonderful Valley, Putnam.
Parrish, The Great Plains, McClurg & Co.
Muir, Our National Parks, Houghton, Mifflin & Co.
Smythe, The Conquest of Arid America, Macmillan Co.
Ralph, Our Great Southwest, Harper & Bros.
Van Dyke, The New New York, Macmillan Co.

Smith, Charcoals of Old and New New York, Doubleday.
Abbott, Old Paths and Legends of New England, Putnam.
Bacon, Historical Pilgrimages in New England, Silver, Burdett & Co.
Cook, Picturesque America, 3 vols., Coates & Co.
Fraser, Canada As It Is, Cassell & Co.
Finck, The Pacific Coast, Scenic Route, Scribners.
Taylor, Alaska and the Yellowstone, Jacobs & Co.
Wright, Greenland's Ice-Field, and Life in the North Atlantic, Appleton.
Peary, The North Pole, Stokes.
Van Dyke, Nature for Its Own Sake, Scribners.
Van Dyke, The Desert, Scribners.
Van Dyke, The Opal Sea, Scribners.
White, The Mountains, Doubleday, Page & Co.

www.ingramcontent.com/pod-product-compliance
Ingram Content Group UK Ltd.
Pitfield, Milton Keynes, MK11 3LW, UK
UKHW022002190726
13853UKWH00004B/1678